Searching for Ezra

a ragbag
of
frustrations

Searching for Ezra – a ragbag of frustrations

Michael Glover

Copyright © Michael Glover 2025
The moral rights of the author have been asserted.

www.1889books.co.uk
ISBN: 978-1-915045-43-0

Other publications by Michael Glover

Poetry :

Measured Lives (1994)
Impossible Horizons (1995)
A Small Modicum of Folly (1997)
The Bead-Eyed Man (1999)
Amidst All This Debris (2001)
For the Sheer Hell of Living (2008)
Only So Much (2011)
Hypothetical May Morning (2018)
Messages to Federico (2018)
What You Do With Days (2019)
One Season in Hell (2020)
The Timely Lift-Off of the Famous Harlequin-Fish (2022)
The Skittery Zipper (2023)
Mistaking You for a Shower of Summer Confetti (2024)
Where We Left Off (with Jason Heroux) (2024)
Vincent's Poets (2024)

Others :

Headlong into Pennilessness (2011)
Great Works: Encounters with Art (2016)
Playing Out in the Wireless Days (2017)
111 Places in Sheffield You Shouldn't Miss (2017)
Late Days (2018)
Neo Rauch (2019)
The Book of Extremities (2019)
Thrust (2019)
John Ruskin: an idiosyncratic dictionary (2019)
Rose Wylie (2020)
Whose? (2020)
The Trapper (2021)
Nellie's Devils and Other Stories (2022)
794 Mini Sagas (2023)
111 Hidden Art Treasures of London (2024)
Cambridge Central Mosque (2024)

As editor or contributor :

Memories of Duveen Brothers (1976)
Goin' down, down, down: Matthew Ronay (2006)
Between Eagles and Pioneers: Georg Baselitz (2011)
Robert Therrien (2016)
Monique Frydman (2017)
A Garland of Poems for Christmas (with Martyn Crucefix) (2022)
Van Gogh: Poets and Lovers (2024)

*For Ruth, Loving Bearer of
the Dandelion Clock*

E.J.Thribb finishes off Ezra's Cantos

Why I Dislike Ezra Pound so Much

Why not try on yet another mask for size, sir? Ezra is not really anybody or anything much at all until, quite wilfully, quite deliberately, he transforms himself into somebody else. Emotionally speaking, he is always a conspicuous lack. He is insubstantial, marshmallow-centred. When he emerges into our common world of baitings and sneerings, his satirical spits and spats are usually small, tepid and poorly written, unconvincing bits of posturing.

The Cantos are scraps, bits, gobbings out. Why these scraps? And why now? Why not that after this rather than this after that? Why is he not telling us more? Why is he not telling us enough at least to understand what we read, and why we should be regarding it as significant? The entire enterprise represents the upending of a great, cacophonous sack. It could only ever be unfinished business.

He is the most tedious of pub gab-abouts, forever buttonholing you with news of his favourite thing, tweezered out from goodness knows where. How can anyone pretend to know as much as he pretends to know, or be capable of making sense of his floors-deep filing system? Why does not the fund of our common knowledge ever seem quite to suffice? Could it be that his primary ambition is to humiliate those woeful millions of know-too-littles, of whom I must always count myself one?

Has there been this decades-long rage to accumulate and accumulate so that, in the end, he will have convinced himself that he has been a Maker – perhaps even a *makar* – of a thing on a truly momentous scale, of a biblical heft, no matter how unruly, no matter how uneven in quality, the mere writing may have been? Oh to be seduced by a mere object!

Words Used by a Range of Impassioned Voices
in Dispraise of Ezra and his Work:

Chaos. Dullness. Incoherence. Mad. Jabber. Insane. Obscurity. Muttery Humming. Fascist. Anti-Semite. Psychotic. Traitor. Propaganda. Hate-Tracts. Arrogant. Hollow. Intolerably boring. Verbal mimic. False Prophet. Archaic. Authentic American Monster. Flagrant bohemian.

Why I Tolerate – and Even Like – Ezra Pound as Much as I do

Who could not be in awe of his energy, the scale of his ambitions? Conquer literary London? Why not! Sit at the feet of an Eagle called W.B. Yeats? Why not? Bring on Paris!

I have never failed to admire, and been a little in awe of, the tombstone-granite-blackness of the cloth of my Faber hardback edition of *The Cantos*, first seen on a table top near the entrance to Ward's Bookshop, Chapel Row, Sheffield, in the 1960s. How could such a weighty book *not* contain entire worlds of wisdom and enlightenment? Why, it was almost as fat as the collected prefaces to the plays of George Bernard Shaw.

Funeral Pyre – the Beginning of the End

Ezra Pound is for mugs. I hate his self-puffery, his strutting, his excessive didacticism, his cock-sure, bar-room-brawler manner. This is why I have decided to burn all my copies of his books, rid myself once and for all of the words of this gullible, intemperate, boastful idiot! I'm going to make a list of them all before I burn them, of course – if I can be bothered. But perhaps that would be to pay them too much attention, give them too much credibility. The whole point is to put him behind me, put the look and the idea of him behind me, be rid of him at last. I've bought the paraffin, and a new box of Swan Vestas matches. But what exactly would I be leaving behind? And what brought me to this desperate pass anyway? What exactly does it amount to, this obsession with a writer that one has never met? I *could* have met him. He died when I was 23 years old. As a tyro editor back then, in the summer of 1972, I could have made the effort. What does this fealty really mean though?

It's not that I even admire much of the writing. In fact, I'm often shocked by how bad, how *tedious* so much of it is. He often wrote too fast, and he had neither the gumption nor the wit to correct his own slovenliness. Why though? More to the point, what fool was I to get myself into such a situation as this one? And what sort of a condition am I in now? Do I feel pleased to be almost on the brink of being rid of him? Well, rid of his books at least… Or am I in mourning for the imminent loss of an entire world of illusion? So it's all my own fault then. He never asked me to pay him any attention. Perhaps we're too much alike. But only in certain very limited respects.

Beginning Again, Once Again, in July 2022

To hell with it though, why not begin again? I buy my new, bright-shining, paperback copy of Ezra Pound's *Cantos* – its laminated black cover gleams like a coffin lid – at the London Review Bookshop in Bury Place, just across the road from the glooming, neo-classical facade of the British Museum, one balmy, intermittently sun-struck Saturday morning in early July of 2022. Let the whole absurdity re-commence!

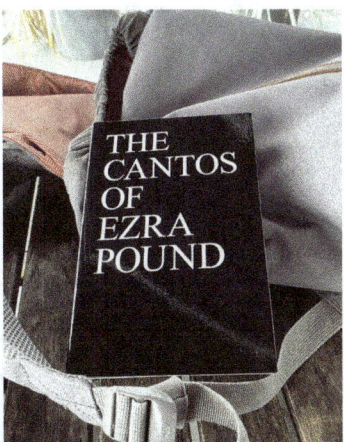

My wife and I are just about to go away to a hotel on Lake Maggiore. I would take it with me. Rather a new copy than my old hard-cover edition, bought in the Students' Bookshop in Silver Street, Cambridge, which was now more than fifty years old, and would not take kindly to bruising encounters with baggage handlers.

Why such sentimental attachment? I love that book, and I wish it no harm. It is in a fine state of repair. Not quite the same can be said of my relationship with its fifty-odd-years-dead author, with whom I have been having scratchy, one-to-one conversations, of the kind that tends to happen between the living and the dead, for more than half a century. I have even been trying to write a book about him. This is it then, that book I knew I would fail to write, an odds-and-sods of a thing, more a grump and a snarl than a hymn of praise. It's been chugging along, up hill, down valley, like a wheezy old steam train, for decades. Enough is enough! I finally decided. Open up the lumpish sack and let it all tumble out! That's my current state of thinking.

I am sitting beneath a huge green umbrella in the bookshop's inner courtyard. The man opposite is reading Ngaio Marsh in paperback, holding it high, tweaked open between his fingers, as if to part-conceal his face. That's the best way to read a crime novel, surely. Others are idling through the weeklies – Henry Kissinger is in the news yet again, in this week's *Spectator*. He has just published a new book, on the subject of six great world leaders, all men that he has known. *The Spectator* is running a long interview with the crusty old sage, by Andrew Roberts. Henry is still fairly cogent for a man of ninety-nine. He has just been stirring things up in Davos, telling the Ukrainians how best to conduct their affairs. Henry knows that he knows. He has seen it all. Well, most of it anyway. Thinking of Henry leads me back to thinking of Ezra. When he was interned in a camp by the Americans in 1945, one of his requests was that he should have a meeting with Truman, to sort things out on the world stage, deal with the problem of Japan. Hubris in abundance! That's Ezra for you. Unstoppable.

Is Ezra Pound Dead or Alive?

Is it better to be dead than alive? An odd sort of a question, I'm aware, but a matter of some importance when I think about my on-off relationship with Ezra Pound, poet and man, the two inseparable, of course. You could say that I missed him by a whisker. I visited Venice for the first time in the summer of 1972, driving my body through swarms of greedy pigeons in St Mark's square, more than a little wonder-struck – as all those ambassadors must once have been. Sun-struck, too. The campanile, in all its immensity, rose up at my side, its great bell jangling the brain when it chose to toll. St Mark's itself, bearing its fistfuls of plundered treasures, harried me from behind. It was almost a little too much for a single earthly afternoon. A *paradiso terrestre* perhaps. Pound died in a little gondolier's cottage in the Calle Querini, Dorsoduro district, just a few months later, in November of that year. That was just across the water from where I was standing. I was not even aware of his presence there. It has always been an on-off sort of a relationship.

But a personal encounter is a small matter, neither here nor there really. It is the work that counts, and what the mind has made of the man. And a relationship with the work of a writer is a difficult thing to contemplate. Are the dead easier to contend with than the living? To a degree, yes, because they are contained and complete. They have nothing more to add to their story All that is now required of we survivors is for us to circle them, on and on, like vultures, picking them apart at our leisure. They can no longer surprise us by re-inventing their story by extending it.

Not true though. Much may well have survived, from texts in trunks and drawers, to the recollections of others, which often come pouring forth with such eagerness, so ready are the memorialists to cash in, spill the beans, now that Libel has drifted off to the Underworld…

Lexington Street, Soho, London

Oh these miserable, rain-slicked streets! It's an early evening in March 2020, and I'm sitting at a small, candle-lit table beside the window of the Andrew Edmunds Restaurant in Soho, staring down at a menu, trying to decide between the lamb chop and the halibut, between that which stumbles ahead on all four legs, nibbling or mother-nudging as it goes, and that which noses like a blade through unchartered waters. The candle-flicker, for all its charm, makes reading none too easy. The interior feels dark, small, secretive and a little pent, ideal for assignations. In a room upstairs, at an hour much later than this, there promises to be a drinking club for private members only. Will the late Muriel Belcher, once the powerful doyenne of the Colony Club, be presiding? Or will she just be keeping an eye on things?

Unchartered waters! Adrian, he who sits opposite, art critic by trade of a similar vintage to myself, is not very pleased with me. He regards me as a bit of a blundering, reckless fool. Give it up! he says, slapping the palm of his hand hard down on the table. *Who reads Ezra Pound nowadays? Nobody.* I nod in wary agreement. Inwardly, I know that in time some part of me will cock a snook at Adrian, and pledge inwardly to do otherwise. I will not give up on Ezra. We talk about other projects. He is reading Gombrowicz's *Diary*. We discuss John Rothenstein, the subject of his latest book, and the paintings by Sir Joshua Reynolds in Brooks's, his club. I'd love to see them, I make that clear. He needs to make that possible, he tells me, firmly. No Brooks would want me as a member.

Ezra's proud ghost, half a century dead, walks by just then, in his cape and his Borsalino hat, same old grizzled beard, slightly stooped now, leaning on his cane. He's just spent the entire day hammering down furiously on the keys of his old Corona typewriter in some rented upstairs room, in Venice more than likely, giving the world what for...

Lago di Maggiore I

Pound's *Cantos*, in all their new bright-shiningness, travel with us, to northern Italy, where having disembarked from a plane at Milan/Bergamo airport, we take a long journey by car to the little resort of Cannero on the edge of Lago di Maggiore, the lakeside road narrowing and narrowing the further we travel, and the wooded mountainside rising ever more steeply beside us, as if almost urging us sideways into the water.

The sight of these mountains in Piedmont reminds me of a postcard I once saw in a book written by Pound's publisher, James Laughlin, called *Pound as Wuz*. It shows an aerial view of Rapallo on the Ligurian Coast just below Genoa, cupped neatly into the shapely bowl that is the Tigullian Gulf. The mountains, topped by umbrella pines, rise just as steeply there, too. That was the place Ezra made his home after leaving Paris in 1925. He would have been the first person to jump into any lake unbidden in those days – he once sent his friend William Carlos Williams very careful instructions on how to make a small pontoon boat which you could use to row yourself far enough out into the water to swim with pleasure. That note was sent from Rapallo. Why choose to live there though? Because he liked the swimming so much.

Only a little promenade separates the Hotel Cannero from the waters of Lago di Maggiore. The elderly signore – the hotel has been owned by the same family for almost a century – greets us in her pearls. Two newspapers wait on a low table in reception: *La Stampa* and the *Allgemeine Zeitung*. The dog sleeps outside in the courtyard, enjoying the cooling breath of late evening.

The room is on the third floor, and it faces the lake. The curtains are closed against the next morning's prying sun. I stack my Ezraical matter in a tidy heap in the corner, together with my several notebooks. The wardrobe will shade them.

Pound as Car Crash: a Homage by E.J. Thribb

Something went very badly wrong with Pound the poet and Pound the man. Why? How? Was it those deaths during the Great War, when so much talent was lost, so many upon whom the future seemed to depend for its intellectual and artistic vitality? If you listen to Pound's pro-fascist, Radio Rome broadcasts of the early 1940s, you encounter a species of raving and raging, an unpleasant combination of the two. This is as far as you can get from that exactitude of terminology he had always demanded of others. These were not words chosen with care. They were intemperate and ill-judged frothings at the mouth.

One way of dealing with the exasperation that prolonged encounters with the writings of Pound induces, is to laugh at him for his absurdities. Take *The Cantos*, for example, the enterprise he regarded as his crowning achievement. So much about its manner of proceeding is ridiculous. Fortunately, the poet E.J. Thribb has caught the measure of the man in this newly written homage called Canto CXVIV…

EZRA POUND

Canto CXVIV

Y'd be nuts too!"
Sitting in the tap room di baggio Firenze
Sending Tom them clauses you cut."
                            F&F to E.Z. passim
Not withstanding. Not with. The pact signed by
        Sultan Mohmammed Khudabandah (Mr. to most)
                &
        Them boys from YONDER
            An ol' Brig. Gen. Leonard Covington
(Fatally wounded at the Battle of Beach Farm)
                                            1813

πιάσει ένα αστέρι που πέφτει

Jus' look how done took all them IDEAS
You gave him an' all them   notions
        For turning @
      rags
into SILKS
An' him a YANK same as you and him putting
    IN all them Greek words and Latin dohickeys
    To spice it up.
    Not to mention Chinaman talk."
Wang Bang Dang

    Inky Pinky Parlez Vous
....
    On his death bed
    Marco Polo said
    Good night Irene.
                              CACOETHES SCRIBENDI
To the Captain of the *Saucy Lady*.
Order fresh water for the pigs and goats."
                      Girart de Montcorbier. 1455.
      (and the g'd for nothing, Comte von Hopp)
Taking a mouthful of Sol's cherry cheesecake . . .
:USERY
LXV   Old Tom got away with it and you went nuts."
      C'd not tell Sweeney from a jar of pickled eggs."
        CANTO CANTAS CANTAT
      Ain't that just the end?"

Make it Old, Boys!

What sort of a being was Pound, what sort of a tissue of awkwardnesses and cussednesses? Ever a wanderer, shuffling backwards into the future, wholly engulfed by a past of which he continued to be a part as long as he had the breath to breathe, wandering the byways of a long gone France, an excessive nostalgia for the old ways and the old gods. And all this in spite of the fact that he was forever shouting: Make it New, Boys!

Is Ezra Pound Dead or Alive? Part Two

A dead writer's words change and change again, in the reading and the re-reading. As more is read, so new discoveries are made. The longer the familiarity, the more nuanced the response, the higher the aerial view?

I remember my first flashes of anger and bewilderment with the man. I had bought a paperback copy of his *Selected Poems*, edited and chosen by his publisher, T.S. Eliot, the magus himself. It was a grey book (by which I mean that the cover was grey). Grey for solemnity. Grey for seriousness. Grey for elderly be-suitedness. The grey of a day of sombre sunlessness, when pleasurable walking declines into miserable foot-drudgery... All that greyness struck me as odd. Why? The idea of a writer often runs excitedly and pell mell ahead of the experience of actually reading him.

When I was a school boy in Sheffield, Pound by reputation (the little that I knew of him that is, which was very little indeed) was the outsider, the disrupter, the American maverick. A man well outside of the syllabus. A man irreconcilable with the interests and the preoccupations and the tolerances of the poet who taught me to marvel at the words of the three Johns (give or take an 'n') – Ben Jonson, Jonathan Swift and John Donne – at my Northern grammar school. Make it New! That slogan was my youthful distillation of Pound. How then to reconcile such a rallying cry with a word that I read in the poem that had been chosen by Eliot to be the very first in the book? It was called 'The Tree', and it was a tale out of Ovid, very briefly told, of an act of magical transformation – a human changes into a tree. The narrator is that tree. He is telling his own story. What went wrong for me happened in the last two lines, and it was one word alone on which my mind snagged, and keeps on snagging whenever I return to it – rather in the way that a tongue simply cannot help catching on, and worrying at, the sharp edge of a damaged tooth. It was that irritating, that perplexing. The word was NATHLESS – which is an antique version of nevertheless. I capitalise it because Pound himself was so fond of CAPITALISATION. That habit, generally speaking, meant that he was in a mood of rising anger and indignation, frothing at the mouth once again, as he so often did, and increasingly so as he aged.

Nathless! Nathless! How could a poet who was said to be a *beacon of the new* resort to a dead archaism, a bit of faux-ancientness, such as NATHLESS? What direction was he facing in? Little by little, I discovered that Pound, for all his sloganeering, slept soundly with the old gods life-long, even as he gestured towards the future. In short, he was a mess of contradictions.

The Invention of the Bardic Voice

How to account for the voice of Ezra Pound in old age? In 1966, at the age of 82, eight years into his freedom from that ten-year-long incarceration by the American authorities at St Elizabeth's Hospital in Washington D.C., he read from his *Cantos* at the Spoleto Festival in Umbria. The cover of the record of that reading, released by Caedmon two years later, shows him slumped into his chair behind the microphone, a grizzled, antique being with scrubby beard, long hair washed and relatively tamed, the skin of his face scored, seamed and crumpled. He is a sack of bones, held together by a relatively elegant shirt, which puckers at the wrist. His skinny right hand, fingers bent into a claw, rises to scratch at his cheek. The look is that of a sage, lost and sombre in the contemplation of his own inwardness.

The voice, however, is something else altogether. You could say that it rises to the occasion of his singular appearance. Pound reads very slowly, and as if he is gargling gravel as he speaks. The voice is distant and meditative, as far from that small town in rural Idaho where he was born almost an entire lifetime ago (he was to die in Venice six years later) as you could possibly travel. This was a decade when Pound was relatively esteemed by the poets of America as they rose up almost as one in opposition to the folly and tragedy of Vietnam. Pound was the maverick outsider then, who did not follow the rules. Who then *had* he been following? Whose does the sound of this reading voice suggest?

Pre-eminently that of W.B. Yeats, the poet Pound had travelled to Europe to meet, and whose secretary he became in 1913, at the beginning of the First World War. Pound and Yeats, the younger man filling the role of the older poet's secretary, had spent three hard winters together in a small cottage on the edge of the Ashdown Forest. Pound would have listened to Yeats, day after day, reading his poems out loud – tremulous and electrifying in its way – absorbing Yeats' intonations, listening to that magnificently self-preening bardic delivery, admiring the perfections of the stage Oirishman. But there is more than a poteen-ful of vatic Irishry in Pound's voice. There is also, in its burr, an admixture of Scottishness too. His voice is fully European, more ancient than modern, and that is what Pound would have wanted, surely, to hear himself as a European bard.

And yet that is not quite true, not really. Pound had indeed damned America as a half-savage country, but he was not an insider, not really, anywhere. He had no wish to become a svelte, aristocratic European in the mould of his friend and publisher T.S. Eliot. Unlike Eliot, he had not arrived in England with an esteemed name and a fistful of calling cards. Unlike Eliot, he had not studied under Bertrand Russell at Harvard, and could not therefore benefit by being slotted into the exclusive literary coteries of London. When he travelled East on his first great European adventure in 1908, the loss of him mourned over by his younger poet-friend H.D., he had no influential wind in his sails. Instead, he chose to dress like a gypsy in the drawing rooms of London for the sheer defiance and bravura of it all. His would be a pound, always, and never a gentle rap rap.

Lago di Maggiore II

Lakeside, mid-morning, July 2022. Having stepped down from the terrace of the hotel where breakfast is served at a leisurely pace for hours on end, we are now seated in our wicker armchairs facing the lake, admiring the blaze of brilliant red geraniums in their terracotta planters, which nod, vaguely and pleasingly, in the general direction of some Etruscan original. A Land Rover rumbles across the cobbles at our back. A cormorant is drip-drying its wings on the top of a tall mooring post driven a few feet into the puckered surface of the water. Below us, an assortment of water fowl drifts haphazardly by. Swallows zip furiously in and out of a nest tucked into the underside of a raised landing stage. A solitary swan snubs a moorhen, and then passes regally on, quite beyond caring. Next to us is the *sportello* where crowds are gathering to buy their tickets for the ferry stops to the islands: *Isola Bella, Isola dei Pescatori*... A small craft out on the water – it looks, being in shadow at the moment, like an ugly wooden door wedge – is slowly nosing its way – why so indolently slow though? I'm asking myself – across Lago di Maggiore.

A little shop next to the *sportello* readies itself for disappointingly slow commerce today (it being so hot again). Pleasures in store include plastic swim shoes (pink and blue), postcards of the places we are all looking at, colourful balls bouncy enough to provoke bursts of laughter when a favourite child falls over, and relatively fashionable brown sun hats, made of paper, which come drizzling coquettishly errant ribbons.

All of a sudden, the ferry arrives with a rumble and a roar – the landing stage gives a few fearful judders. The crowd surges forward, and moments later it is sucked onto the lake, quite gone. Silence descends. Those who remain behind (such as ourselves) have no plans to go that far – unless reading is a species of travel, which it is, of course. In fact, there are quite a few of us, I notice, travellers from cities most likely, who have blinked awake this morning to uncustomary warmth and the lulling pleasures of a lakeside prospect...

This hotel is the sort of place to which people return, bearing last year's memories along with them. The elderly feel themselves a little younger again, a little more *sportif* perhaps. The females are wearing flimsy white tops and blue canvas shoes. Old customers greet the same old retainers – what a miracle it is that we have all survived to greet each other again with such a mutual warmth of recognition!

I open my old copy of Pound's *Guide to Kulchur*, begin to tune in to its spitty prose, that characteristic mood of extreme exasperation. It was published in 1938. He wrote this book in Rapallo, not too far from here, where, as Yeats reported when he visited him there in 1928, he had a room overlooking the Ligurian Sea. Yeats called Pound *irascible*. Spot on, I am thinking as I read. He's got the measure of the man. Yeats also tells us that Pound's art is the opposite of his own. Only the affection of a long acquaintance still bonds them.

The book is dedicated to Louis Zukofsky, a young Jewish poet who enjoyed – endured – an intermittent correspondence with Pound during the 1930s and, ever more intermittently, on. Zukofsky quickly learnt to write back to Pound in the way he was being written to: snappy, laconic, slangy, lightly peppered with ridiculous contractions or mis-spellings. We two, Pound tells him in his dedication, are strugglers in the desert. What exactly does that mean? Loners. Backs up against it. Implacable hostility on the part of the Establishment. Fighting back against STUPIDITY.

It's rough and ready stuff, pugilistic, is *Guide to Kulchur*. He's getting it all down, without taking a breath. Pound rants on, as would always be his way, about exactness of terminology, and especially so when he himself was being at his least exact. Deference is also, curiously, part of the mix from time to time. Confucius is his mouthpiece. The exposition is partial, intermittent, but also reckless and puzzling in its extreme brevity. He is so exasperated that he cannot express himself with clarity. He's thundering out the words on that typewriter of his. He wore out six or seven of those rat-a-tat word machines during his lifetime.

The time for guardedness and reflection is over. He casually refers to Pauthier. Who the hell be he? A nineteenth-century translator of Confucius into French, just in case you are asking. He sketches in the history of Western thought. He writes as if his fevered brain is just about to explode. Everything being said about the past is loose and wafty. And there is no one looser and waftier and more intemperate than Pound himself, we find ourselves thinking as we read. His own boasting fogs his mind. Usury has contaminated Western thought, he thunders. Civilisation is corrupt, rotten at the core.

There are two kinds of ideas, abstract and concrete, the ones that remain afloat in a vacuum of abstraction, and the ones which lead to ACTION. The Greeks and Romans lacked social responsibility, they were highbrows.

Usury corrodes public order. Usurers have no wish to have knowledge circulated. Maintaining public order is the first duty of the state.

I look up. The cormorant's wings are at rest now. A waiter is finically laying tables for lunch around our table. Is this a mild-mannered gesture of hostility, a wish to see us gone from here? I flash her a look of unredeemed Poundian irascibility. She melts away with due deference. I feel momentarily ashamed, and then yoke myself to Pound's forward-thundering chariot yet again.

Amidst all the hysterical and harried half-sense, there is also, from time to time, clarity and searing insight. What does any poet have the right to discuss? Pound asks, flinging it out like a challenge. Why exclude philosophy and economics from general educated conversation about culture when obscure cosmologies and abstruse metaphysical musings are permissible?

After all, had Pound not spent quite long enough in the company of W.B. Yeats? Only he who writes with the utmost simplicity can expect to be understood. Stick to dog, horse and sunset.

Polemic! More polemic! On he goes, scattering the faint-hearted as he rants. He taunts to bamboozle and mislead. He who inveighs against looseness of expression is most culpable of it, again and again. His prose is scatter-gun, water forever on the furious boil. It's all part memory, or reckless reportage loosely based on memory – as in a fleeting description of a visit to the Prado that wisps by like so much else. And Usura runs through it all, that poisoning of the well.

As I read, seated at that table in the open air on a warm summer's morning in Piedmont, and stare across the lake, I think about Pound presiding over his own table in Rapallo, watched over, at table's end, by the great hieratic head of himself, carved from a single block of marble by French sculptor Henri Gaudier-Brzeska in 1914, that man who was to die so young, like so many of Pound's friends.

It's year XII of the Fascist calendar that evening, and Pound the pedagogue is presiding in his mind over his own Ezuversity (as he called it) at his very own table, and probably boasting of how close his ideas were to those of Mussolini, and also recalling with some pride that single meeting he had had with the thug he intermittently called The Boss, as if he's sitting in some dive in the Lower East Side, doffing his cap at the local Capo. What a meeting that had been! Ezra could see in his face the greatness of the man, the quality of the mind, how fast-moving it was…

I glance up just then. The cormorant has not stirred. I wonder about Ezra as cormorant: the ungainliness, the preposterous showmanship of it all. I close the book with a snap and stare down at the cover. Bull's eye or maze? It could be either.

My Confession

Let me begin by making a confession. Every few years, I have found myself in the grip of what I can only describe as a psychological spasm of sorts. Some urge seizes hold of me that feels quite familiar when it strikes. It is an urge to write a book about Ezra Pound. His face, with that grizzled beard, probably at the age of sixty or thereabouts, swims into the mind's eye, as if beckoning me to pay it some attention. When that happens, I am usually thinking about a photograph of Pound in early old age by Richard Avedon that I still have propped up in front of me on the desk of my study in Clapham, and which at some point in the distant past disappeared, emerging years later from behind a central heating radiator, looking almost as bruised and battered as that image of the poet himself.

Perhaps it was all the more powerfully haunting when it was not present to me in actuality… His eyes are screwed up. He looks tense, lost, the very embodiment of anguish. It is a poet's face all right, enthrallingly inscrutable. I recognize the type. And when it comes, it does so with all the force of a tiny earthquake experienced inwardly, and by no one but myself. Recognising it for what it is, I find myself willingly embracing it. When the mood strikes, prompted just a few weeks ago by something slightly different – the sight of an old book on a shelf at the London Library, and, in the reading room of that same institution on the same day, a reference to a newly published edition of some letters to and from Pound referred to in a literary journal of which I had until that moment been unaware – it seems almost inevitable that it should have returned. It was just a matter of biding one's time. Ezra always does return.

Why do I want to write a book about Ezra Pound anyway? Why should I want to add my voice to the chorus of attention that he continues to receive from poets and critics, in spite of the fact that he has been dead for more than fifty years? For a start, I sense that the two of us have things in common. I want to get to the bottom of all his impassioned and convoluted thinking about poetry matters for myself. Like Pound, I too write and care about poetry, and I too am exercised by the fact that it is not esteemed or noticed as much as it deserves to be. We both come from unpromising backgrounds.

Like Pound, I came from a situation – a small, terraced house in north-east Sheffield – which had, by and large, passed poetry by. Poetry was as little talked about or spoken out loud in the streets of Fir Vale, Sheffield 5, as it had been on that street of non-stop saloon bars in Hailey, Idaho, where he was born. Like Pound, I had had to go elsewhere in my pursuit of it. Less adventurously, it has to be said. I went to university, in England, the country of my birth. Pound did something similar at first, but he soon made even greater leaps of faith and distance. He came to Europe, and he spent the greater part of his life there. The country he loved to spend time in most of all was Italy, and one particular place in Italy: Venice.

Other aspects of this man fascinate me too. There was something wild, erratic, untameable about Ezra from first to last. He was a provincial who wanted to slough off the dreary mediocrities of provincialism. And yet he never smoothed away the rougher edges of the pioneer. He wanted sophistication, but he flung his punches like a sullen kid in a rough house. His letters were wild from first to last, his spelling eccentric to the point of ridiculousness. Some of his earliest letters to his parents, written when he was little more than a child, are already eccentric, with evidence of a strange wilfulness that seems almost indistinguishable from ignorance or even stupidity. He was no infant prodigy. All this has always intrigued me about him, the fact of his being such an oddball. If he had been more conventionally clever, less wayward altogether, he would not have been half so interesting.

Perhaps the book ought to begin with a bit of doggerel as an epigraph then, something like this:

An Epigraph

To the memory of Ezra Pound

You are standing at my shoulder again,
Advising me on my literary opinions.
Your voice is high and shrill.
You will not take no for an answer.

You have read the best that there is.
You have witnessed the worst of mankind.
And now you demand some attention.
You will not tolerate an empty room.

I look up and stare at you.
Your eyes are red-rimmed.
There is dust on your shoulders.
I would sweep it off if I dared.

Hectoring

That little fragment of a poem of sorts is an attempt to get to grips, in verse, with the hectoring man who so often seems to have been hovering at my shoulder, observing everything that I do, commenting upon the words that I am writing, pointing towards this or that imperfect phrase, for almost half a century. Sometimes he is standing in his *peignoir*, wearing a worn pair of house slippers. At other times, he wears that black cloak, the borsalino hat he was modelling when he walked past the window of Andrew Edmunds' restaurant in Soho just a few brief pages ago. If it's an evening and he's going out to dinner in Venice, perhaps after opera at the Fenice, he may well be wearing one of his velvet dinner jackets of the kind that his mother, the very upright Isabel Weston, used to insist that he wear at table in Wyncote, Pennyslvania, after the family had fled east from Idaho in pursuit of a little more respectability of the kind that his mother felt to be her due. In the early days the hair flamed up red, complementing the small slash of a goatee beard. Beard and hair look best when you see his face in profile, proud and fierce as a young god. Years later, the beard was still there, but it had become more abundant with age, more straggly and unruly, more prophetic perhaps.

A Spasmodic Pursuit

This is an account of a spasmodic pursuit then. Its subject is my frustrating inability to write a book of any consequence about a man who was born in 1885 in Hailey, Idaho, a little frontier town in the American mid-west with a single street which, according to Pound (whose grasp of facts could be shaky), boasted forty-seven saloons and one hotel. One of his grandfathers, the famous Thaddeus Pound, had been in the lumber and railroads' business. Others of his forebears had come over on a boat from England which was definitely not called the *Mayflower*. His mother's side of the family was related to the poet Longfellow, but Pound keeps that famous literary forebear well out of the picture. The story of his life is that of a spasmodically gifted, outsider poet with an increasingly tainted reputation, a reckless man of singular gifts who plummeted headlong into folly. This is the man who has preoccupied me, on and off, for nearly fifty years.

No, Pound and I did not meet. This was one of my life's many lost opportunities, and it was amongst the saddest and most significant, I always tend to think, as one is inclined to do if one has an appetite for fantasy. It is perfectly possible that such a meeting, had it happened, would have changed my life. It would certainly have radically modified the contents of this book. It may have meant that this book would have turned into the one that I wanted to write about Pound rather than the story of my partial failure to do so. No one will ever know. Least of all myself.

Promising as a theme? Unpromising?

Who Was Ezra Though?

Ezra Pound was one of the most controversial poets of the twentieth century. He lived in Europe for much of his life, and it was in Italy, during the Second World War, that he delivered a series of notorious broadcasts over Radio Rome, warning America against the foolishness of engaging in war, inveighing against what he perceived as her political crassness and lack of sound judgement. At war's end, these broadcasts led to his arrest, his imprisonment in a cage outside Pisa, transfer to America, indictment on a charge of treason, and to a thirteen-year period of incarceration in St Elizabeth's Hospital for the criminally insane just outside Washington D.C. Had Pound not suffered the humiliation of incarceration, he may well have faced the death penalty – there were many who called him a treacherous Fascist, and bayed in public for his blood. He was tainted, lifelong, by this perceived act of betrayal of his native country. Upon his release from St Elizabeth's, Pound returned to Italy. When he arrived back at Naples harbour, it was reported that he gave the Fascist salute (his apologists call it a harmless wave), and declared that all America was an insane asylum. He died, in Venice, on 1 November 1972.

Ezra Pound was a man born on the margins, physically and culturally. He regarded America as a backwater, a half-savage country. It had to change. He would not remain there for long. The civilizing lure of elsewhere beckoned. By the time he was a teenager, poetry was his passion and Europe his destiny. W.H. Auden once said that poetry makes nothing happen, and that it exists only in the valley of its making. This was not Pound's cast of mind. Pound was a pedagogue with a mission. He was a man determined to cause a stir. He regarded poets in particular and artists in general as vital forces in society. They were the antennae of the race, he once wrote. They showed us how to live. They purified the language of the tribe. And so his love of poetry included a kind of unwritten global mission statement which could be baldly summarised as: poetry changes the world.

Pound was close to his father, Homer Loomis Pound, and less so to his mother, Isabel (née Weston). To his father he confided his literary ambitions, and he kept in close touch with him when he was away from home. His mother dressed him in velvet at the table as a child, and she expected more of her son than vague literary aspirations without a definable or respectable social end. In 1889, Homer became Assistant Assayer in the Pennsylvania Mint, which gave him enough money to be of use to Ezra throughout his son's life as a writer. As a young teenager Pound had travelled to Europe in the company of his father's cousin, Aunt Frank. Pound determined to establish himself there. In 1908 he was in Venice, preparing his first book of poems for publication. Soon after that, he would arrive in London where he would settle himself for several years. His first ambition was to meet the Irish poet W.B. Yeats, to sit at the feet of an acknowledged master.

Ezra always wanted to be a poet. He had the courage of his convictions from a very early age. His mother, on the other hand, didn't think it was a suitable profession for a son of hers. In fact, it wasn't a profession at all. It lacked respectability. Financially, socially, it was a nowhere sort of place. Why not the diplomatic service instead? she wondered aloud. Why not an American diplomat to the Court of St James? she asked, and even more noisily when she learnt of his plans to go to London in 1908. Oh those innocent days of pre-World-War-One England! Oh no, it wasn't *that* that he was going to England for, mother. He was going there to meet a man who happened to be a very venerable poet indeed.

Ezra regarded Yeats (aka. 'The Eagle') as the greatest poet currently writing in the English language. In 1909, the year of their first meeting, he himself was a young man, twenty-four years of age, in a hurry, with much to do, much to achieve. Soon he was sitting at Yeats' feet, at the older poet's Sunday evening literary soirées in London's Bedford Row. A little later still he was dominating those proceedings with his loud and confident talk. With his flaming red hair, goatee beard and extravagant manner of dress, he looked and behaved every inch the poet. By 1913, the year before war broke out, he was the older man's private secretary. He had also invented a poetic movement during those London years. It was called Imagism.

Ezra was determined to make his mark on the twentieth century.

Lago di Maggiore III

Upper Terrace, late-morning, July 2022. Where exactly to re-read my pristine copy of *The Cantos*? There were the lakeside tables for dining, or the swimming pool inside the hotel, enclosed by a courtyard, overlooked by a sundial, that was heavily overpopulated by children with their inflatables, who would jump and yawp and yell and thrash about.

Was that a safe place for an un-thumbed edition of Pound? Could bespatterings by random drops of water be avoided? We opt for a terrace, still overlooking the pool, two long, steep flights of steps up from all that leaping madness. If we keep close to the wall, we can outwit the blazing sun too.

And so to begin…

Is it an epic? That's what Pound had wanted to write. It is steeped in the matter of epic. Like Dante's *Divine Comedy*, it begins part way through – much has clearly happened already; much is still to come. The first words tell us as much: 'And then…' Where exactly are we? And what will be our direction of travel? And why epic anyway? Why aspire to write one? Does not the very idea strike one as weirdly anachronistic for a man who forever wanted to Make it New? Perhaps, were he to succeed, it would be a guarantee of greatness, a guarantee that a boy from a small town in Idaho would have a name to come…

The story of that first canto is full of drama. Winds are pushing a craft out into the waters. The harried craft is Circe's to control – we are in Homeric country. There is much lamentation, hubbub, weeping and confusion on board ship. Sacrifices are made, repeatedly. The souls of the unquiet dead begin to emerge, needy souls, pleading to be heard. Elpenor is amongst them, yearning to be noticed and remembered. He had died by accident, having drunk excessively. Then comes blind Tiresias, who now addresses the narrator of this first canto. That narrator is Odysseus, part way through his agonisingly long return from the Trojan Wars. Then, with abruptness, the story peters out. Pound makes it clear that we have been listening in to his version of a fragment of a 16th century translation of the *Odyssey*. The canto ends even more abruptly than it had begun, with a colon:

Throughout, there had been a tremendous roll call of classical names. We can almost feel Pound, that noted mimic, rolling them across his tongue. His trajectory as a writer is already clear to us: his aspirations to achieve literary greatness are on the rise and rise He has set himself on the same stage as the Homeric heroes. Out go the shorter lyric poems of this youth, in comes the lifelong toil of wrestling with the idea of the Epic...

That Epic first began to emerge with the publication of *A Draft of Thirty Cantos* in 1930, though they had already been many years in the writing and the re-writing. The title suggests that the words we read are to be regarded as provisional, subject to change, and perhaps even to infinite extendibility. It is a form of chronicling which will also take in the matter of Pound's life and his preoccupations. It will become, in time, an enormously unwieldy compendium of this, that and the other. That other will include History...

Anatomising Ezra

Chewing Over What's Left of Ezra
– a Conversation with Alistair Davies
on 3 August 2022

We met in the gutter (where better a place?) to talk about Ezra, then changed our minds.

The gutter in question was in Monmouth Street, Soho, just outside the Monmouth Street Coffee House. The people who ran that exquisite gem of an establishment had got into the habit of putting a few rackety picnic tables out in the street, just off the pavement, and then cordoning it off. It was a Covid measure which stayed when the restrictions were lifted. Most people seemed to like it. Except me. Too noisy. The chairs were too flimsy for comfort.

So no sooner had the coffees been ordered than we left again. Where better than one's own back garden in Clapham, even if the back lawn did look like a snatch of the Tennessee Dust Bowl during the Woody Guthrie years? So that's where we sat and talked of distant Ezraical matters, underneath the big green umbrella, sun-dodging. And could there be a more capacious a place to start than a continent called Walt Whitman?

'I regard Pound as Whitman re-born,' said Alistair, making a bold first strike. (Too bold and reckless by half, I was thinking.) '*The Cantos* are his version of *Song of Myself*. The subject matter's different, of course. Whitman responded more to places and people, Pound to artefacts, ideas, things he had read. And, of course, Pound was highly critical of America. It was a "barbaric yawp," or in 'Hugh Selwyn Mauberley': a "half savage country, out of date." He both wanted to make himself a European *and* retain his own Americanness, but was embarrassed by it – ill at ease inside his own national identity. He never fitted in. He also made no concessions.'

'He expressed himself in such ridiculous ways in his letters to other people, spelling his words phonetically, stretching vowels and consonants, the perfect stage Amurrrikan... He set himself up for a pummelling by the critics, for his supposedly slapdash scholarship, and his theories about the relationship between sound and word in Provençal poetry.'

'And yet, what he argued about that relationship between sound and word is standard thinking now: scholarship has pretty well caught up with him – his estimation of himself as an original scholar.. The interest in Provençal poetry at university level is now in America, not Europe – you could call that a legacy of sorts.

'If you think about how his 'Homage to Sextus Propertius' was received – they shot him down! The poet didn't even know his Latin – the version was full of elementary howlers.'

'One of them implying it was so bad that Pound ought to seriously consider committing suicide!'

'How could it not be full of 'howlers' when it contained a 'patent frigidaire'? But that, for me, is the funniest line. They just didn't get what kind of thing it was: a wild version, a mouthpiece for Pound himself, a kind of Robert Lowell imitation decades before its time – another of his many, many personas...'

'Yes, they hit him hard… But, I think the event that may have hit Pound harder than almost any other though was the death of Gaudier-Brzeska – such a talent snuffed out so young! I think it stoked his hatred of London, Paris, the Great War, and his anger with the war-mongers. I think it contributed, in general, to his incendiary, gritted-teeth mood.'

I asked Alistair why he thought Pound was so consumed by the subject of usury, particularly given its original meaning in the Middle Ages, as I understood it, of nothing more than lending money at interest. 'The man is completely crazed on the subject.'

'I think, when he came to London, he would have encountered people who were advocating various forms of social credit. There were extensive discussions in literary circles about the proper role of money in society, stimulated in part by London's being the centre of capital, and in part by the extraordinary gap between the rich and the poor and the ostentation of the super rich.'

'His father was an assayer at the Philadelphia Mint. He would have smelt the reek of money from his very early days…'

Alistair said there was something Oedipal about Pound's obsession and how given his father's work, he would have been used to appraising money from a very early age. But that there were all sorts of matters which added to his fury – the terrible persecution of the Cathars in the Middle Ages – Pound regarding them as guardians of special knowledge. 'But as you see in the 'Hell' *Cantos*, his principal fury was directed at those in Britain who had made huge profits from the First World War, either through banking or producing arms. As outsiders, he and T.S. Eliot saw it as a war of trading empires.'

I suggested there was a link to Dante, who condemned Usurers to the seventh circle of Hell. Dante being one of Pound's touchstones… though he didn't quite manage to write one hundred and twenty cantos, the writing just petering out in odd sputterings… 'One of the things that troubles me most about Pound is how slovenly the writing could so often be – which seems to be so completely at odds with what he preached as a young critic: exactitude of terminology; avoiding the slush and the slip and the slither of the worst of the Victorians. He makes such ridiculous generalisations. He's at his worst in the 1930s. Always writing too fast –

not even pausing to correct himself. Making careless, half-cock attempts to remember the name of a person or a date, and then just leaves it at that! It's as if he just can't be bothered. He's in too much of a steaming hurry to correct his own sloppy behaviour! That's no way for a pedagogue to behave. No wonder he wore out so many typewriters. So much for Dr Johnson's advice: write fast if you must, but don't forget to correct it later.'

'The man's mind was scrambled – seeing everything in conspiratorial terms – he'd probably be writing material for QAnon if he were alive today. There's something very American about this though, isn't there? – stretching back much further than Trump: this predisposition to suspect conspiracies everywhere. It's been going on a very long time. And think of Pound's obscenities, too, which were quite deliberate. He was breaking the bounds of *politesse*, chucking any notion of correctness in writing onto the scrap heap…'

I replied that he held positive beliefs as well: his obsession with Confucius came to mind, which began with his acquiring papers of the scholar, Ernest Fenellosa from his widow. 'This precipitated the marvellous 'Cathay' poems, which I think are his greatest achievement. It also set in motion a life-long fascination with Confucius the sage, model for a perfect kind of governance… I don't know what was it about Pound and China. A wholly different place then, of course: Qing Dynasty…'

'China was very backward, with a largely agrarian economy. It could be construed as a model of simplicity, an example of living in harmony with nature and one's fellow beings….'

'The polar opposite of Pound in all his ostentatiousness and weirdness..'

Alistair went on to talk about how neglected Pound is now. 'It wasn't always the case. In the 1960s with Vietnam and other crises, he was esteemed – by poets especially perhaps – for the fact that he didn't follow the rules, and for being proudly anti-establishment, no celebrant of the status quo.'

'One of his problems was that he had such a high opinion of himself. Asking to see Roosevelt in person when he went back to America in 1939? Roosevelt didn't oblige, of course, though Pound did get to see a lesser political being. And then there was his belief that Mussolini – who Pound once met – would take him seriously and even appoint him as a kind of court poet. He genuinely believed that to have a poet close to the head of the Fascist administration would be a matter of some importance. None of this was true, of course, because Mussolini was a thug and a boor. Pound read too much into the fact that Mussolini had casually pronounced the book he gave him *interessante...*'

'You know, I think Yeats should shoulder a lot of the blame for Pound's drift in the direction of totalitarianism. Although Yeats was the greater poet – his mastery of the phrase must have influenced Pound – he was unpleasant in all sorts of ways. He was a terrible sponger, who would outstay his welcome, and, according to one less than admiring witness, drain a man's cellar without batting an eyelid. Major Robert Gregory, Lady Gregory's son, detested him for dining royally at his expense.'

'I find that relationship with Yeats fascinating. He fondly remembers that cottage on the edge of the Ashdown Forest in the *Pisan Cantos*.'

'Being an "alien," Pound had to report to the local police every week once war broke out. They saw soldiers in training in the forest. They witnessed how society was becoming militarised. Yeats convinced Pound that an aristocratic government was the best option, so much better than the flawed democracies of Britain, France and Germany which had entered the war with popular consent. And so it is perhaps unsurprising that when Pound, in the *Cantos* of the 1920s, comes to look for models of good governance, he praises the ideal of the Renaissance prince. And he came to regard Mussolini, the power-hungry thug who was very good at silencing dissent, as the Renaissance prince *de nos jours*. And Pound, being drunk on his own importance, believed he could influence events! Much else was in the air then of course, feeding into Pound's thinking, on which we haven't even touched: the influence of Nietzsche, for example...'

'One of the extraordinary things about Pound – that voice of his when he reads his poems – did Yeats influence that, do you think?'

'Well, anyone listening to Yeats for three long winters was bound to fall under the influence of his extraordinarily flamboyant and histrionic reading style – the voice of the Irish bard speaking forth, in a dirge-like drone, from the Lake Isle of Innisfree... So tremulous. So electrifying...'

'There are some good things to be said about Pound, though, aren't there? The fact that he and his mistress Olga Rudge, revived the reputation of

Vivaldi in the 1930s by collecting manuscripts from all over Italy and establishing a Vivaldi archive. And then there are the *Pisan Cantos*. There is so much near unrelieved tedium in *The Cantos*, but least of all perhaps in the *Pisan Cantos*, his work whilst incarcerated for treason…'

'Yes, I think that the *Pisan Cantos* are the best of them. They have so much emotional intensity – unsurprisingly perhaps – written when he would have been weighing in his mind the very real prospect of ending up on the end of a rope. It's not surprising that Villon, another man often in trouble with the law, gets more than a mention. The entire sequence is in part a series of flash-backs to a pre-war world, in which Pound is trying to rescue people and places from oblivion, beginning with a lamentation for the death of Mussolini – at the beginning of the first canto, he has Mussolini and his mistress Clara hanging upside down, tethered by the heels, in a public square in Milan. There is so much human sympathy for American soldiers held in captivity, artists, even the birds that he can hear singing beyond the cage. Even though he is depicting himself as a victim, unjustifiably held in detention in that terrible cage in the open air beneath the broiling Italian sun, it's the least self-pitying of his poetic moments… Pound's remembering is an act of retrieval, a witness to poetry's survival against the forces of violence. He would have been very much aware of the bombing of Monte Cassino by the allies in 1944.'

'Olga Rudge mentioned to me Eliot's treachery: the fact that he would praise Pound in public, but in private tell his friends that there weren't more than two lines of *The Cantos* worth reading. You think there's more to the story than that, don't you?'

'Yes. Eliot did a lot for Pound – he quietly supported Omar Pound, for example. You could also argue that it was very courageous of Eliot – and of Faber and Faber – to carry on publishing Pound so soon after the war and his support for fascism. Eliot would have been hugely influential in arguing that Pound should be kept in print when, in many circles, he was an unmentionable figure. Eliot was also on the jury of the Bollingen Prize, awarded to Pound for the *Pisan Cantos* in 1948. Eliot's presence would have been important, bringing with it the authority and the esteem of the latest Nobel Prize winner. Geoffrey Faber – conservative, Anglican, Fellow of All Souls, independently wealthy – would have been involved too. Eliot's generosity also extended to Faber and Faber, his employer – he bailed the company out in 1952 when it was on the point of collapse.'

'Where did Eliot get all his money from?'

'The impact of the Nobel Prize and the commercial success of the plays. When Eliot came to England, he was already very well connected – his very name marked him out as the member of an American elite. He had studied under Bertrand Russell at Harvard when he had ambitions of being a professional philosopher, and when he came to London, Russell introduced him to all the best people... Remember too that *The Waste Land*, which Pound edited to its great benefit, made Eliot a literary celebrity at the heart of the British and European cultural establishment, while Pound ended up a peripheral figure. Like Wyndham Lewis, who suffered a similar fate, he was to some degree overwhelmed by anger, spite, envy, intolerance because those he had promoted enjoyed the fame and attention he craved.'

'It was perhaps his character that let him down, then: his impetuosity, his failures of judgement? You could also say that it was never easy for Pound, the outsider... Like when he finally returned to Italy after serving his time at St. Elizabeth's Hospital for the criminally insane: supposedly giving that Fascist salute as the boat pulled into Naples Harbour... seeing himself as some sort of reincarnation of Homer's Odysseus. He certainly believed himself to be engaged in an epic enterprise, by his own lights anyway. Compared to Eliot he was a nobody who had it all to do. Not a nobody in his own opinion, however.'

Seeking Out Circe at Birling Gap

Usury

Usury is a filthy, tri-syllabic word. Its ugliness when spoken out loud – in fact, it is very difficult to speak out loud – almost defies and defiles the tongue: YOO ZJHOOER REEE… It gets clogged inside. It's not easy to drive it out of the mouth. It's too big and unwieldy. Its sound – the way it emerges with such slow and twisty-turny-churny reluctance – is all over the place. Easier if you could spit it out, clean, in one quick gobbet, like an oozy ball of phlegm. Usury is the death-worm in life's bud, the disgusting slug that the hooded man who has tied you to the chair in that godforsaken garage invites you to swallow, whole, when you start to emerge from your miserable drugged condition. Usury is an apocalyptic notion. It divides one human being from another with all the brutality and the brutishness of an axe. It sets the world of the civilised *polis* – that fantasyland – on fire. It makes the world move too fast. It is a perversion of nature. The idea of it drove Pound to distraction, and into a mood of hysteria. It stained and vitiated his poetry. It helped to destroy his reputation as a man of letters with serious things to say about poetry matters.

I have wanted to be rid of Pound so many times. This is why I scored a thin line of erasure through five pages of a notebook of mine dated 2021. Those pages consisted of themes to be developed, little *aperçus*, markers on the way ahead. Then I crossed them all through, quite lightly though, as though even then, at that moment of withering dismissal, some part of me knew that the unwritable book would not stay dead for too long. At that moment though, I could see no way ahead. Pound the book was unthinkable, unworkable. I could no more make it cohere than he had been able to make his *Cantos* cohere. My book was a mass of tangled nonsense.

And, when I turned up that notebook the other day, looking for something else needless to say, I noticed that one of the entries on those pages had to do with USURY. This is what it read:

usura = a murrain [a plague]

Pound regarded himself as being in good company when he condemned the usurers. Hadn't Dante banished them to the seventh circle of hell in the *Divine Comedy*? Had he not described seeing them, in that dream-vision of Canto XVI of the *Inferno,* squatting on the extreme outer edge of the circle, in order to avoid the flames that were greedily lapping at them, flailing about with their hands, rather like dogs pawing at their snouts as they try to defend themselves against the fleas and the gad-flies of high summer?

Can good come out of bad? Was usury really as bad as all that? There are incantatory passages in Pound's *Cantos*, passages which many critics regard as the poem's finest moments, when he seeks to drive home his hatred and horror of usury. *With usura hath no man a house of good stone*, he fulminates in Canto XLV. This is Pound, moralist of outrage, in full flood. Usury blocks off the creative impulses, keeps the weaver from his loom, the painter from his canvas. All comes to rack and ruin thanks to the blight of usury.

I was never so sure that this level of hysteria was really justified. Wasn't usury everywhere, going about its daily business? Didn't high street banking depend on it? Didn't usury help my own mother earn a bit of money on the side by selling clothes, household items, and even long playing records through her Freeman's catalogue business? You enjoyed the pleasure of having something arrive through the post, which you then paid for, week by week, with a little interest added. If that was usury, how much harm did it really do? And anyway, if the world did indeed move too fast, was not that perhaps more the fault of the internal combustion engine, which therefore amounted to the curse (or the blessing) of human inventiveness in the end?

The Invention of Imagism

…When Ezra arrived in London in 1908, he regarded Yeats as the only poet of value in the English-speaking world. In fact, Edwardian London was no place for a young and energetic poet to be at all if the truth were known. The feeble energies of the 1890s were long spent; poetry seemed all lush and loose, faint after-echoes of the piping of mindless Swinburnian muzak. Ezra set about to change all that.

By 1912, he had formulated a set of principles for the writing of a new and more vigorous kind of poetry that would be equal to the demands of a new era. These principles would have an enormous influence upon the way poetry would be written and discussed throughout the 20th century. In Ezra's opinion, there were three cardinal virtues: precision – poets must be precise and concise in their use of language; vers libre – free verse – should be used as a way of liberating the poet from the trammels of dead metrical structures; but, above all else, the poet should employ hard, clear, concrete images. Abstract formulations had had their day.

The movement was brought to birth in the British Museum tea rooms in June 1912. Ezra had been joined in London by Hilda Doolittle, a childhood friend. He asked to see some of her poems and, leaning over her shoulder, he corrected them in accordance with his new principles. Then he signed them for her: 'H.D. Imagiste'. A movement was born; and so was its most representative poet.

H.D. remained faithful to the principles of Imagism for most of the rest of that decade. Her poems were just what Ezra seemed to have ordered as a tonic for the scribbling tribe: hard, clear and short. In spite of the fact that they were usually set in Grecian landscapes and concerned themselves almost exclusively with figures out of Greek myth, there were no needless ornamentations, no quaint devices, and no archaism. And H.D. the Hellenist, introduced and sponsored by Ezra, became a fashionable commodity in pre-war London, where Greekness seemed to be everywhere: it was modish to go about in sandal-shod feet; to purchase sculpture with Greek curls; and to be seen reading Andrew Lang's translations of Homer.

***

Did it ever really happen, that encounter in the British Museum tea rooms? Had Ezra *really* imposed his will upon his young American friend in this way, declaring her poem to be 'Imagist', a fine example of a piece of work that would define a literary movement created by the very man who had named it into existence? Is it not all a little too pat? And is not my own account of it a little too slick and superficial too – and perhaps especially the bit about Andrew Lang.

I wrote that feature called 'The Invention of Imagism' for the *Financial Times* (hence the fact that it is in italics), and it was published in 1992, eighty years after that fabled encounter. Had Ezra co-opted Hilda Doolittle, turned her into a part of his story? And when was the account first written down anyway?

I am wondering about their friendship all over again, trying to piece together its details, in a high, dramatically sited garden at a place called Birling Gap on the south coast of England. I am also holding a copy of *End to Torment* in my hands, a brief memoir written by H.D. in 1958, almost fifty years after Ezra had pigeon-holed her and defined her as the founder member of a new movement that came to be known as Imagism.

He and H.D. had been childhood friends in Pennsylvania. She had been devastated when in 1908 he left for Europe. A little later she had joined him there. The memoir, part journal, part essay, is a document of drifting pain, sadness and bewilderment. H.D. is writing it in Kusnacht, Switzerland. She is in poor health. Her mood is fragile. She is thinking back to things that happened almost half a century before, to the actions of a young woman who was just beginning to find her own way as a poet. She has been urged by others to write down her memories of the Pennsylvania of her youth. She is setting all this down in the 1950s, which is a terrible time for Pound. The old friend she once judged to be either a *predatory cat* or a *hidden emperor* is still being held in a hospital for the criminally insane in Washington D.C., a prisoner in all but name. Was he an ogre who had never quite put away childish things? Or a magpie? Or perhaps a phoenix? One or another of those choices, certainly. For all that, she still feels much residual affection for him, that, yes, together with a sense of helplessness, an inability to *do* anything on his behalf. Few felt a similar degree of affection at that moment. Few were rising up in his defence. Her mind wanders to W.B. Yeats, those early portraits, in which his bow tie looked as fluttery as a butterfly. He has been dead almost twenty years. At least Ezra is still alive. Such dear, gone days…

Birling Gap, elemental and mysterious, is a good place to be thinking about the sadness of ageing poets, I am thinking to myself as I raise my eyes to the magnificent white chalk cliffs, so buttery and crumbly, that face the sea just along the coast from Beachy Head, a favoured spot for those seeking the quick exit of a leap into oblivion. There is nothing to stop them. This is nature wild and untamed. There is a pathway, dusty and scrubby at the moment, because there has been so little rain in the past few months, that leads up the side of the cliff. From where I sit, I can see the walkers climbing it because, as the name Birling Gap suggests, it is just here that the land slopes down, and opens up and out into a natural inlet. So I watch all these walkers – and there are many of them – as they ascend the broad, ragged track that will take them up to the top-most point. All this land is part of a national park called the South Downs, and the owner of the section that takes in the very edge of the land and these cliffs is the National Trust. And it is unfenced. Though it is still early morning, they are already ascending the track in packs and clumps, small and busy as ants, and some are already standing perilously close to the edge, and even peering over… These ever shifting, ever crumbling cliffs of chalk, which pass, depending upon the time of day and the ever shifting light, from a brilliant white, to beige, to a smudgy yellow, leave white dust on the palms…

H.D. writes compellingly and confusedly. Her thoughts keep on circling back on themselves. She thinks back to Ezra as a young man, operatically showy, with his ebony stick, cutting a dash in the midst of a circle of disciples. Then, in 1908, exactly fifty years ago, he had left, for Europe. She had followed him and, at a certain point, some years later, he is visiting her at a clinic in London. There is a child being spoken of. Whose child? Hers? Theirs? Was he not already married? Were they ever engaged to be married? And if that engagement was thwarted, who did so? Such confusion!

Circe's Ingle Emerges in East Sussex

Women? Pah! They were all one to Pound. In fact, in much of his writing (his satirical light verse is the exception), he doesn't much deal in women of flesh and blood at all. His women are usually idealised shapes, goddesses, creatures of myth, fantasy or idolatry, Circean temptresses elevated above the common ruck.

I am thinking about these matters as I walk to and fro down the beach, over which the great white chalk cliffs called the Seven Sisters rear, where the Downs meet the sea at Birling Gap in East Sussex. The sea's immensity is always humbling, its unboundedness, its mica glitter, its ceaseless changes of colour, the way it is never not pushily oncoming, from horizon to horizon.

I am on a level with this sea, on the beach now, yards from the rock pools through which my son's tireless powerhouse of a small Jack Russell noses and noses (he is called Vincent in homage to a painter from across the water), leaping across or weaving between one deliciously odoriferous rock pool after another with tremendous agility. Monet painted many of his seascapes well above such a sea as this one, up hill and behind his aunt's sea-facing house in Le Havre, so that the water's immensity, its awe-inspiring breadth and ceaseless shiftingness, seems in his paintings even greater and broader in scope and general impressiveness than ever.

Here at Birling Gap on the coast of southern England, the Dieppe ferry is leaving a shifting line of white in its wake as it moves with stealth out into the sea, from right to left, easing out from the port of Newhaven, that down-at-heel place. The cliffs at my back, for all their tallness, look so fragile by comparison with the sea's litheness and muscularity. They are such unstable structures. Sheets of blinding white chalk fall away from them when they are assailed by wind and rain, which settle in great heaps on the rocks beneath. All that buffeting by the elements has a knock-on effect, of course. There's really no telling when the side wall of one of the few remaining fisherman's cottages will give up the ghost and hurl itself with reckless abandon onto the beach.

And out of that sudden absence of chalk, improbable shapes reveal themselves, sculpted, scooped out, without the need for any intervention by human hand. As I go to throw yet another ball for my breathlessly eager canine companion, I glance at the portion of cliff behind where he stands and quivers in excited anticipation. Circe's Ingle! This recently arrived, deeply carved bowl is surely Circe's Ingle, where Odysseus found himself in such peril, that sorceress to whom Ezra draws our attention in the very first canto...

A Serious Discussion in a London Square in 2023: Could an Imagist Poem Get Away with Likening an Orange Giraffe to a King Tricked out as a Roman Soldier?

It is a cold March morning in the public garden at the centre of Golden Square, Soho. This is a congenial location. Somewhere at my back, on the upper floor of his brother's haberdashery shop, William Blake had his only public exhibition. That would have been in 1809. It was a failure, needless to say. The man who regularly conversed with angels found rapport with his fellow man, whether as artist or human being, much more challenging. Just off Golden Square, in Beak Street, a blue plaque marks the house where Antonio Canal (better known as Canaletto) once lodged, taking a break from the monotony of painting idealised scenes of Venice for aristocrats on the Grand Tour in the eighteenth century.

There are handsome wooden benches around the garden's perimeter, occupied by very few today. Where are the furious Chinese bat swingers who usually monopolise the ping pong table? Two public monuments stand on plinths facing me, one of King George II acting out the role of being a member of the Roman soldiery, the other a yellow giraffe with cheery orange splotches down its long neck. They face away from each other, as if acknowledging the absurdity of their proximity. Seeing them there, so weirdly juxtaposed, makes me think of Ezra's Imagist enterprise and, in particular that famous poem of his, just nineteen syllables in length, which pulls together two quite distinct images: various random faces in a crowd, and some petals on a wet, black bough. Is there any electricity between those two ideas? I ask myself more than half a century after I first read those words. I'm probably thinking about it too because just a few minutes ago I was emerging from Leicester Square underground station before beginning to thread my way through the streets of Soho to this bench on which I am now sitting.

The other day I picked up a thin anthology of Imagist poetry edited by Peter Jones in 1972, the year Ezra died, and the year that I graduated. Ezra's attempts to mould an unruly gang of individualists into a movement failed, of course. No one was quite biddable enough. What is more, the meaning of the word Imagist itself was hotly disputed. And why, when Ezra first used it, did he add an 'e' to the end, as if it were something French, and not the invention of an American who loved nothing more than gathering disciples around him in defence of a hot new cause? The most disappointing aspect of the whole enterprise was that so much of the work in that slender little paperback seemed such thin gruel, emotionally and intellectually, I discovered, when I read it at Gatwick Airport a few days later. It barely deserved to be read all over again.

A great deal of stodgy prose has been written about the origins of Imagism. It fomented a lot of anger too, much of it Pound's. You see, someone stole his baby soon after it was born. It was snatched out of the pram by the formidable, and formidably wealthy, Amy Lowell, who then turned it into what Pound witheringly described as Amygism.

Ezra could always turn a withering phrase. He was so good at fluff and blather and off-the-cuff put-downs.

Ezra Goes to Sea in a Coracle

Deal, on the Kentish coast, at the edge of the North Sea, is a hard-bitten place, where no amount of prettification (old, beach-facing houses newly slathered in pretty pinks and heavenly blues, for example) can disguise the fact that many a long dead smuggler's wrongs have not yet made for a right. France is plainly visible – and even the clock tower of Calais – when the light and the hour of the day oblige. I am in the company of two archaeologists, old and tried friends.

The house itself where I am staying, long and low-lying, almost sits on the shingle. It has been theirs for upwards of a decade. A narrow path, busy with walkers on their way to elsewhere (except for when they spot the teddy bear in the corner of the window) keeps the two apart. Look up and you notice that its roof level is rimmed by a white wooden balustrade from which you can observe, had you world enough and time, the many tragedies that have unfolded down the centuries along the treacherous Goodwin Sands. A handsome white telescope is at the ready, close to the upstairs window, cocked in the direction of the night sky.

It's the sea that's your main preoccupation though as you try to stare it down from that elevated spot. One hard nudge from the god of the winds, and you'd be up to your neck in salt and brine. The North Sea certainly takes an interest in the basement of this house at times of high water, slopping lazily around as if it were a friend fresh dropped in, and always so sluggishly reluctant to leave again.

It's late afternoon now, and a roseate blush hangs over the sea, as it prepares to play host to the blood red moon that will, to our astonishment, brim the horizon line part way through the eating of supper a little later. Could this place be the ultimate romantic option? A fanciful dream. The trouble is that the North Sea lacks pity, and always has. You're at the mercy of forces beyond your control. I stand in the guest room, staring down at the contents of my suitcase. What use are these red beach shoes against such murderously sharp and uneven underfoot stuff as you find on this beach?

The next morning, we all plunge down what looks and feels to me like an alarmingly steep cliff of shingle, and stumbly-venture in. As I swim, I begin to notice – others are being pulled away from me at alarming speed by a mightily muscular tide – that Ezra Pound, no less than he, young looking and red-bearded, is in the water beside me. But he's in a boat. I call out. He's working on his version of *The Seafarer*, he tells me. He's doing literature. I'm doing life. When I read his version some hours later, in a volume called *Personae* that I'd remembered to pack in my suitcase before leaving Clapham, I recognise that his prosody, choppily alliterative, had indeed taken its cue from the buck and the swing of the waves that morning. What a frail thing that boat of his seemed to be though, more a spinning coracle than anything else…

Archaeologists such as my friends make so much of fragments. They set them apart, raise them up, see so far into them. And so it is here, at the entrance to the front garden of this house, and all so prettily arranged in a giant terracotta bowl – a broken bottle, green as the depths of the sea, its cork stopper intact; a toppled kilner jar; a pine cone; the broken triangle of a Wedgwood plate; pebbles large and smooth as a child's fist, and all gathered inside a huge ceramic container, big enough for an elephant to slurp from, and all as if offered up to the elements. The sea is mightily audible from here, but beyond the reach of the camera because it repels the camera's eye by the relentlessness of its dazzle.

And all this early-morning wonder is playing out on a patio directly in front of me, whose outlook feels like the end of some branch line that Dr Beeching, that brute, failed to notice in 1963. The buffers are sited where the black and white tiling ends, aren't they? And when the steam from the still gently sighing locomotive disperses, the raspberries – two varieties, the red and the yellow! – will swim into view, and I shall eat them immediately before someone else, equally deserving, hoves into view.

Pound constructed his *Cantos* from a myriad of such fragments as the ones that fill this bowl in front of me, I'm thinking to myself as I lever in a mouthful of my host's late-morning porridge, made all the more delicious by a rich, dark, clotty sediment of Costa Rican sugar, but those words of his do not lie on the page reposeful, as do these fragments in this summer morning garden. They are jagged, rebarbative. He defended his writing method with reference to the challenges of modern art. Cézanne was such another, he counter-argued, when Yeats described *The Cantos* with mocking bewilderment following a visit he made to Rapallo in 1928.

The Sweepings

Yes, when Pound described his ongoing epic to Yeats over those long conversational evenings overlooking the Ligurian Sea in 1928, he aligned it with the tidal waves of The New. It would be like the art of modernity, he said, the art of Cézanne and Kandinsky, for example, in that it would be an art of fragmentation, an art of taking apart, and then of staring down at a heap of rubble. Vibrant rubble, of course. How could things be otherwise? How could anything of scale and pretension, any piece of writing which strove to regard itself as the equal of its historical moment, be otherwise? The century had been a tragedy, a horror. A modern poem could not but reflect that fact.

Unfortunately, he also described it in such a way as to suggest that the enterprise would not in fact be that at all. It would also be something monumental, with a reputation to come, engulfed and defined by the classics, by the story of Odysseus and his descent into the underworld, by Ovid, by Dante. The folly was to believe that it could ever be finished, tied up neatly, as Dante's *Divine Comedy* had been. It was inevitable that it would forever remain akin to a heap of broken bits in a terracotta bowl, unfinished and unfinishable. There was no longer a stable world order to underpin it. It was constructed from so much that was disparate, cobbled together recklessly, fragmentary memories, things snatched from the air. It could never have been an ordered whole. It could never be a monument. Instead, it became in the end a testament to one man's folly.

The Seduction of the Image

The idea of the image, something sharp, hard and uncluttered, held great appeal to me as a young poet. Ezra had fought for it, recommended it as an antidote, a way of freeing oneself of bad writing habits. I became a little obsessed by it too. It would turn poetry into something much sparer and keener-eyed, as Ezra promised, preached, fulminated. All the rhetoric, the fluff and the flummery, would fall away to reveal something pure and of itself, something disentangled from the puff of rhetoric, the incessant drone of story-telling, the boring to-and-fro of argument... This required careful study, a degree of quasi-scientific investigation. That was how I thought of it then, I, who knew nothing of scientific method. And so, at twenty-two years of age, during my final year as an undergraduate at Cambridge University, I did a thesis on Pound's idea of the image, written for the most part in a bay-windowed front room of a house in unfashionable Cockburn Street to the east of the city, furnished with rackety, self-made book-shelving of the kind that Ezra himself might have been eager to construct, he too being a whittler of crude wooden furniture.

Ezra in Queens' Lane

It was at Cambridge University that I began to get to know Ezra a little better, that man who would prove to be a maddening, on-off companion life-long. With my first term's grant and college bursary combined, I acquired: a fine Hacker record player with grey and black veneer; a complete boxed set of the *Collected Recordings of Anton Web*ern (as directed by Robert Craft) from the Cambridge Music Shop, a hushed and most rarefied emporium opposite the gates of Trinity College; a black opera cloak with a lemon silk lining from Ryder & Amies on King's Parade; a pair of wide-bottomed, violet trousers known as loons; brown, elbow-length gauntlets (plastic), and much else that was either flamboyantly Wildean or particularly taxing and highbrow.

I was teaching myself to be an intellectual *flâneur*, and such a person was required not only to look distinctive when walking along King's Parade, but also to have a wide appreciation of the works of Schönberg, Berg and Webern, no matter how alarmingly dissonant and unpleasant those products of the twelve-tone system might sound on first, second or even tenth hearing. I also began to acquire a multiplicity of books by or about my new obsession, Ezra Pound. Pound too had struck a pose in the literary salons of London. A poet must cut a dash, we both agreed on that.

I have these books by me as I write, the *Collected Shorter Poems*, inscribed 'Queens' College April '69', and, somewhat later, an edition of *The Cantos* and *Drafts and Fragments* of the last cantos that Ezra ever wrote. To swim in the waters of Pound's mind was bewildering at first. His earliest poems seemed to be completely at odds with his strident pronouncements as a critic. His early criticism talked good sense much of the time. A fledgeling poet could profit by it. His poems, on the other hand, and especially those youthful ones, seemed curiously archaic in theme and diction, throwbacks to the Victorians whom he was said to despise. He seemed to be not one but a whole range of people, and all talking at cross purposes to each other. Could these various Ezras ever be reconciled?

Acquiring Ezra

I can see by my own small, hand-written inscription on the first of the book's preliminary pages that I acquired my copy of Ezra Pound's *Drafts and Fragments of Cantos* CX-CXVII in the Student Bookshop on Silver Street, Cambridge, which was directly opposite the end of Queens' Lane, within spitting distance of the medieval gatehouse of Queens' College itself, in February 1970. That was my college, and in 1970 I was living there, within a minute's walk or so of this bookshop, which I visited, daily, to examine the poetry shelves – in order to discover what else might have arrived overnight that deserved – demanded – my immediate attention. This bookshop was a haven of books published by the smaller poetry presses – Fulcrum Press and the Grosseteste Press, for example – and it was therefore of great emotional importance to me. I was already a poetry fanatic in those days, and I have remained one life-long. The acquisition of new poetry was somewhat akin to the infusion of new blood. I would pale and wither without it.

The bookshop itself must have obtained the copy from Faber and Faber in London just days before I grasped hold of it – someone at the shop has written 13.2.70, in very faint pencil, on the very last page of the book. How eager I must have been to read it! The fact that I had bought this book – which represents the end point of more than half a century of work on what proved to be a tragic epic – suggests that I was already in the habit of buying almost anything I could find which bore the name of Ezra Pound. I say this because I had certainly not read the rest of *The Cantos* with any thoroughness by this point in my journey into the mind and the character of this exasperating man. I knew, already, that I was taking him on trust, that at some point soon I would want – be compelled – to read this book too because it was a part of a greater whole, which it would be necessary for me to encompass sooner or later. Such was the nature of my early commitment to my idea of the man, and all that he represented, which was by no means entirely clear to me. Call it irrational if you like. Irrational or not, it was already a compulsion.

What did I find in this book? What kind of a thing was it? For a start it was disappointingly slender, more a fumbling stutter of a book than anything else. The text began on page 7 and ended on page 32 – a mere 25 pages in all. As the title of the book suggested, several of these texts were fragments of cantos or notes and addenda, and even the ones which were complete were unusually brief. The tone is regretful. He speaks of incoherence, and of losing his centre, of the man who seeks good and does evil. Was it the author of those raving broadcasts over Radio Rome that he was thinking about when he wrote those words? All told, this is a mind at the end of its tether, as he declares.

This is the very same Pound who, in old age, had invited a young disciple called William Cookson (and his mother) to Schloss Brunnenburg, Pound's daughter's house in the Tyrol, then set him the task of trawling through scraps of lines and sentences just in case Cookson could find something worthy of preservation. In short, Pound could no longer trust his own judgement.

Ezra Let Loose in a Sheffield Classroom

What was it then about me and Pound? Why did we think that we would get on like a house on fire? I had first come across Pound at school, in a poem that caught my eye. It had happened during an English lesson, when

I was about eighteen years old. It described an encounter with a beautiful woman – more a vision of a woman than a real encounter, as would often be the case with Pound – in London's Kensington Gardens, and how she looked, as he put it, with such delicate memorability, like a *skein of loose silk blown against a wall*. Substantial as a something and as flightily, fleetingly insubstantial as an almost nothing. Simultaneously. I loved that image. I often think about it to this day. The slightly mysterious, Nordic tang of that word *skein* particularly appealed to me. And that idea – that image – of a loose piece of fabric blown against a wall, of a shred of fabric lifting off, caught by the wind, assuming a wind-sculpted shapeliness which would disappear again no sooner than it had arrived – stayed with me.

Years later, I would adopt a pseudonym under its influence: Jake *Foulard*, the wearer of a neck-hung scarf, worn with a carelessly jaunty fashionableness. Jake, like Ezra, would blow carelessly, affectedly, through the literary salons of London. Perhaps. In 1909, Ezra took a stroll through Kensington Gardens with his friend, the American poet William Carlos Williams. Williams later reported that Ezra always walked a step or two ahead of him.

The poem, half way through, introduces us, rather unexpectedly, to a group of children of the very poor. Until that moment you are rather thinking of Kensington Gardens as a place of fading refinement, with its fashionable people adrift in it, rather in the way that a *foulard* is borne along by the wind. Then these surly street kids shoulder their way in on the act and change it all. Pound refers to them as sturdy and unkillable. I was rather shocked by the brutality of that description, and by Pound's remark that such children would inherit the earth. He seemed to admire their tough-mindedess. I sensed that he preferred their bullishness to the anaemic refinement of the lady. Perhaps they reminded him of himself.

This fragment of engaging, rather acidic reportage was like no other poem I had ever come across before. The speaking voice was casually conversational, the line lengths variable. The verses seemed to find their own shape. The words were not boxed in by metre, rhyme. It managed to stand proudly upright on the page without metrical scaffolding of any kind. I was soon able to put a swanky French name to this kind of experiment in the modern manner: this was an early encounter with *vers libre*. What is more, it sounded utterly unlike the tum-ti-tum rhythms of 'Horatius at the Bridge' by Lord Macaulay, which was the only poem I had learnt by heart at school. We used to recite it, *en masse*, during dull Latin lessons. It still dins, like the regular feet of men tramping through Flanders mud, in my inner ear:

> Lars Porsena of Clusium,
> By the Nine Gods he swore
> That the great house of Tarquin
> Should suffer wrong no more.
>
> By the Nine Gods he swore it,
> And named a trysting-day,
> And bade his messengers ride forth,
> East and west and south and north,
> To summon his array...

When I re-read Pound's poem now, I recognise that its discovery in that English class at Firth Park Grammar School was the beginning of a new life-pursuit. An alternative religion was beginning to present itself to me which might loosely be described as the inward life of literature, and Ezra was to be one of its new deities.

A Hopeless Task

For better or for worse, the work by which the world remembers Ezra Pound is a long poem called *The Cantos*. Its title pays homage to Dante Alighieri, who wrote his *Divine Comedy* in groups of cantos or songs. Ezra Pound's *Cantos* were to become one of my new sacred texts, and Pound himself a figure of inscrutable authority. In fact, the inscrutability of Pound – what struck me at first was the near overwhelming impossibility of getting to grips with him at all – added enormously to his appeal.

To understand the *Cantos* would be the project of a lifetime – rather in the way that Christianity itself had seemed to me to be the project of a lifetime when I had been engulfed by it as a young teenager. His words – and especially the words of *The Cantos* – were thrillingly beyond my reach. I loved the idea of him, of his world, of his literary accomplishments, but what use was an idea on its own? What hope was there for me here? He had, it seems, encompassed so much: abstruse languages living and dead, knowledge of ancient civilisations, Oriental and Occidental. He seemed to have sprawled with such scholarly ease across so many fields. Would I ever be sufficiently well read to confidently seize hold of everything that he had thought, said and written, let alone find myself in the position where I could stand above him and pronounce upon his works and opinions?

Those who wrote about his *Cantos* – I had begun to read a pioneering study of Pound and his poetry by the Canadian critic Hugh Kenner at the kitchen table in Sheffield, quite ostentatiously, perhaps hoping that my relatives might read a word or two over my shoulder, and then back away, nodding their heads and sighing, a touch awe-struck – were almost as opaque as the poem itself.

Hugh Kenner's book, written six hours a day over six feverish weeks, and published in 1952, at a time when the poet was incarcerated in that hospital for the criminally insane in Washington D.C., was a pioneering study. Twenty years later, Kenner would write *The Pound Era*, which would once again argue that Pound was the most significant figure of the great Modernist experiment, greater even than T.S. Eliot, the man whose reputation, in the opinion of most critics, stood much higher.

I swum, wonderingly, in the waters of Kenner's prose, impressed, bemused, astonished by his recondite vocabulary. One thing became immediately evident to me: the critic of the works of Ezra Pound would never be expected to write clearly and simply because Pound himself was not a clear and simple writer. In order to prove himself the equal of the master, the disciple must match him in obfuscatory erudition. The authentic disciple had to sound like the master. It was incumbent upon him to be hectoring, gnomic, and a bit of a scold. It almost went without saying that he would also have to be very well read, and the absolute master of a range of abstruse vocabulary. In that book, I read words that I had never read before, and I dutifully wrote them down in my notebook in preparation for the future. The list included such specimens as these: *enchiridion, canorous...* Words as delicious conversation-stoppers.

Getting to grips with Ezra was an immensely difficult and often frustrating task, and yet the very fact that I was trying was of great importance to me, and a source of personal pride. I already sensed that to declare oneself a Poundian would be to discover that others were in awe of you because you were committing yourself to climbing a mountain that so few others had tried to climb. You belonged to a priestly caste, a small band of initiates.

Weighing the Gravity of *The Cantos* in Ward's Bookshop, Sheffield

When I look at my five-decades-old copy of *The Cantos* now, weigh its heftiness in my hand, admire its heavy, austere blackness, pick my way through, still quite tentatively and reverentially, its hundreds of pages of text, I am reminded of all that the idea of the book in general has meant to me. Seriousness. Inward questing. Secretiveness. Books, as objects, are sacred things, not to be treated lightly, not to be misused, not to be allowed to share the same physical space as messy foodstuffs. Their spines are not to be broken or put under needless pressure – I remember how I used to wince when I saw someone bend a book back on itself, as if it were a helpless contortionist being put through its paces by a mad and vindictive imposter of a personal trainer fresh off the streets. How could that person do such a thing to a book? Odd though it may sound, I have never really reconciled myself to the idea of the seriousness of paperback books. A paperback, essentially, is a piece of brain-jangling triviality: the inane, bibulous burblings of a fading starlet, page after page of fleetingly eye-beguiling puffery... Books need to have hard boards in order to express, confirm and sustain their trustworthiness, their indomitability, the sheer physical and emotional weight of their wisdom, their stiffly compacted knowledge.

When I first saw that copy of Ezra Pound's *Cantos* in the flesh in Ward's Bookshop down Chapel Walk in Sheffield, it was lying beside other serious-minded books on a table. I had already heard of it. It had been spoken of at school. I had read references to its great length and impenetrability. My appetite had been whetted for the terrible challenges that it posed. Its title, though I did not quite understand its significance, had already lodged itself in my brain as a milestone/millstone of sorts, something not to be avoided or got around – as the poet Basil Bunting also once said, when he wrote, in 1949, the year of my birth, on the fly leaf of Pound's *Cantos*, these words: *'There they are, you will have to go a long way round/if you want to avoid them./It takes some getting used to. There are the Alps,/fools! Sit down and wait for them to crumble!'*

I used to circle it on a Saturday afternoon, eyeing its quasi-biblical authority on that table, pivoting about its presence there in fascination and wonderment. Yes, the blackness of its cover always lent it such an authority because... well, were not Bibles black, always black? And I had

had my dealings with Bibles all right. My Christian adventures began when I was thirteen years old. I began to commune with a new friend called Jesus, whispering my prayers to him night and day, but especially at nights, after the lights were out. There was nothing odd about this. It was called prayer. It was what any devout Christian was obliged to do. It was his direct line to the Deity. Other rituals took place at bedtime. I would sit up in bed with my Bible and my Biblical commentary, the second being a little green booklet of explanation and exegesis. Each book of the Bible, and each segment of each book, was picked apart and served up fresh. All irregularities, inconsistencies and jarring strangenesses were smoothed away by that devout, faithful, faceless interpreter. This habit of studying the Bible, word for word, night after night, led to a settled mode of thinking about books in general: books were things to be studied, and studied hard. They were not to be fleeted through or scampered over. They were to be dug into like hard, rich, peaty earth. Only then would they yield up their riches.

I was carrying this reverential cast of mind with me when I stared down at that hefty book on Saturday afternoons in Sheffield in the late 1960s. And, later on, I would take the bus back home to Pitsmoor, up hill and down dale, and always on the fuggy-with-fag-smoke top deck, with grey, drifting, slithery fag ash settled underfoot, for the view's sake – still in a mood of restless wonderment, still pledging myself to that long and toilsome journey through *The Cantos* at some date in the not so distant future. It would be a spiritual journey of sorts, I recognised that. The name of the god alone had changed.

I see now that my discovery of this poem would be the beginning of a new life-pursuit, one which led me first into folly and unhappiness, and later in the direction of self-fulfilment. My old religion, that evangelical Christian faith of my early teenage years, had gone by the time that I first encountered Ezra, never to return. And now an alternative religion was beginning to present itself to me, the inward life of literature, and he was to be one of its new deities. Yes, this was not a monotheistical faith by any means.

The Puzzling Fascination with What's Difficult...

The fascination of what's difficult. These words appear in a poem by W. B. Yeats – they are both its title and its opening line – and they have always had an extraordinary pull for me. Ezra too is difficult (and especially his *Cantos*), and he is undeniably fascinating. Not always, of course. Sometimes his writing can be both flat and very boring. But is he fascinating precisely *because* he is difficult?

Wait a minute though. Why *should* what is difficult have more appeal than what is easy? Furthermore, why should words which are difficult to understand seem to promise more than words whose meanings are, it seems, immediately apparent and therefore instantly gratifying? Is it that the idea of a riddle muttered by some roadside sphinx must necessarily go hand in hand with the idea of profundity and the promise of a conclusion to some important quest? And why is Ezra so difficult anyway? He often introduces words, phrases, symbols and pictograms that mean nothing to us at first glance – until we make an effort to discover what they mean by referring, for example, to *The Guide to the Collected Cantos of Ezra Pound*. Is this not a little outrageous though, that we should need to buy a book in order to understand another book? Not necessarily. No scholar of the Bible or the Talmud would think it wrong or reprehensible. They might describe it as exegesis. So many sacred things are hidden from view, they would probably argue, precisely in order to conceal them from the eyes of the vulgar or the undeserving ignorant. *To he who has ears, let him hear*, as we read in *The Bible*. But are not Pound's writings mere prose and poetry? *Mere? Mere!* I hear his acolytes howl in disapproval. Not at all. Poetry is an elevated thing, and always has been! Are some of Pound's writing somewhat akin to sacred texts then? Pound also refers to things which only he could know – small events in his life, familiar names, etc. Why is he doing this? He seems to be suggesting that these private things are important precisely because he himself and his own writings are important. He has raised them to some level of importance by doing so. What is more, if we do happen not to know what he is referring to, it is our inadequacy. What a puzzle. What a riddle. What a conundrum…

To return to Yeats, that opening line to which I referred does not *commend* the fascination of what is difficult to us. Not at all! Quite the opposite in fact. It tells us that it *freezes the sap from the bone*, and turns life joyless into the bargain. Are Pound's obscurities likely to lead us into joylessness after all then? Oh dear.

The Lakeside Madonna Breezes by

Lago di Maggiore IV: July 2022

The lake-facing facade of the hotel is squeezed on each side by a narrow, twisty street – more rising alley or *salita* than street – which ascends steeply in the general direction of the upper village. To the left is the Via Guglielmo Marconi, and to the right the Via Massimo d'Azeglio. The street sign of the latter is in the pleasing shape of an armorial shield. Little happens in these streets during the daylight hours because it is almost too hot to climb them – even the small dogs are transported in their own little pushchairs lest they turn breathless from overmuch use of their legs. Much better to walk along the flat, part-cobbled, lake-facing promenade in front of the hotel, as so many do, at the much later, and much cooler, hour of the *passeggiata*.

The hotel staff are particularly exercised by the topic of unremitting, moistureless heat this morning. 'There have been so many perilous months of drought here in Piedmont – even the great River Po has run dry,' Nora, our regular waitress, tells us as she walks towards us with cafetière and cups precariously balanced on a silver tray. She raises her hands to the skies in supplication when we speak the word rain, having first set down the coffee. Another morning she is not quite so lucky: coffee spillage, meltdown, grief and shame, all Italian style.

That morning, we do the climb, part way up the Via Massimo d'Azeglio, and then take a cross street, on an unanticipated diagonal, until we meet, at the junction just below the unlovely market square where cars park when the stall holders have all gone away, the little 16th-century church of San Rocco. San Rocco himself, that miracle-maker and doer of endless good works (he was said to have devoted most of his energies to caring for victims of the plague), was born in Montpellier, and in later life he spent time beside this lake. When he too fell victim to the plague, an angel turned up to cure him. Oh the great good fortune of the godly! He got into some trouble though. When he arrived at the shores of Lago di Maggiore, someone – perhaps even several – took him for a spy from Angera, and even imprisoned him for five years. Spying on whom though? And why?

I am wondering these things as we walk into the little church. His effigy stands behind the high altar, a surprisingly handsome travelling saint, accompanied by a dog who seems to be forever turning and turning at his feet as San Rocco raises his eyes heavenward. There are a number of other effigies in niches in this small, rectangular, morning-sun-struck interior, and they are all the more affecting, if not alarming, for being almost life-size. One of them we will see again, after darkness falls.

We descend to the lake shore a little later by Via Guglielmo Marconi, the little street on the other side of the hotel. Paintings by local artists hang mid-street, held in place by wire that is almost invisible, some feet above our heads. One, quite a good copy of a Magritte, is of a man in a very heavy, formal suit and bowler hat, more suited to a dark, chilly day in Belgium, where Magritte was born. As we pass beneath the bowler hat, we notice that we can see into the hotel kitchen, where a great deal of furious preparation for greedy lunching is already being done – by all but our waitress Nora, who is enjoying herself by telling a story to a man with his back turned away from her. He is wrestling with a giant squid.

That evening something religious happens. We had read about it in the church earlier that day. It is an annual procession which involves carrying the statue of the Madonna del Carmine (in her role as patron saint of the Carmelite Order) from the church down to the lake's edge, presided over by Padre Giuliano, with prayers to the madonna offered, and a blessing of the lake. The first we know of it is the sight of a play of tiny, flickering lights on the waters of the lake, magical pin-pricks of floating illumination. At first we are puzzled, thinking it a strange trick of the moonlight. It is only later that we walk down to the lake side and stare down at all the floating candles.

Madonna del Carmine

A little later we are standing in the place where we ate breakfast that morning, above the little promenade, facing the boat stop. The procession begins, but not quite in the usual way. We seem to have arrived part way through. Perhaps they have been walking round and round and round…

The children straggle into view first. They are mainly taking pleasure in the little candles that they are cupping in their palms, hoping that the wind will not blow them out too soon. Then some tourists and parishioners surge untidily by, chatting happily as they go. And, finally, there appear two rather anxious looking and slightly dishevelled priests at the head of the procession, chanting as they go: *Madre di Dio, Prega per Noi! Madre di Dio, Prega per noi!, Madre di Dio!…* – that specious hope that beloved and time-tested words, spoken until exhaustion sets in, will make things right for us all, in the end.

It is only now that she passes us by, the statue of the Madonna del Carmine which habitually lives in that niche in the church, rather precariously balanced on her wooden trestle, which is being carried by four burly young men, one at each corner. Her blue outer garment, which looks wind-flurried, is punctuated with gold stars. It is that lake scene all over again.

They are all gently moving forward in a desultory and rather distracted sort of way. The lights bobbing on the lake look magical, there is no denying that. It's a kind of enjoyable mid-summer pageant really. You can take or leave the religious bit. No wonder the priests looked rather tired and anxious, and their vestments somewhat in need of ironing, if not cleaning. Is there much piety or godliness on display here this evening? Surprisingly little.

Did Ezra have much to do with religion? Was he godless or godly? Somewhere in between perhaps. One evening in Rapallo, walking up the little *salita* towards the little house where he had deposited his mistress Olga (he and his wife Dorothy were domiciled in the valley), he had a vision of gods in the air. Gods are everywhere in *The Cantos*, of course, afloat on the azure air, sources of wonderment. He once, as a young man, wrote what amounts to a kind of credo called *Religio*. Gods, he wrote, are states of mind, forms we conjure into being…Sometimes they take form, especially when they manifest themselves as the gods of antiquity – Apollo, Diana, the Cytherean goddess. Sometimes it feels as if they are standing behind us. You can humour them, and even feed them, with flowers…

Poems Made by Words

At Cambridge University in the late 1960s, the idea of thinking of a poet in the context of his or her own life story, of regarding a poet as a human being who suffers pain and may even show emotion from time to time rather than as a brilliant word machine, felt wholly alien to one's nature. When we engaged with poetry then, we studied and nit-picked over words, not poets. Poets were their words. Poetry was written by language, and not by human beings. Anything other than those words on that page were an irrelevance and a distortion. Hadn't Hugh Kenner said as much in his early study of Pound, that the biographical element was an irrelevance?

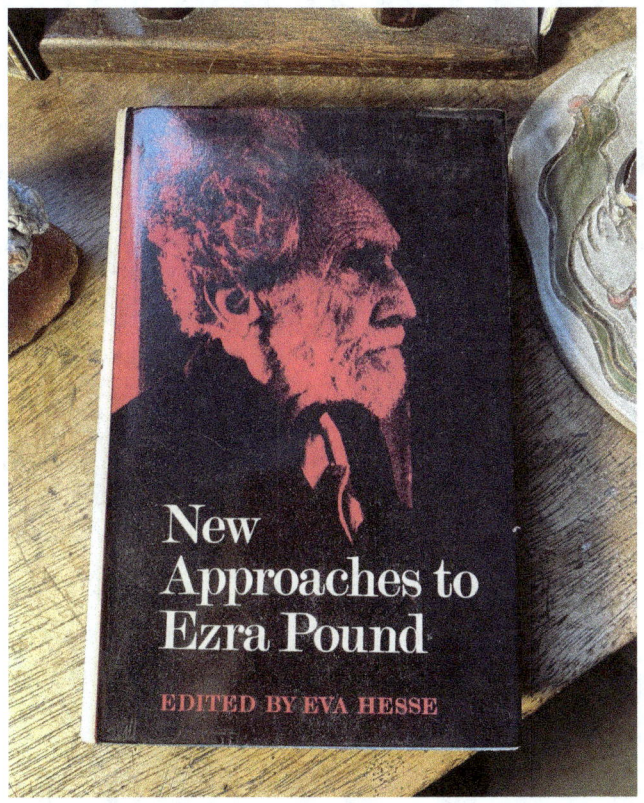

Ezra was one of those disembodied spirits, uttering words that were both timely and timeless, wholly set apart from the span of years through which I – or he – happened to be living. Is this quite true though? In fact, it was his *image* in old age – shock-haired as if floating through ether, reproduced on the cover of a book called *New Approaches to Ezra Pound*, I remember staring and staring at as I sat one afternoon beside the River Cam close to a pub called The Mill, steadily drinking pint after pint – which gave him much of the meaning that he had for me then: distant, hieratic, inscrutable. That image induced in me, on that sun-struck afternoon, a state of near mystical reverie. This man had clearly communed with the gods, which (loosely) included Dante, Homer and Confucius. I did not know then that he had banged out his words on a Corona typewriter (he wore out quite a few of these). Nor that he was a practical man, who had made his own furniture. In photographs, you can often see him sitting in one of those very uncomfortable looking, hand-crafted wooden chairs. He was not averse to the various latest manifestations of modernity either – when he first saw a film of Mickey Mouse, in Italy during the 1930s, he was as thrilled as all the rest of the onlookers. Even Ezra's life as a prophet and a scold could also allow a little space for levity.

What is more, many of the older poets writing at the end of the 1960s seemed rather similar to each other, abstracted, even standardised, in their use of language. You could almost imagine that the same machine had written all the poems that they had written. At least, that's how it rather seemed, though if we had expressed that idea out loud to ourselves, we would have recognised immediately the absurdity of such a notion. Poems were machines made out of words, and it was our task to analyse their intricate mechanisms, how all those cogs and all those wheels interlocked, to take them apart and marvel at each separate bit. This practice was called close reading. It was a serious pursuit, and the fact that it was so serious meant that the subject itself – the study of English literature – became serious too. We weren't just idly leafing through books like the commoner beyond the walls. We were engaged in the serious analysis of great literature in the company of experts.

Yes, books were written by language, and not by human beings. The physical fact of them, their inviolability, their unchangeability as objects, gave them an authority and an objectivity. It scarcely occurred to me in those days before I myself became an editor and a writer that bookmaking was a human process, that books were subject to late changes of mind by vulnerable, uncertain, self-correcting authors. In fact, I remember very clearly the moment that this fact was brought home to me. It was almost a revelation when it happened.

Many years later, early in the 1990s, I found myself reading the unbound proofs of a new collection of poetry by Seamus Heaney. I was preparing to interview him for *The Economist*. The book was called *Spirit Level*. I needed to think about it before finished copies were available from the publisher, and so I had been sent a set of page proofs to work from. Leafing through them one morning, I was suddenly brought up short by the sight of a correction, in pen, by Heaney himself, the scoring through of a phrase, and its replacement by another. At this late stage in the publishing cycle, he had decided to revise a line of one of his own poems. To this day I remember my shock at the sight of this oh-so-human intervention. Poems were not unbudgeable monuments after all then. They were man-made things, forever in the re-fashioning, until they were finally abandoned.

It was years later still that I discovered an even more extreme example of late editorial decision-making, and of how the most fragile and despised of materials can bear a huge freight of meaning. Ezra wrote one of the most important sections of his *Cantos* in the summer of 1945, during his months of incarceration by the American authorities at Pisa, before he was returned to America, charged with treason. As he wrote, he sent sections of it to his daughter Mary for typing and preservation.

Any poet knows the importance of the opening lines of a poem, how those first words can set a scene, fix a mood, announce a theme. Pound added new opening lines to the first poem in the *Pisan Cantos* that would give it an edge of great political significance. In homage to Mussolini, recently captured and hung by the heels alongside his mistress Clara in Milan, Pound evoked that scene of public humiliation in order to draw attention to his abiding Fascist loyalties. The lines themselves were written on a fragment of lavatory paper. Many of those *Cantos* were first written in the pages of a child's schoolbook that a Jewish chaplain at the camp gave to him one day.

Poetry in the 1960s

It is quite difficult to think back to how poetry was regarded in the 1960s when I first began to read Pound's words as a schoolboy in Sheffield, and later as an undergraduate at Cambridge. Poets – even poets such as Ezra – were less newsworthy then. There were no big poetry prizes in those days. Poets were not generally talked about. Poetry readings, and the selling of books through such events, was not common, although the year 1965 – three years before I went up to university – had seen the beginnings of the kind of mass readings' culture that we are all so accustomed to enjoying (or enduring) now. That was the year the first Poetry International was staged at the Royal Albert Hall in London, an event which brought together Allen Ginsberg, Lawrence Ferlinghetti and others of the Beat Generation. It became the stuff of legend.

The more massively authoritative the book, the more it seemed to crave my attention in those days. I remember returning repeatedly to look at the fat spines of George Bernard Shaw's *Collected Plays* and *Prefaces*, two hefty volumes which were quite as thick as a Victorian Bible or the *Collected Plays* of Shakespeare. I yearned not so much to read Shaw's words as to have read them. Shaw was not an especial favourite. I didn't drool over the possibility of seeing his plays at the Sheffield Playhouse, though I would dutifully buy my ticket when new productions of the plays turned up. No, what appealed to me was the massiveness of the books themselves, and everything that massiveness represented: authority, knowledgeability. I knew that he had been a hugely opinionated man. I wanted to have encompassed these books so that I would feel thickened out with Shaw's literary knowledge, facts, opinions. A thin boy at every age except babyhood, I lived in horror of being too thinly read, of having nothing to say when the moment came to declare oneself.

Ezra Pound v Stanley Cook

There were certain difficulties associated with the idea of Ezra, quite separate from the daily struggle of understanding his writings. My burgeoning allegiance to the idea of him and what he represented had, even when at school, found itself at odds with another important influence in my life, and in fact in direct conflict with a man who had quickened my appetite for the writing life, and nurtured my ambitions to be a poet more than anyone else. This man was the poet Stanley Cook, my English teacher at Firth Park Grammar School in Sheffield. It was Stanley who showed me how to begin to make my own small way in the world of poetry. He commented on my work, he introduced me to the names of some of the poetry magazines to which I could send it. He began to teach me a certain doggedness of application.

Stanley Cook

As a practising poet, Stanley Cook could not have been more different from Ezra Pound. Stanley was a poet who cherished the idea of the local: local habits, local people, local locutions. He wrote of Sheffield, its particular people, and the way they lived their lives. He saw in the local the essence of human life. He saw in the ordinariness of the day-to-day the utterly extraordinary. He practised a writing which deliberately lacked lustre, flamboyance, and any degree of self-conscious swagger. He would never have introduced a word from a language other than English into his poetry. Stanley Cook, I believe, distrusted and perhaps even despised the Americans who had arrived in England in the early decades of the twentieth century to show the English how to practise the ancient craft of poetry in our times. Did we really need to be taught to suck eggs? No, we needed no such teachers as Ezra Pound and T.S. Eliot, with their spurious learning and their self-conscious internationalism. Our native traditions were quite strong enough to sustain us. That was his position. Ezra, in his view, was little better than a loud-mouthed soap-box orator from an alien, unhistorical elsewhere.

And so my fascination with Ezra, which grew and grew as I read and re-read a grey paperback edition of his *Selected Poems*, a volume with an introduction written by his publisher T. S. Eliot, was obliged to live a half-buried life at first because I admired Stanley so much, and I had no wish to be in open conflict with him. He had so much to teach me by example, as writer, thinker and human being.

There was another man who played an important part in my writing life from a very young age, and he too caused me to harbour life-long suspicions about Ezra and the way he expressed himself. This man was Jonathan Swift, who amazed me by the force and simplicity of his words, the bite of his humour. Swift's incisiveness and simplicity haunted and impressed me mightily from the start, the ability to cut through, to deflate, to level a deadly humorous barb, to eviscerate a fool... How could a man of the early eighteenth century have written so clearly? Why had the Victorians, living so long after, chosen to write such long and complicated sentences by comparison? Surely words have a duty to be clear and direct. Why, then, had Ezra too chosen to be so un-simple? Was it to do with the poetry of our time or the nature of poetry in general? Or was it something about Ezra as a human being? And yet even that was not quite true. Ezra was not always obfuscatory, I discovered. When he was writing prose and not poetry, he could use words like a weapon that struck to the heart.

Where to Read Ezra

Where exactly did I read Ezra when I was an undergraduate? The place itself was always important to me. I had an abhorrence of reading casually, and perhaps even of being seen to read casually; of sitting, for example, on a bench in a public park where un-seriousness or the casualness of daily life, complete with its fragmentary conversations, its human squeals and its pram squeaks, all life's trivial inconsequences, passed by. I did not wish to see or to hear noisy young children pleading for attention from their mothers. I wanted to be enveloped in all the solitariness and the silence of serious study.

And so I opted for Queens' Old Library, which had once been a rather lugubrious Victorian chapel, with its severe central aisle and its metal book stacks to left and to right, and, tucked in beside each stack, a small wooden table with a chair, suitable for one reader alone. I remember it was there that I first began to get to grips with such wild works of Ezra's middle years as his *Guide To Kulchur* (1938), which seemed to seethe with anger at man's follies and failures of judgment. I read it until midnight was fast approaching, until my eyes burned in wonderment and admiration and much incomprehension, while those hot strip-lights crackled and fizzed high above my table, as if I were an egg in a pan. Needless to say, I was often the last to leave.

The Appeal of Elitism

Pound was an elitist, unashamedly. He had no truck with mediocre writing or second-rate thinking. Words, for Pound, were in the care of the *literati*. It was their task, collectively, to keep the language clean and precise, to ensure that words described things accurately. There was to be no compromise, no slide or slither. I knew that, and I welcomed it. It struck me as being both rigorous and admirably idealistic. If it also meant that it condemned the sloppy, indifferent majority to the waste bin, so be it.

What is more, our unpromising beginnings made such an idea appealing, to both of us, I sensed that. Why *not* stand accused of behaving with arrogance and stridency? We had nothing to lose, and everything to reach for. Ezra had acquired all that he knew by his own efforts. He had often behaved badly – by the standards of the day. In 1907, for example, he was dismissed from a junior post as teacher of French and Spanish at Wabash College, Crawfordsville, Indiana for having a woman in his room overnight. A hungry burlesque performer, he had happened upon her in the streets of the town, and had brought her back to give her some shelter. Unfortunately, having a young woman in your room – even if you were sleeping on the floor and she was occupying the bed – was a dismissible offence at the turn of the 20th century in the educational establishments of the mid-west.

Pound had been a noisy, overbearing, cocksure man, and I made a list of some of the words – nouns and adjectives – that might best describe him, wondering to what extent any of these words might just as well describe myself: ranter, pedagogue, campaigner, fixer, outsider, know-all; impatient, tetchy, quarrelsome, pugilistic, tireless...

When he judged, he did so fiercely, intemperately. He swung the axe from the shoulder. He was never suave or polite or polished. He seemed to enjoy handing out reading lists. He scolded, barked at his readers for not knowing enough, telling them that they should be looking not *here* but *there*... He pulled strange texts out from obscure corners, and told us that this was the essential reading, not all that other stuff endorsed by mainstream judgment. In short, he was his own self-trumpeting Ezuversity. Unlike T.S. Eliot, he never pussy-footed around his own judgments. He never minced his words. And yet his judgments were often couched in such a way that they seemed carelessly provisional, as if, in spite of all the bluster and the rancour, he too wanted to hedge his bets. Perhaps some part of him recognised that he was going at it too hastily, too impatiently, to arrive at a settled and fully defensible view. He swung a punch at us, and then stepped back a pace or two...

He was always too reckless to be a scholar of the more conventional stamp, too lacking in carefully-does-it, inch-by-inch sobriety. I forgave him for that. It all seemed very human – and thrillingly unnerving in its way.

Reading and Writhing

At university, my attitude towards reading and writing became more and more defining of my character. Ezra played his part in this, the elusive density of so much of his writing, and the fact that I admired him, increasingly, for what often, at times, appeared to be his deliberate bouts of obtuseness tending towards perversity. A significant part of him does not quite want us to know what he wants us to know – in spite of his critical pronouncements as a young man, which might suggest that the opposite ought to be the case. It has often been said that good poetry poses peculiar emotional and intellectual challenges to the reader – think no further than Shakespeare, for example. But it seemed that the poetry of the 20th century offered more challenges than most. And I admired it for that reason, for the fact that it seemed so set apart from its readers, that it yielded up its meanings so grudgingly, and only after the application of such effort. Poets, it seems, belonged to some kind of a priestly caste. To become an initiate would require a long and arduous journey.

I think of these things when I reflect on some of the essays I wrote in those days. Though a common enough, acne-scarred boy myself from the most humdrum of social circumstances, I craved to belong to a world which was completely uncommon. Part of me wanted my words to be beyond the understanding of the average reader. And it was for this reason that I wrote, in part at least, in order not quite to be understood, in a hectic, fragmentary, laconic fashion. All this was quite deliberate. I would define my own ideas in ways that caused even me to be slightly baffled by them. I was slightly beyond the reach even of myself. Similarly, the poetry

I came to admire most of all was often only semi-comprehensible, full of ambiguous turns of phrase. Why was this so good? Because it was a reflection of the fact that reality itself was extremely difficult and complicated – and there was nothing more complicated and difficult than the perplexing inner nature of twentieth-century man himself. It followed therefore that the only authentic writing, the only kind of writing that was faithful to the nature of today's tortured reality, would be dense and difficult too. All the rest was froth, un-seriousness, popular entertainment.

Gaudier's Ezra

There was one other place in Cambridge where I found Ezra, on one particular summer's afternoon, after I had taken a slow cycle ride to the end of Queens' Lane. At the eastern end of that lane, just as you reach the traffic lights, you can still see a small row of modest, interconnected cottages on rising ground to your left. This was – and is – Kettle's Yard, once the home of H.S. Ede, who had in the 1930s been a curator at the Tate Gallery. Jim Ede had been an art collector throughout his life, and his marvellous collection of paintings, sculptures and objects – pebbles arranged in a semi-circle on a table top, for example – was lovingly and tastefully dispersed throughout his home, which consisted of these three seventeenth-century cottages knocked into one. Displayed on the walls of the attic room of one of these cottages, I discovered a whole series of pen-and-ink drawings by Henri Gaudier-Brzeska.

Gaudier sculpted the marble bust of him in London in 1914 which became known as the 'Hieratic Head'. Before he carved the bust itself, Gaudier did hundreds of drawings in his studio beneath the arches in London, with his tempestuous model, Ezra, sitting patiently in front of him, uncharacteristically at rest. Most of these drawings are now lost. One of the few to survive is in Kettle's Yard, Cambridge. It is severely angular, almost mechanically so. You can see a slash of goatee beard, experience for yourself that ferociously concentrated gaze. He bears more than a passing resemblance to Trotsky on that day – which, had that been pointed out to him in later life, would surely not have entirely displeased him.

Aside from that drawing by Gaudier, I knew almost nothing about Pound the man until much later. He was an abstraction to me, words on a page, not someone I might ever have met in a pub or engaged in conversation. He was the sum total of his words, and of the general ideas that I was striving to extract, with considerable difficulty, from those words. It was proving to be as difficult as having a tooth pulled in the days before the invention of anaesthetics.

Walking in Ezra's Shadow in South Kensington

I left Cambridge with a heart-felt sigh of relief in the summer of 1972, having written a thesis on Ezra and the origins of Imagism in my final term. Times were favourable to the young graduate in those years of full employment. Within weeks I had landed my first job as a junior editor, in South Kensington – the salary was £1,600 a year, which struck me as a marvel back then. I was also within relatively easy walking distance of Church Walk, that tiny clutch of houses at the foot of Kensington Church Street, where Ezra Pound once lodged as a young man in the teens of the 20th century. He too had once arrived in London and pursued a career of sorts as poet and editor.

His slash-and-burn tactics with T.S. Eliot's *The Waste Land* had worked a treat, for example. He had trimmed a prolonged fit of garrulousness into a masterpiece. To be an editor was to find oneself in a position of great power and influence, and what is more, it was a power that could be exercised behind the scenes. An editor, like a poet, could be an unacknowledged legislator.

Welcome to the Serenissima

I Arrive in Venice for the First Time in 1972,
Unaware of Ezra's Presence There

In the summer of 1972, that year of my graduation, I had also been in Venice for the first time, and therefore closer to Pound physically than ever before in my life, a fact of which, alas, I was completely unaware. My partner and I had travelled all the way from London in an old blue Ford van that did not quite survive the ordeal of covering such distances. We abandoned it, radiator smoking, beside the road in Ingolstadt on the way back, piled what we could into a pair of oh-woe-is-me rucksacks, and headed north. Had I knocked on the door of Pound's modest home that summer – 252 Calle Querini, that former gondolier's cottage in the Dorsoduro, a quarter much colonised by the English – I might even have hoped to say hello to him. Unlikely, as it happens. Pound would live for just a few short months longer, and he was most reluctant to speak to anyone in the last years of his life. In fact, he had become notorious for his taciturnity. It would be another dozen years before I entered that house, and then it would be his mistress that I would be talking to, Olga Rudge, whose father bought that cottage for them in 1929, on the eve of the Great Depression.

Ezra's Obsession with Venice

Ezra Pound could never get enough of Venice. He went there for the first time in 1898, as a boy of thirteen, in the company of his Aunt Frank, who lived in New York City most of the time. That first European trip was an ambitious one. It took in Paris, Brussels, Cologne, Mainz, Nuremberg, and then Venice... He was ravished by the magnificent physical decrepitude, the stupendous after-life, of this once great city, suspended on water, simultaneously embodied and dream-like. Yes, to experience it was a little like experiencing a dream of itself.

He was right, of course. Almost everyone in the civilised world has always agreed with him. Venice is undeniably more agreeable, as Ezra once wrote, than Wyncote, Pennsylvania – or even than Madison Avenue and 47th Street – and he returned there again and again. He once made a list of the years in which he had paid some of those early visits: 1898, 1902, 1908, 1910, 1911, 1913, 1920. So, at a conservative estimate, Ezra had been there seven times by the time he was thirty-five years old.

Who would not wish to do so though? The sight of Saint Mark's Square as you approach it from across the lagoon on a sunny day for the first time is like nothing else on earth. Forever after you wish that you could repeat that first experience of pure visual theatre. No wonder the world's ambassadors were awe-struck and intimidated. That is, of course, precisely what the Venetians wanted to happen. They wanted the visitors to bow down and worship, to undergo what is still an almost unearthly experience. It looks – and it feels – ravishingly unreal. Millions have thought so, and continue so to do. Entire anthologies could be assembled – entire anthologies *have* been assembled – from the words of great writers singing their praises of Venice. This is why Venice is always so crowded with milling, jabbering groups of awe-struck onlookers.

In 1908 Ezra published his first book there, at his own expense – well, it was more likely at his father Homer's expense. (His father gave him generous financial support life-long.) One hundred copies were printed, by A. Antononi. The book was called *A Lume Spento*. Translated into English, that means: *With Tapers Quenched*. Pound lodged at Calle dei Frati 942, in a room that overlooked the San Trovaso Canal (the building's door is in a side alley), overlooking the 'squero', an old boatyard where gondolas are made and repaired to this day.

All Mortar and no Bricks – or the Voice of Silence

Another traveller with Ezra Pound on his mind arrived in Venice in 1972, that year of his death. He was called Alan Levy, and he had travelled across all the way from America with a photographer called Horst Tappe in tow. Levy had something of a reputation as a journalist, best known for his in-depth profiles of writers puzzlingly described as 'living immortals', which means those who were still certifiably alive, and had reputations which were almost certainly bound to grant them immortality in the end. A bit of a guessing game? What the hell. These profiles were published in *The New York Times Magazine* during the 1970s.

Levy's grand plan was to interview Ezra on such matters as these: Pound's work and influence; the meaning of *The Cantos*; the writers he had championed; the poet's engagement with politics, economics and Fascism, etc, etc. A broad and far-reaching agenda. He would then write up their conversations first as a feature, and then as a book.

That grand scheme would in due course be published in book form, eleven years later, as *The Voice of Silence*, but it was surely not the book that Levy had hoped and rather expected to write. Alas, it did not go to plan. Pound could not have been less willing to talk to him. And yet the book exists. It is short, one hundred and fifty pages in length. And how much of it are the spoken words of Ezra Pound though? Levy found Pound to be in a mood of hyper taciturnity. My guess is that Pound's contribution consists of approximately one hundred words, which means two-thirds of a word per printed page.

How then did the book manage to be so long? Padding is the answer. There is, for example, a detailed bibliography 'from Hamilton College to Hallmark Cards', as full and as garrulous as the author could possibly make it, which runs to forty-six pages. Then comes the chronology of Pound's life (ten pages); a comprehensive portrait in quotes (by other people, of course, ranging from friends like William Carlos Williams, to implacable opponents such as Irving Howe); and, finally, Levy's own guide to Pound's work in poetry and prose (he even advises us on which audio recordings to listen to, and in which particular order). He tenderly holds your hand through all the challenges, the screaming frustrations, the be-puzzlements, advising you on what to read and when, and what to leave until the very end, in order to try to guarantee that your enthusiasm will not sag or disappear altogether in mid-ocean. That section adds another twenty-seven pages.

Setting aside for a moment the matter of his death, 1972 was a strange year altogether for Ezra Pound. In that year an immense, encyclopaedic book was written about him, his world and his influence, by Hugh Kenner, the Canadian who had been the most loyal interpreter of his gnomic world. The book itself was called *The Pound Era*, and it sets him at the centre of a group of great literary achievers – a quotation on the back of the cover of the paperback edition gives their names. Needless to say, they are all men.

In other respects, 1972 was a year in which Pound was wilfully ignored. In January of that year a professor of English at the University of Maine called Carroll Terrell nominated him for an honorary degree. (Eight years later Terrell would publish a standard doorstop called *A Companion to the Cantos of Ezra Pound*). The proposal was later withdrawn. A whiff of treachery still hung in the air. It was also in the year of Pound's death that he was nominated for the annual Emerson-Thoreau Medal (worth $2000) for distinguished services to American literature, awarded by the American Academy of Arts and Sciences in Boston. He had many supporters, but the governing council held a special meeting and vetoed awarding the medal to Pound on moral grounds. The man was a fascist, one of the opposition told the *New York Times*.

The most interesting moment of Levy's book withholds as much information as it seems to wish to offer. He, Olga and Pound have just returned, in the dark, to the gondolier's cottage after a long evening out at a local restaurant. Ezra, exhausted, has gone upstairs to bed. A siren sounds the *acqua alta* alert. They are stacking books and other valuables onto high surfaces, out of harm's way. Levy thinks he recognises a book that Olga seems to be intent on concealing inside a damask napkin. It's by Mary de Rachewiltz, the child born out of wedlock that she and Ezra put out for informal adoption to a farmer in the Tyrol. In 1972 Mary had published a memoir called *Discretions* – that title is a knowing nod in the direction of Ezra's *Indiscretions* of 1923, and its peppery, staccato delivery reminds you much of her father's hectic manner of address. Levy asks Olga what she thinks about the book. Olga flies into a rage of anger and grief and love and frustration on the subject of Mary. Levy tells us that much, and nothing more. Much to his regret, his mouth must remain sealed as to the details, he tells his readers, causing us all to howl in frustration.

Mary remained Ezra's standard-bearer life-long. She translated his *Cantos* into Italian.

Selective Taciturnity

Was Ezra's silence selective? Did he say so little to Levy because he did not especially *like* him? Did he find Levy tedious or irritating? Did Pound sit up in bed in his pyjamas in that upstairs room and watch Levy, head bowed over his reporter's spiral-bound notebook, breathless with awe, leafing through his huge list of topics, and loathe the very idea of him? Was he sick of answering the same old questions over and over again? Had he done with all that guff, all those slick headline-hunters?

The fact is that this was not always the case. Pound did talk to a few. Perhaps if Levy had been someone else altogether, someone Pound found more congenial, the response would have been quite different. Could youth, a little more charm, and less of a relentless agenda have helped perhaps? That seems to have been the case with a young Irish poet called Desmond O' Grady.

O'Grady first heard from Pound when he was 21 years old, and living in a Cistercian Monastery on Caldey Island, just off the coast of Wales. Pound was enquiring about a little book of poems that O'Grady had written. O'Grady was astonished that his hero should be in touch. Pound was still incarcerated in Washington D.C. Where had Pound found his address? It was like a visitation from the Holy Ghost. The young man's response was admiring, close to idolatrous. To be in touch with the Master, the greatest poet since Dante! Their friendship gathered pace – Pound and Olga went to stay with O'Grady when he later lived in Rome. In fact, Pound moved in with him for a while. O'Grady stayed with Pound and Olga in Venice.

He even accompanied Pound to the Spoleto Festival in 1966, remarking (in a fond memoir that he wrote after Pound's death) upon the fact that Pound refused to be introduced by Stephen Spender, such was his likely contempt for the man. O'Grady speaks of nothing but good behaviour – which seems to have included words in plenty – from the crusty, cussed old sage, and even a conspiratorial partnership: at one moment, Pound makes it clear to O'Grady how tiresome he finds Olga's fussing over him. Needless to say, he was with Pound at the end.

There is a pattern to be observed here. Pound liked nothing more than young admirers. He loved to be loved by acolytes, to take pleasure in the reverence of those who were in awe of him, to bask in the glory of being the sage who had survived against all the odds. Who would not? The young are so much easier to deal with than one's contemporaries, who might include neglected wives or former friends who have experienced the full force of one's fury or betrayal or casual indifference. The slate is clean! Pound plied the young with advice, gave them readings lists, steered them along. He liked nothing better than to be Papa Pound, set apart as a magnificent survivor of the worst that fate could possibly throw at a man. And this is how we so often see him in Venice, in his twilight years, a magnificent monument, in cloak and perfectly calibrated hat, poised and posed beside a gondola, Titan amongst the Poets, as the plaque now reads above that door in Calle Querini, so cherished by the eager eye of the camera.

Lago di Maggiore V:
the Soothing Balm of a Postcard Scene

I wake up in the hotel room on that first morning beside the shore of the lake with this odd Ezra word swimming around inside my head, the Greek adjective he often used to describe Odysseus: *polumetis, polumetis*. It means many-minded, a man of many talents, a man smart in so many different ways. Irritation begins to rise in me at the thought of Ezra's clownish absurdities, not least his claims to be a polymath, if not an all-encompassing genius. Was it not Ezra who, according to his publisher James Laughlin, thought that he could solve the war in the Pacific by trading Wake Island for a complete set of the classic Noh plays? What to do about my sad and incurable addiction to a man capable of such antics?

I put the postcard on the bed, the one I'd picked up in reception when we arrived. I lay it down on the counterpane with great and solemn care. It shows the lake shore, with the tidy wedge of the little village of Cannero pushing itself down towards the water as if sun-thirsting, lake-thirsting, and the wooded mountains rising behind. The hotel itself faces onto the lake, with the mooring place for the boats to the islands in full view directly in front of it. The restaurant, with its awnings to enable outside dining when the sun is at its most tormenting, is in the closest building of all.

When the heavy, brocaded curtains of our bedroom are thrown back, the counterpane is suddenly enriched, thickened by sunlight. This little postcard scene, in all its aerial serenity, seems to rise up towards me from its rich orange ground, as if almost afloat above the dense weave of the grounding fabric. It is an entirely people-less view, stunned into the utmost tranquillity by sunlight, as an aerial prospect must always surely be because our eye is too distant to see any scurry of human life. How pleasing to be rid of all the human torment, and to see nothing but that little quay protecting, as if with a loving arm, its half dozen boats, with the village rising as if to greet the tower of a church, and the mountain side rearing up beyond and above, so green, so deeply green and wooded...

Reviewing Ezra in the 1980s

How do you begin to make any living of sorts as a writer? What about book reviewing? Wasn't that a part of it? I did a great deal of that in the 1980s and 1990s, and less so after that. Why did I do it anyway? To earn the pitifully meagre sums you were always paid, which generally meant that the more prestigious the outlet, the smaller the reward would be? (Beware of being offered anything being loftily ascribed by the likes of, say, Oxford University Press, as an *honorarium*. That creature is the cruellest and meagrest joke of them all.) To acquire books for free that you would otherwise be forced to buy with money that was needed more pressingly elsewhere? To keep up with your private literary obsessions? A little of all three.

In 1991 I talked to Anthony Burgess at the Savoy Hotel about book reviewing (amongst many other things), and the moment that has stayed with me longest was when he exclaimed, with such spitty vehemence, after the tape recorder was turned off needless to say, that book reviewers were *such cheats*! Did that mean that he was? I wondered, without ever quite asking. In my earliest and callowest writing and book-reviewing days, I was too serious and solemn faced, too slavishly dutiful and boringly serious-minded, to be a bare-faced cheat. I read every word of every book, cover to cover. I also made voluminous notes in a hand small enough to be barely legible. And when I came to write the review itself, much of it consisted of the arduous stitching together of threads of themes I had discerned, interspersed with quotations from the text itself. Ah, the text, the text! That's what it was, a near sacred thing – if, that is, I had managed to snatch from the hands of other greedy reviewers books that I knew would contribute something to my own burgeoning writing life. I often managed to do just that.

Burgess had told me that when he had reviewed a batch of books, he would sell them, immediately. That was not my way. And it was Pound that I wanted to review most of all, new books by him or about him.

And so during that first decade or so of my writing life, I found myself reviewing books by or about Ezra pretty much as and when they were published, and most often for magazines such as *Books & Bookmen* and *British Book News*. The article that I wrote about Ezra for the April, 1984 issue of *Books & Bookmen* was in fact a review of a collection of his letters. To my amazement and delight, the editor chose a magnificent photograph of Ezra in old age for the cover of the magazine. Sitting in a gondola in that cloak and black hat, and set against a gorgeous backdrop of the Grand Canal near the Rialto, he looked every inch the poet/sage.

I convinced myself that the editor had featured the book on the cover because she wanted to draw attention to my name and the quality of my review. I now have the good sense to acknowledge that she probably did so because the photograph was so ravishing. The chance sighting of the cover of that issue when it was published, on a news-stand in the centre of London, left me with a swimming head. It was all I could ever have wished for at that stage in my writing life, which had barely begun. It seemed to herald my coming of age as a reviewer. Was I not a talent to be watched for and remarked upon? It also inwardly strengthened the bond between myself and Ezra. It seemed to represent a kind of unspoken pledge that I should – and would – do more for him in the coming years because we were so indissolubly connected. I even imagined that there might be letters of appreciation from readers. Just a few, that is, because I was aware in my high-minded way that this book was not for everybody. Like almost all pieces of writing that appear in newspapers or magazines, no matter how self-consciously contentious they strive to be, the review was greeted by a deafening silence from the reading public, and I soon settled back into my quiet life of gentle, semi-impecunious obscurity in a damp corner of south London.

These writing commissions paid me £10 per review, but they kept me up to date with what was happening in the Pound industry. And to call it an industry then was no exaggeration. Pound, to slightly misquote the man himself, was news who stayed news. This has been the case for as long as I can remember, and it continues, although much more sputteringly now, to this day. A few months ago, I scanned the number of books by or about Ezra that the London Library currently held. There were more than a hundred of them. In spite of what Adrian thought, some of us still can't get enough of reading about Ezra, and there is always more of him to be read. He never stops turning up. Books, pamphlets and articles aside, his correspondence was extraordinary, voluminous, and the more the scholars look, the more they seem to find. Barely a year goes by without the discovery of yet another cache of letters. Or so it once seemed.

And as the books about Ezra came and went, the critical studies, the biographies, the prolonged examinations of his controversial behaviour, I began to ask myself: what should I do about Ezra? Would there be a niche for me? And what would be the shape of that niche if there were to be one?

Dead Men

Ezra stayed put in Kensington, a prosperous and fashionable district of London, during much of the First World War, agonising over the deaths of his friends, but otherwise unscathed. He had lived amongst illustrious artists and men of letters, some of whom left and never returned, lost to the barbarism of that conflict. My grandfather Harold Hickson's dead comrades, on the other hand, were all local men from Sheffield, trainee cutlers like himself, draymen, shift workers in the rolling mills, but also teachers and accountants. To both men, it was to be a defining moment of their lives.

Back of postcard reads: 'Some of the Lads at Redmires Camp Nov 1914' The faint X and W, added in black ink later, marks the dead (6) and the wounded (4). Harold Hickson is third from the right in the top row.

Ezra's response to the meaningless loss of life during the First World War was poured into the first part of a long poem called 'Hugh Selwyn Mauberley', written between 1917 and 1920. It is a precious, over-wrought, self-consciously literary piece of work about the attitudinising of an aesthete for the most part, which seems to thirst for a fat wad of interpretative notes (which critics, needless to say, have generously provided), but not entirely. When the First World War swims into view (it was still happening as he wrote), Ezra seems to let down his guard, and write from the heart of the sense of betrayal of those who returned from the war, coming home to old lies, new infamy, and liars in public places. He was only ever a spectator at all this senseless waste.

My grandfather Harold Hickson, was photographed in uniform before leaving Sheffield for the Somme beside his young wife Mabel, a milliner. Harold never rose to heights of eloquence about that conflict; in fact, he barely spoke of it at all. Occasionally, he would unfasten his garter, pull down his stocking, and show off a bit of shrapnel, lumpishly lodged in his lower leg. It felt oddly magical to the child that I then was, like a kind of party trick. On another occasion, he might break into a couple of words of pigeon French (never more than a couple) to show us exactly how he had told a farmer that he would love a couple of chickens just like the plump little bird that was running back and forth across the farmyard in front of his eyes: *deux comme ça!*, he would say, making a comically jabby V sign with his fingers. It was either a matter of silence – or a burst of laughter, to which we all laughed along, thinking of sunlight and of the comedy of fearful, scurrying birds in a French farmyard.

Not so my grandmother. She received official notification of the names of the men from the battalion who had died, and it was her job to give the families back in Sheffield the news. Harold was one of the few members of the Sheffield Battalion to survive, and his survival was due to the fact that he served principally as a cook and a runner. Ezra received news of the Western Front from his friend Gaudier-Brzeska, who had felt compelled to serve, and paid the price for it. News of what was happening to him was sent to Ezra by letter.

Had Harold expected gratitude, uplift, the warmth of an old and familiar world returned to? Or might he have experienced some sense of betrayal because the same liars were still monumentally settled in the same public places? Perhaps the second. He soon discovered that the only work available to him would be blustery and out-of-doors – on the roads, in a high, cold, desolate part of Sheffield called Redmires, wielding a pickaxe. Rather that than return to the cramped and filthy conditions of the cutlery factory, which was little better than a sweatshop. In later life he became a groundsman for the YMCA, guiding a magnificent drayhorse called Tommy as it pulled a giant roller across the windy field where the cricket pitch was sited. Mabel made the cricket teas in the wooden pavilion.

And what of Ezra? The deaths of those friends of great literary and artistic promise – the philosopher T.E. Hulme, the young French sculptor Henri Gaudier-Brzeska – helped to drive him mad. Gaudier's early death touched him especially. He kept Gaudier's 'Hieratic Head' (which now lives in the National Gallery of Art, Washington) with him, life-long, at table's end when in Rapallo, presiding over the assembled members of the Ezuversity, the two or three of them. It cleaved to him. It defined him as a maker.

But how exactly? What is the significance of any portrait bust to its sitter? And what if that sitter were to be Ezra Pound?

The Hieratic Head

Poets are difficult to characterise. No one quite knows what species of being a poet is, not exactly. They can inspire reverence, awe, and even a touch of fear in the soul. If you were introduced to a poet at a party, what would be your opening remarks? Is a poet a seer, a memorialiser of the race? Perhaps, in days gone by. Think of Homer. Or Blake. Is he also perhaps a healer of sorts, a doctor of the soul, a source of emollients or curatives? We are often inclined to reach for a poem at a funeral. And what about the *look* of poets? Should that cause us alarm? Tennyson, like Ezra himself in his later life as a taciturn, be-cloaked Venetian sage, sported a tremendous, moons-of-saturny, broad-brimmed hat, and when G.F. Watts, memorialiser of so many of the great Victorians, came to sculpt a full-length portrait of his old friend in the company of his faithful dog Sirius (the one that used to pull the cart containing the various brothers Tennyson around the Lincolnshire Wolds), that hat played a large part in his representation of the character of the man. The right hat sets off, adds mystery, *gravitas*. It also part-conceals the truth. Of baldness, for example.

And what of this strange portrait bust of Ezra by Gaudier-Brzeska? There are so many versions of Pound the man. He wore so many different masks, in poetry as in life. When very young, smitten as he was by a penchant for archaisms, he often sounded so old, as if he was digging up poems from ivied graveyards. The 'Hieratic Head', on the other hand, possesses a chilly, austere magnificence, the clean-lined austerity of Modernity. It was sculpted in 1914, not long before Gaudier-Brezska went to the Somme, where he died less than two years later. Pound was twenty-nine years old when Gaudier hand-carved it from stone, but its look is timeless. He did about one hundred preparatory drawings for this bust, of which ten survive. Some of them are hard, swift and geometrically severe. The one that turned up recently in a house in Shepherd's Bush was quite different. It had a yielding softness about it. It seemed to linger over its subject. It showed us a young man of a quite specific age.

Not so this portrait bust. In this bust, Pound could be construed as young, but he could also be old. Like a representation of some god, he is beyond the reach of all temporal considerations. That is probably what pleased him so much about it. And it undoubtedly pleased him a great deal. When he decamped to Italy in the 1920s, it eventually followed him to a garden in Rapallo. He loved to be in its company. It would sit at the end of the dining table in the open air, keeping watch over proceedings – rather in the way that the shrunken head of Jeremy Bentham would preside over meetings from the end of *his* table at University College, London. As Pound warmed and warmed to the idea of Mussolini, his beneficence, his clarity of thinking, the bust's stark lineaments would nod sagely back at him, in quiet approval of his growing hysteria.

In short, the hieratic bust gives solidity to his character. It makes him more and other than he ever was. It raises him to a higher level. It sets him apart from all the rest. It puts him on a level with the gods. It monumentalises and aggrandises the man, simplifying his features until they are nothing but brilliant, hard facets. It tricks him out for all eternity rather as the Emperor Augustus was tricked out on those Roman coins. In short, Pound has become so much greater than himself in this Vorticist portrait bust. Pound said that he wanted the portrait to look 'virile', and so it does – to a degree (from the back it looks rather like a limp penis). And yet there is much more to it than virility. It is also a carapace or a helmet of sorts. It has a kind of brute, martial vigour. It is forever on the march.

Ezra and Venice

About fifteen years into my preoccupation with Pound, I discovered that no one had written a book specifically about the man and his links with Venice. By then I knew a great deal more about his life and works. In addition to the reviews of his books that I had written, I had also read around the subject fairly serendipitously, which had included various recent biographies and critical commentaries. I was beginning to see him in the round in a way that would have been impossible for me as an intense, tunnel-visioned undergraduate relentlessly engaged in an analysis of the meaning of the image, and whether or not English poetry had developed in surprisingly different ways around the year 1912 as a result of the influence of a young American roustabout. I knew the names, the reputations and many of the works of some of the writers and artists he had known in England. I knew where he had spent his time, and how and where his life had ended – in his beloved Venice. I knew, in short, that he was a human being with rages, passions and foibles, a man of strong opinions fearlessly expressed, who had frequently caused other people's hackles to rise. I also discovered that someone who had been in touch with him – yes, with the Master himself – lived about two miles away from my own home in Clapham. This was a turning point. To meet a man who had corresponded with Pound would change everything. He would become much less of a slippery abstraction, a thing glimpsed from afar. A more concrete Pound would come into being.

Cookson, Poundian

William Cookson edited a small literary magazine with a large reputation to those who knew about such things. It was called *Agenda*, and it had begun publishing in the 1960s. I had devoured it as an undergraduate. Cookson had started to edit the magazine at Oxford, ably assisted by a friend of his, the poet Peter Dale. Ezra Pound was at its heart. Cookson was a Pound specialist. In fact, he was a fanatical devotee, and would remain so throughout his life. Someone once told me that even at the end of his life, when alcoholism had taken its toll, he could still recite every word of Pound's *Cantos* flawlessly, all eight hundred pages of them. I have no proof that this is true, but it does not sound entirely implausible.

As a boy at Westminster School, Cookson had written an enthusiastic and perceptive review of *Rock Drill*, a late section of Pound's epic poem, for the school magazine, of which he was the editor. He had sent the review to Pound, and he had received an appreciative reply, which developed into a correspondence between master and pupil. Pound gave Cookson a bruising, brow-beating education of sorts in politics, economics and world literature of the kind in which he specialised. Cookson swallowed it whole. What is more, it was Pound who encouraged Cookson to launch *Agenda*. Pound, in short, was its presiding spirit, its reason for being.

In the summer of 1984, I went to meet Cookson at his first-floor flat on Albert Bridge Road, overlooking Battersea Park. I was there for two reasons. I was keen to review books for *Agenda*. My life as a literary reviewer (principally of poetry in those early days) was just beginning, and I needed to make it prosper. As a writer, reviewing was one of the few ways of earning a little money from one's writing. There was also a second reason, which was just as important to me. I wanted to meet the man who had known Pound, albeit principally as a correspondent. I wanted to touch the hem of the garment of the man who had touched the hem of the garment of the Master. There would surely be a transfer of magic of some kind.

I met Cookson on a sunny, mid-week morning. The room overlooking Battersea Park where we sat and talked in a slightly awkward, desultory and pause-punctuated sort of way – this is how conversations with Cookson always went, I later discovered – was much as I had expected, untidy as pleasingly literary spaces tend to be, the walls lined with bookcases into which books were jammed vertically and then horizontally, every surface burdened with books, letters, papers, unopened mail. Down the length of the hall, made particularly dark and narrow by yet more bookcases, there were unsold copies of *Agenda* magazine, with their distinctive white spines, in their thousands. I inwardly thirsted to own them all. There was also a lovely, sprightly and slightly unruly, crotch-curious dog, which made Cookson snort with pleasure when it misbehaved.

After Cookson had set down the mug of cooling coffee that he had spent quite a long time preparing in a sunless kitchen at the back of the flat, we talked a little about reviewing. Cookson was charmingly diffident, bashful, rather child-like, and inclined to blush a little when he spoke with any emphasis, so much less forceful and decisive in conversation than on paper – a trait which he holds in common with many other writers. He let his head loll sideways against the back of his chair when he spoke, as if he did not quite know what to do with it. In fact, he looked a little penned into his chair, as if some part of him would have preferred not to be there at all. In appearance, he reminded me a little of Dylan Thomas. He looked cherubic, flushed of cheek, and innocently young for his years. He had a carefree giggle. His curls were untidy, a touch damp looking. I left with two or three very slim volumes of poetry to review. They were my choices from amongst the many tottering piles. Nothing was organised in that room. Books sprouted from odd corners of the floor like hairs from an old man's ears. Cookson didn't have strong opinions about many of them. They had turned up, uninvited, craving a little attention, waving at the editor half-heartedly. By and large their authors were unfamiliar to him, and, after I had looked my fill, he seemed pleased, and even a little relieved, that I had chosen the ones that I had chosen, I felt. He quite liked the idea of the magazine being trenchantly up to the minute. He was curious to know whether I would have strong opinions of my own about them in due course. He wished me well with them.

I remember asking him how he decided which poems to choose for his magazine. That was a question which had always fascinated me – how editors decide what to publish. Of course, poems have to reach a certain level of competence in order to be worthy of consideration at all. But after that? 'What are your criteria?' I asked William, fairly gently. It would have been no good at all to bark at him. That would have probably sent him scuttling back into the half-murk of his extraordinarily messy, sunless kitchen at the end of his bookcase-lined corridor. 'If they move me,' he said, with a half-smile – he was always very good at quick – often very quick – half-smiles, which ended almost as soon as they had begun. I waited for the next two or three paragraphs of critical guff and puff. They never arrived. He had said all that he had to say.

I was flabbergasted by that response. It sounded so…oh, what exactly is the word I am looking for? Amateurish? Casually subjective? Slightly unprofessional? Slightly crude? And yet I know exactly what he meant. You read thousand upon thousand of poems, and then something catches your eye – no, it catches at your mind and your heart simultaneously. It is a little like a burr adhering to a jacket down a country lane. The bloody thing's caught at you – and it sticks. The poet A.E. Housman, that exquisitely embittered classics' scholar, once said something similar, in a letter: 'I can no more define poetry than a terrier can define a rat; but he knows a rat when he comes across one; and I recognise poetry by definite physical sentiments, either down the spine, or at the back of the throat, or in the pit of the stomach.'

I left William Cookson's flat in a mood of extraordinary serenity. This was what I had dreamt of so often: to acquire new books of poetry without having to pay for them, and then to write about them, and even to be paid a little for doing so.

The reviewing didn't work well on that first occasion. (Later, matters improved a little.) I took against one of the books I had been asked to review – no, one of the ones that I myself had chosen to review, let us be perfectly clear about this. I worked myself up into a silly rage against it, and cracked all kinds of inappropriate and barely comprehensible jokes at its expense. As far as I can remember, I never came close to addressing its themes or even to describing its contents. My keenly bladed knife was out for its author, who was getting more attention as poet and reviewer than I felt he deserved. Which meant, of course, that he was getting much more attention than *me*. I, of course, was receiving almost no attention at all in those days, and quite deservedly so. I had published nothing but poems in magazines. Weeks later, after a tentative enquiry as to whether or not he had received the review, Cookson said something vague, waffly and mild-mannered about it – something to the effect that the reviews' pages were a little over-full at the moment. He spoke with a casual airiness, as if those pages were some distant thing over which he had little control. Neither of us was in any doubt about what he really meant. I then spent a day or two feeling thoroughly ashamed of myself. A few mornings later, my full vigour returned, and I was ready to strike out again with my huge, magnificently unwieldy paper sword. Perhaps a little less rashly? I do hope so. Sooner or later, I matured a little.

That slight disagreement was not the end of our acquaintanceship by any means. We liked each other. Cookson enjoyed the fact that I admired what he had been doing with his life. The magazine had a small – well, not too small – Arts Council grant, and a significant proportion of it was supporting him in the manner to which he had grown accustomed over the years. Perhaps I would have aspired to do exactly the same if I had been in his position. Our obsessions were remarkably similar. At a later visit, we talked about Pound in some detail, and I told Cookson that I was planning a trip to Venice. He asked me whether I would like to meet Olga Rudge, Pound's companion, the mother of his daughter, Mary de Rachewiltz, who had translated his *Cantos* into Italian. I knew Mary's name all right. She had published a memoir of her life during the time I was at university. I remembered having thumbed through it in the English Faculty Library. It had made me feel slightly irritated because it was too self-consciously Poundian by half.

Though elderly now, Olga was very welcoming to Poundians, he explained. Was I one of those? I asked myself. Was I a disciple in the way that the name seemed to suggest? Not quite. I had too sceptical, too irreverent a cast of mind to be a disciple. On the other hand, I knew that I would be very pleased to meet Olga, and that I had for years been toying with the idea of writing a book about Ezra...Olga loved to meet writers who were interested in Pound, William told me. She loved to talk about the poet, to keep his flame alive. He even offered to write to her on my behalf. I accepted without a second's hesitation. I was on my way to a meeting which would bring me closer to the reality of Pound's life than ever before.

The last time I saw Cookson, he was lying horizontal, having the time of his life. His legs were pumping the pedals of a go-cart in Battersea Park on a sunny Sunday morning. He grinned at me and gave me a tiny, twinkly wave with the fingers of one hand. I wonder to this day whether he ever really memorised all of *The Cantos*, and whether, if that were true, he could still have recited the entire poem even when he was too alcohol-soaked to care. It's an absurd thought, of course. Who would ever have had the patience to sit with him in that book-overwhelmed, first-floor room facing the park, or have the hours and the days to spare to listen to it happening? Who would have volunteered to step in from time to time with the necessary sustenance to keep us both going? Surely not his long suffering wife. His frisky dog would certainly not have held out.

Stepping Over the Marble Stoup

Meeting Olga in a Venice Under Mist

On 28 December 1984, Venice was something of a Whistlerian scene: phantasmal beings emerged through the mist, ragged, spectral, half-formed. There was a terrible chill in the air. The atmosphere felt heavy, funereal, a little like one of those late views of Venice by J.M.W. Turner.

The first thing that Olga Rudge did after she had opened the door of 252 Calle Querini to us was to point out the near-half-metre-high marble step that had been set there to keep at bay – for a time at least – the rising waters of the lagoon. Having made high, exaggerated leg-lifts over that barrier, we entered the tiny living room of the gondolier's cottage that Olga had shared with Pound until twelve years before our arrival. As she watched us climbing over the tall, thin marble step, she told us of flooding, that ever present threat. 'In '63, it rose as high as the table,' she said, quite cheerily, as if throwing down a challenge to the waters of the lagoon to repeat the trick if they dared. 'We didn't mind. It was lovely, so peaceful. Only the sound of lapping water. I cooked upstairs on the open fire.'

Olga was very gracious to me and to my wife. She gave us two hours of her time, at the end of which yet another Poundian rapped on the door and swelled the band of acolytes – this was Professor Singh, biographer of the critic Q.E.Leavis. Olga's anecdotes – doubtless often re-told – evoked a vanished world of literary giants: T.S. Eliot, W. B. Yeats, E.E. Cummings, William Carlos Williams, Ernest Hemingway. My sadness was that I felt that, in the end, I had disappointed her. In spite of what William had said, I felt in my heart of hearts that she did not want to meet yet another young poet and admirer of Ezra from London, nor to answer the same old questions about who Ezra had known and when. She had said all that before, too many times, during his lifetime. Hadn't they all come queueing at this door, all those journalists from America, notebook and pencil in hand? She wanted someone tougher and meaner and better connected altogether, someone who could make something happen out in the world

– a Senator from Idaho, for example or, at worst, a darned good lawyer of any description. In short, she wanted someone who would clear Pound's name of that enduring taint of treason. That was what obsessed her, that yearning to clear his name, and to condemn once again the behaviour of those who in her opinion had betrayed him. Other stories from the distant past were of less importance to her. What enthralled me most of all, then and now, on the other hand, was the life that Pound had lived in its totality, with all its triumphs and its failures.

It was a marvellous place, that dimly lit room where we sat, no less than a shrine to Ezra, and I drank it down to the dregs with my eyes as I listened to her. Olga, small, light, bird-like, flitted about around us as she spoke, proffering huge slabs of *panettone* which were slightly on the dry side. This was the woman who had played the violin to Mussolini, who had delved into the archives and discovered hitherto unknown works by Vivaldi. Logs were burning in a grate beneath a stone alcove. An ancient flat iron stood on its end at the corner of the grate. On the high mantelpiece above it, there was a pair of plaster life masks of Olga and Ezra, taken in 1929, she told me.

There were Chinese ideograms behind glass, framed extracts from *The Cantos* with their first letters picked out in red like illuminated psalters, a pen-and-ink self-portrait by Wyndham Lewis in the corner, and a Gaudier-Brzeska nude, in marble. At the back of the room, a steep staircase with a simple wooden balustrade led you up to a tiny upstairs bedroom, and then up again. It was in that upstairs room, directly above the one in which we were sitting, that Pound spent much of his time in his last years, in bed, saying almost nothing, regretting far too much past folly.

'Yes, I have lived here on and off since 1929,' she told us as she poured out weak tea from a child-size teapot. '252 Calle Querini, San Gregorio, Venezia.' She said it emphatically, and in full, as though we were ignorant of where she lived – in spite of the fact that we had just arrived there, quite successfully, and were sitting in front of her listening to her words. She spoke to us rather as if she were speaking to a slightly tiresome official at the post office who may or may not have been just a touch hard of hearing.

'My father gave me the money. He was in real estate. It was a good job I asked him then because, a year later, the year of the Crash, he would not have been able to give me a penny. I had not even seen the house when I

bought it, but I wanted a little house in Venice – who doesn't? – and American friends who lived on the Fondamenta – we used to go to dinner with them – said that these three little gondoliers' cottages were up for sale. So I wrote to my father and asked. We lived in Paris then. *Capito?*
That was an oddly engaging touch – to ask two English people, in Italian, whether they had understood what she had just told them in English.

'*Si*,' I replied. In spite of the fact that she had been born in America, Olga's English accent was impeccable. She had had a good English education. At other times, she would conclude her sentences with the word '*ma*'… It trailed away. I mentioned this to her.

'If you begin a sentence with '*ma*', she explained to me, 'it shows doubt, hesitation. They used to say – as a joke – that if you were caught by the Fascists saying such a thing, they would take you straight off to the *confino*, no questions asked…Mussolini used to collect jokes like that, against the Fascists. He would have enjoyed that one. He had a good sense of humour.'

That was an aside, of course. I was soon listening to what she really wanted me to hear.

'What I want,' she told me, 'is a good lawyer who will take up the case, clear Ezra's name.' What could I say to that? I hung my head in regret, and pouted into the fire.

Her mind shifted back to 1945, when Pound was arrested by the partisans near Pisa, and then detained by the Americans for his anti-semitic, anti-Roosevelt broadcasts over Radio Rome. He was kept in a cage in the open air, with nothing but a Chinese dictionary and a copy of the *Analects* of Confucius in his pocket for company. How could such wounds ever be healed? I was certainly not the person to heal them. At least I could listen, and sympathise….

Confucius Calling
from a Back Garden in Sussex in 2021

What was it about Ezra and Confucius? Why did he have a book by him in his pocket when he was incarcerated in that cage in Pisa in 1945? What exactly was the appeal of this dreadful bore? Confucius, to Pound, offered a model of good governance whose foundation was respect within the family and between the generations. Everyone knew his place in society. Everything proceeded by a pre-ordained plan. In the *Analects* (translated by Ezra in the 1950s), we meet a Confucius who, neither myth nor sage, sounds like a living, sensible (albeit laconic) Chinese man who proffers good advice to one and all, a man who lays down family rules that all must obey, a man who believes most of all in the need to keep one's word and possess clarity of thought. A man Confucian in temper displays modesty, calmness and restraint. He is magnanimous and courageous, wise, sober, bold and humane.

As I read him in my son's back garden at Birling Gap, with Vincent the dog now pawing, with some trepidation, at a ball that has fallen into the swimming pool, I think back twenty years or more to a visit I once made to a Ming-era village in Jiang-Xi province in south-east China, and to the great wooden panels, dating from the seventeenth century, which were still on display on the walls of the temple. This ancient writing, clearly Confucian in inspiration, was the book of rules, ranging from punishment for adultery to simple filial piety, which all, without exception, must adhere to – or be cast into exile, never to be allowed back, reduced to the status of a non-person.

Confucius, that solid, a-religious man, became for Ezra a stick with which to beat the irresponsible know-nothings of Europe and America. Much of it was fairly simple-minded stuff. How to behave yourself. The need to respect one's elders. It was not Confucius alone though who mattered to Ezra. The language of classical Chinese itself was a source of literary empowerment. In the later *Cantos*, Chinese characters play an ever increasing role. What do they mean exactly? And is it really true that they can provide useful lessons for poets now?

Pound's understanding was that when you look at a Chinese character, you see multiple meanings visualised and held in balance. Each character consists of a number of discrete elements. One may be a symbol of the sun, another the symbol of a tree. When placed in conjunction with each other in this way, meanings begin to proliferate... So much is compacted. Much is suggested by very little, and it is all a thing seen in an instant, and then perhaps internalised and reflected upon.

Pound's preoccupation with all things Chinese had set in motion something similar on my part back in 1968. Wherever Pound went, I was duty bound to follow – and when in Cambridge I sought out several aids to understanding.

Fifty years on, I still have Raymond Dawson's *An Introduction to Classical Chinese*, together with an EP in the World Foreign Language Record Series, published by the World Publishing Company of Cleveland, Ohio and New York, called *Chinese (Mandarin)*. I must have had heady ambitions to encompass both ancient and modern. The image on the record sleeve seems to be hedging its bets too: it shows a couple of timeless rural workers toiling in the paddy fields in their sampan hats. Fifty years on, that book and that record still remain virgin ground. They are not for sale or barter. Untouched or not, they still have a hold over me.

Pound's involvement with Chinese poetry had begun in earnest in 1913, when the widow of a Spanish-American scholar of Japanese language and culture called Ernest Fenollosa handed over to him a bundle of documents written by her late husband. She wanted him to make some use of them. They consisted of a short essay about how meaning is extracted from Chinese written characters – how the Chinese understand them; how they bear those meanings and feelings – and a collection of poems written by Chinese poets a millennium or more in the past – the poet Rihaku, for example – in versions by her late husband. These versions by Fenellosa were re-shaped and re-made by Pound unto a sequence of poems called *Cathay*.

Olga Tunes Back In

'Yes, that is what I need, a good lawyer. It was against the Constitution, what they did to him. What are those words? "That one shall not cause a man to suffer cruel and unnatural punishments?" And yet that is precisely what they did to him. The orders came direct from Washington. It was not the local Americans. They were absolutely charming.' She stared at me. I nodded.

The story continued with an account of his handover to the Americans. He went willingly enough, she told me. There didn't seem to be too much fuss and bother. All that rather surprised me. The way Olga told it made it sound as if he was preparing to go out for a social engagement.

'He put on his best suit – his mother loved to see him like that – it was the last time she was to see him. He wanted to walk down to the village to give himself up. I went down first. When I arrived they were all there, the Americans, poring over their maps, not interested in me at all. They wanted to get to Genoa. They had to pore over maps! Why could they not just follow their noses?'

I had no answer to such a feverish burst of irrationality, so I waited for the story to resume, and on it went like the flood of 1966 – which was even greater than that of '63, I recalled – in full spate.

'So I went away, and when Ezra himself went down they had all gone – to Genoa, one presumes – with the exception of one negro. Ezra spoke to him – Ezra was fond of negroes – and the man produced a bicycle. He wanted to sell Ezra a second-hand bicycle! He'd probably stolen it. Anyway, the last thing Ezra wanted was a second-hand bicycle…'

In fragments, that's how she told us the story of what had happened to Ezra forty years ago as the Second World War was drawing to its close, in luminous – or perhaps not so luminous – fragments. Some of these fragments I could not make cohere, not quite. It all reminded me of the onward march of Pound's *Cantos*.

'I knew he had been taken by the *partigiani*, but I was afraid to approach them. So I went to where the English had their headquarters, believing that my good English accent would see me in good stead. The English sergeant-major was helpful, and confirmed that he was there. I asked him to come looking for me if I hadn't returned within half an hour. I found him there. Later, I returned to him with the food that the English gave me – white bread and other delicious foodstuffs that we hadn't seen for years. Ezra and I ate quietly in a corner…'

Pound was then taken to Pisa, where he was imprisoned in a cage by his American captors. That was the terrible part, that they treated him as if he were some dangerous animal, not a 60-year-old American poet whose crazed and inflammatory opinions had got him into trouble. His shoelaces and belt were removed from him. He had nothing but tar paper to shield him from the sun or protect him from the rain. The stockade was illuminated by searchlights, night and day. He had a tin can for a toilet. (Did he also have in his pocket a piece of jade with a smooth bowl carved out of its centre into which a thumb might settle? More of that later.)

The memory of all these indignities provoked fresh outrage all over again. That incarceration would have a terrible effect upon him – it would also shock him back into writing poetry.

'Was it not cruel and unnatural to take him away like that so that none of us knew for seven months what had happened to him? Would they do that to a common criminal? Then why to Ezra?'

Olga's mention of Ezra's fondness for "negroes" led her almost inevitably to an equally contentious matter, Pound's anti-semitism. Those broadcasts had been stuffed with racial abuse against the Jews. Olga smoothed it all over.

'Of course he denounced usury – but not the Jews themselves. The morning after he died, when the chapel where Ezra was lying in state opened its doors, who was the first to arrive but a Jewish friend of his? There were two of them, one on either side, sketching...'

Olga spoke of his friendships with writers and artists – and of the loss of so many of those friendships. Pound had known and encouraged so many great writers, and so many of those writers and so-called close friends had turned out to be not quite as they seemed – Ernest Hemingway, for example, who had been in Paris with Pound and Olga during the 1920s.

'And what about Papa Hemingway?' she suddenly asked me as if I deserved to be ticked off for missing today's headlines. 'Has the story broken in England yet? That he was a double-agent, receiving money every week from the Cubans and working for the CIA? He was as bad as the rest – a rotter. And Bill Williams too. Only E.E. Cummings kept faith with Ezra. He stood by him to the end.'

At this point Professor Singh, who had been listening in silence for the most part, chipped in with yet another story of the untrustworthiness of the writers' tribe. T.S. Eliot, the man Pound had given such support to early in his career as a writer, had proved to be as treacherous as so many of the rest in the end, it seemed.

'Eliot did a very nasty thing. He wrote in a letter to F. R. Leavis that no more than six lines of the *Cantos* were good poetry. He could not bring himself to make such a statement in a straightforward way – and yet he wanted to ensure that those who mattered were aware of his real feelings. It is typical of his weakness, of his deviousness, to behave in that way...'

Olga had the final word on matters of treachery. 'And yet it was Yeats who did the most damage,' she said. 'Ezra always told me that his remarks about *The Cantos* in 'A Packet for Ezra Pound' harmed him more than anything else…'

Did Eliot deserve such condemnation?

A Brief Yeatsian Interlude

Some months later, Professor Singh's heady, whispered talk of betrayal of one writer by another in front of that roaring fire on an inclement winter's day in Venice in 1984 led me to wonder about a poet whose name had also been mentioned in that context: W.B. Yeats. Ezra had arrived in London in 1908 with one quite specific end in view: to make the acquaintance of the man he regarded as the greatest poet then writing in English. By 1913, their friendship had prospered to such an extent that Pound had become Yeats' private secretary, and they were living together in a cottage in the Sussex countryside. Yeats had taken the cottage to facilitate his wooing of Georgie Hyde-Lees, who lived nearby. The two got married four years later.

Which of the two poets, master or disciple, was in the ascendancy by then? You could argue that it was no longer Yeats, but the talkative, swashbuckling young blade from Pennsylvania. After all, does not Yeats' poetry after 1914 seem to have benefited by everything that Ezra himself had been soap-box-preachifying about when he wrote of the need for poets in the modern age to slough off the slush and the slither of Victorian habits? Was it not altogether leaner, tauter and more, well, sharply imagistic than it had ever been in the past? Yes, it was. But what did Yeats himself think of Pound's poetry? Twenty years later, and years into the great enterprise that became known as *The Cantos*, we got an answer.

In 1934 Yeats made a visit to Rapallo, where Pound, by then Mussolini's bosom friend after a single relatively brief meeting, was then living. Yeats wrote about that visit to Pound in Rapallo in the introductory section of a book of much impenetrability called *The Vision*. They would sit together in the evening in Pound's rooms that opened onto a flat roof overlooking the Ligurian Sea, having agreeable conversations about that poem forever in the making of which Pound would never quite be rid – until it gave up on him.

Yeats' words about Pound and his poetry, when he came to write them down miles away from his old friend, were far from impenetrable. He began by informing his readers that he and Pound were worlds apart. And what of *The Cantos* themselves, which he describes as 'an immense poem of which but seven and twenty cantos are already published'?[1] His judgement was far from a ringing endorsement. In fact, his words are those of a man who is floundering, if not drowning, in the presence of a baffling masquerade...

'I have often found there brightly painted kings, queens, knaves, but have never discovered why all the suits could not be dealt out in some quite different order... There will be no plot, no chronicle of events, no logic of discourse... He has scribbled on the back of an envelope certain sets of letters that represent emotions or archetypal events - ABCD and then JKLM, and then each set of letters repeated, and then ABCD inverted and this repeated, and then a new element XYZ, then certain letters that never recur, and then all sorts of combinations of XYZ and JKLM and ABCD and DCBA, and all set whirling together...I may now that I have recovered leisure, find that the mathematical structure, when taken up into the imagination, is more than mathematical, that seemingly irrelevant details fit together into a single theme, that here is no botch of tone and colour...'

The mays, mays, mays seem to have it then...Would it really have the structure of a Bach fugue when the 100th canto was complete?

The future was to dictate otherwise.

My Conversation with Olga Concludes

As we were about to take our leave from the gondolier's cottage, I thanked Olga for talking to us so fully. Her reply was rather enigmatic, which pleased me.

'When he did not wish to talk, I would not talk either. One should not speak for one's husband. Let him speak for himself. I was not much of a talker when he was alive. Now look at me...'

---

[1] 'A Packet for Ezra Pound' (pp 4 & 5), the opening section of *A Vision*

What exactly was she saying when she said those words to us? That she ought not to have said what she said? That she simply had not been able to stop herself talking about him, and that perhaps she ought not to have done so? Would the better part have been silence? Pound certainly opted for that during his last years.

Ezra's Burial in San Michele

Ezra Pound was buried on the cemetery island of San Michele in November, 1972. Jewish friends grieved beside his dead body in the chapel of rest. Thirty-four years later, his companion Olga Rudge was laid to rest in the plot beside him.

Lago di Maggiore VI: One Damned Canto After Another

Day after day I leaf through, drive my eyes across, hundreds of pages of those jitterily lineated *Cantos* again, seated in a comfortable rattan chair beside the lake shore, or out of harm's way on that terrace above the pool, where the kids never cease their splashing and their squealing. This morning's reading hour or two, in the heat-struck summer of 2022, attaches itself to memories of earlier encounters with other men's copies of the book, Ed Rosenfeld's for example, which later got stolen by goodness knows who…

Did I not read it one summer, sunk deep into an old wooden rocker in the backyard of Ed's lovely wooden house in West Hurley, Upstate New York, with some fat orange koi cruising across the surface of a little, man-made pond at my back? Was that the same summer I wrote a poem about Ed's house that eventually found its way into *Impossible Horizons*[2], my first full-length book?

Must reading *The Cantos* always go hand in hand with memories of water moving? Ezra spent so much time beside water, absorbing the lessons of its wayward fluidity, but during those Rapallo years especially, where he built himself a pontoon from which to jump and then swim. Here is the poem about Ed's house, which faced out onto a man-made lake called the Ashokan Reservoir. This body of water, heavily patrolled by cops night and day, provides much of the drinking water for the city of New York.

[2] From *Impossible Horizons* (1995)

The House Above the Ashokan Reservoir

The mellowness of wood on those broad stairs
That made a gentle twist up to the light
Of living space so full of air it seemed
Not comfortable, no, but merely right…

Within that space the sun made gentle play,
But not until the evening, when the light
That danced upon the reservoir's broad face
Shone up into our eyes. And then we bathed.

But was it not the colour of that wood,
The wood he'd used for stairs and parquet floor,
That gave the house its special atmosphere,
An atmosphere of ochre to the core?

And what did ochre in that wood suggest –
If that is not too definite a word?
A balm that soothes anxieties away,
A something that approximates to rest.

When I look up from the page beside the lake shore in northern Italy during that summer of 2022, the Ezra words I have just been reading readily attach themselves to – or bounce off – the things that I see. I notice a yacht fleeting by with *bellying canvas*, just as Ezra wrote in that very first canto. Moments later, I spot two sun-kissed young men standing upright, perfect steersmen, poised and balanced on their fleeting skiff, quite the opposite of Ezra's words, which lurch and teem and wobble, rackety, ungainly, and out of control.

My note-taking becomes more erratic and undecipherable as I lose patience with the man and his methods of sifting and accumulating. It is as if Ezra is pouring in bucketloads of unedited material in order to bulk out the whole, give it weight and heft, lend it the authority of ever more obscure sources. The writing feels under-energised and poorly organised. The words do not feel under pressure. The numbness of tedium sets in. Occasionally the rough-housing gives way to calmness, flashes of illumination, stillness, the soft pad of beasts, meditative reverie that lists here and there as he gathers the gods of antiquity about him; then, in an instant, hard-nosed dyspepsia returns again, mine and his, when he howls and rages at the ignoramuses of Europe and America, the monopolists, the financiers, the obstructors of knowledge. Is this really anything other than one damned attack of biliousness after another? Is the real Pound a bar-room brawler or a light-stepping aesthete? Backwards and forwards he goes, from past to present and back again, lashing and kicking out. It is like listening into – or stumbling upon – the non-stop jabber of a madman as he stirs everything that he has ever read or thought or done or felt into the whirling mix…

Civilisation has gone to rot. And Ezra has gone down with it. That same civilisation has coarsened his impulses. Whatever happened to delicacy, poise, grace, word-crafting? He is beyond all that now. All he knows – all he is left with – is the pitiful, accusatory jab, jab, jab. Does Ezra really have any sense of this poem's trajectory? Or is it a matter of pushing off from shore and hoping for the best? Did he have pleasure in mind for his readers? It's a tragic and unreadable mess.

Today I find myself agreeing with the American critic Irving Howe, who once described *The Cantos* as a 'junkshop of intellectual debris.'[3]

But if this is indeed the case, why have I come back for more? Who is the more to be pitied, Ezra or me? If I regard this desperate, near life-long attempt to give some order to his thinking as a failure, and if I could have put a stop to all my fretting about it forty years ago, why didn't I do that then? Why do I need yet more proof of my own folly now? I needn't go the whole way with him. I needn't even have come this far. Why waste my time? I could have hit him hard in the fourth round and then backed off, thrown in the towel.

A Pilgrimage Across the Waters of the Lagoon to Ezra's Grave on the Isola san Michele, 8 September 2022

Venice has buried many of its most illustrious dead on the walled cemetery island of San Michele, which is just across the lagoon from the

---

[3] *Ezra Pound: The Voice of Silence*, Alan Levy (1983), p.62. First used in an attack on Ezra published in *World* magazine in 1972.

Fondamenta Nove. Seen from Venice itself, the island's long horizon line prickles with cypress trees, which rise behind the entire long length of its enclosing, red-brick wall. The wall is broken intermittently by chapels of rest. The island shines like something beguilingly paradisal on a sunny summer's evening when viewed from the terrace of one or another of the not inexpensive Venetian restaurants along the beautiful broadwalk that is the Fondamenta Nove.

It is a serious matter, a visit to the cemetery island, not a destination to be happened upon by chance. The elderly Italian seated opposite to me on the lurching and water-bouncing vaporetto is reading an ancient and well thumbed paperback edition of an Italian translation of Bertrand Russell's *A History of Western Philosophy*.

The middle-aged Italian in blue shirt sleeves who disembarks from the boat just in front of me after the briefest of brief journeys crosses himself as he steps off the boat and prepares to pass through the cemetery's arched entranceway. Just inside that entrance, on the left, there is a rather sentimental boy-monk fashioned in terracotta, hung about with strings of beads and flowers as if he is a shop dummy freshly dressed. He is clutching the Christ child, almost breathing down onto his tender head, with its massing of curls. Real flowers spill in such abundance in front of them. Art – even the art of a sentimentalist – demands its homage. But what of humankind? I ask myself. Needless to say, the sun is beating down relentlessly. The walk towards the grave is a hot and determined trudge of a journey.

Pound's body was borne here by gondola on 3 November 1972, after a service held in the Palladian church of San Giorgio Maggiore, and laid to rest in a plot in the sector reserved for the Evangelico (Protestants: Recinto XV). The plot itself is by no means easy to find, for all that various signs warn us of its approach, and even seem to be leading us helpfully towards it. The cemetery's little give-away map is both free and perfectly useless, as is the only little book devoted to the subject of the Venice of Ezra Pound, and the places with which his name deserves to be associated.

The cemetery has many of these discrete sectors, kept apart from each other by high walls, and entranceways or exits occasionally patrolled by stone lions. The dead, it seems, can be fussy about the company they keep. One sector is held in perpetuity by the Bembo family. Another is reserved for the military, and others for priests and holy sisters. Yet another claims to be exclusive to the Greeks, but that particular one happens to contain the bodies of Igor Stravinsky, and Diaghilev, a flamboyant Russian impresario. In the Protestant and Greek sectors bodies are either laid in the ground individually, with headstones, or contained within ugly and pompous family mausolea.

Elsewhere, where many of the undifferentiated dead have been laid to rest, there are other arrangements. Bodies are contained within what look like long, uninterrupted lines of tall pale stone filing cabinets. Each subdivision – ample enough to suggest the shape of a coffin – has a little pot for flowers attached to it. The fact that these little vessels are often perched so high in the air means that the cemetery has had to provide a mobile metal step ladder to enable ascent, which waits there, patiently. No one ascends during the short time I spend considering the usefulness of this arrangement.

Many of the older dead in the Protestant sector seem shockingly unloved or forgotten. Crucifixes are toppled; entire tombs have fallen in on themselves. Have they long since outlived the memories of the living? Is there no one alive still to care? Apparently not. And, more to the point of my visit on this particular sunny autumn afternoon, does anyone still care any more that Ezra Pound was buried here almost exactly fifty years ago?

Very few, it seems, and those who have remembered have done so inaccurately. The cemetery's little map tells us that the grave is tucked away in one corner, close to the boundary wall, so we spend much time fruitlessly pacing the periphery. To no avail. The authors of the book about Ezra and his favourite Venetian places inform us that he is buried beneath a laurel tree – perhaps they know in their heart of hearts that he deserves the laurel crown sacred to the poets of antiquity. In fact, the plot is much closer to the centre. Pound and his mistress Olga Rudge are buried in contiguous plots beneath three bay trees, which are so huge and so healthy that the gravestones themselves – inscribed rectangles of marble, quietly modest in size, designed by Joan Mitchell – are close to being totally obscured, Olga's especially – I pull away fronds of greenery, sweep away masses of dead leaves with my hand.

I step back to consider how Pound the megaphone, Pound the loud-mouth, Pound the frothily loquacious controversialist has been memorialised by those who survived him. With a wholly uncharacteristic degree of elegance and restraint. There is no vertical headstone, and no plot to mark out or suggest the length of the body. These modest stone markers contain two undated names – nothing but that. If you did not know the names already, they would be a mystery, half buried in nature. It is as if the two names want to hide away from overmuch public scrutiny. The stones lie almost flat to the earth on which they sit, canted to the smallest of tilts. And what of flowers? Does anyone still pass by and leave evidence that Pound is still remembered by the living? No. There is a single bunch of flowers close to Pound's stone grave marker, but it is so old and so withered that I cannot begin to hazard a guess as to its age. What is more, its withering is very distinctive and, as it happens, quite appropriate. The flower heads are a rich, deep mauve in colour, as if the colour has withdrawn and intensified into an essence of itself – a little like a flower head painted by Cy Twombly.

Pound's grave, in the quality of its neglect, and its lack of posturing, could not be more different from the graves of Brodsky, Stravinsky and Diaghilev. Those three bask in plots which are open to the air, and welcoming of attention. They all command their ground. They have flamboyance. And they are clearly being admired by the living. Stravinsky's has a tight bouquet of cut flowers, newly laid down, bound in silver wrapping, like a tribute to the body of some much admired beauty, fresh flung down in grief. Diaghilev's monument has the enduring homage of several pairs of ballet pumps, all ranged in a row. Brodsky's, quite close to Pound's, well, just swanks. But then Brodsky himself *did* swank.

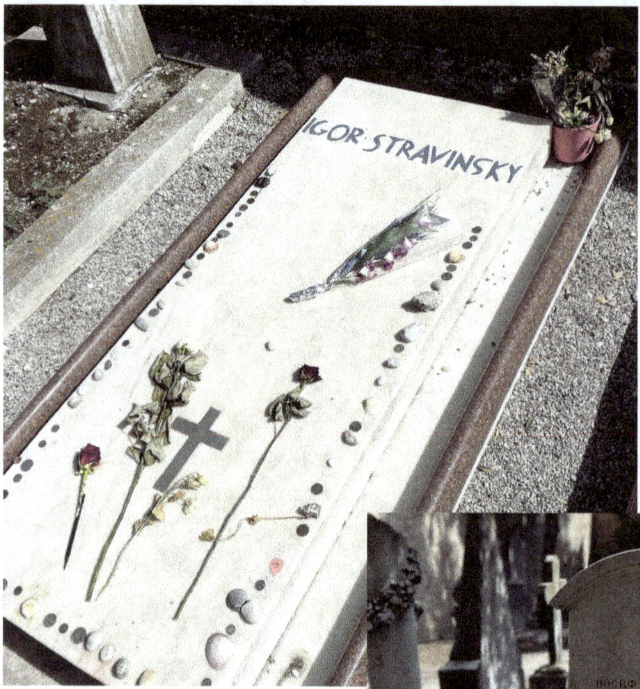
IGOR STRAVINSKY

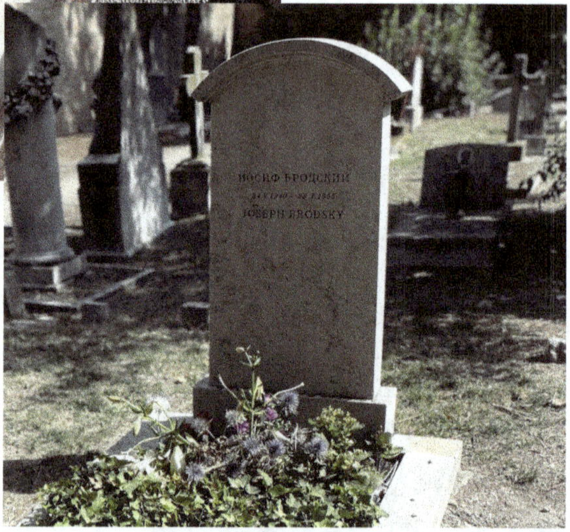
ИОСИФ БРОДСКИЙ
JOSEPH BRODSKY

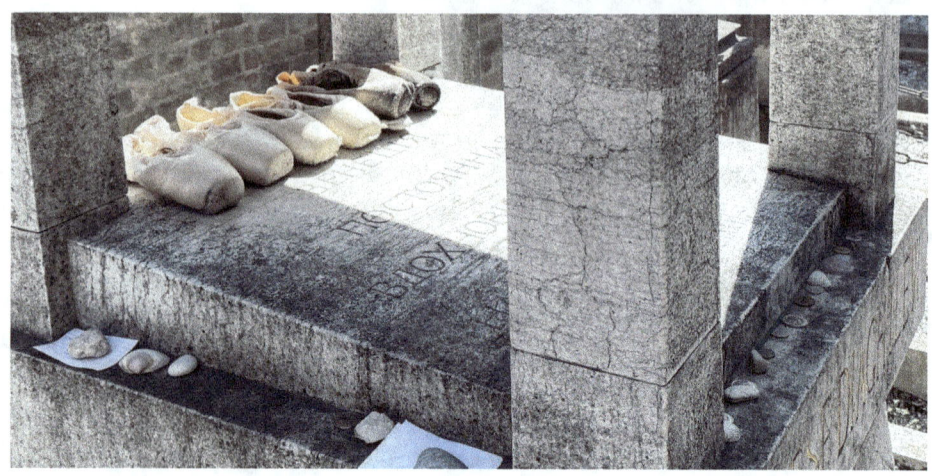

Pound and Venice: a Book Proposal

Early in 1990, six years after meeting Olga, I wrote a synopsis of a book about Ezra Pound and Venice, and one cold afternoon in January, uncomfortably seated on a high stool at a bar in Clapham South, I showed it to a publisher called Ib Bellew. Bellew was mildly interested in the idea – after all, he had published some books of poetry, and even one or two books *about* poetry – but I was my own worst enemy on that day. I also told him that I had several other books that I was interested in writing for him. One of them was a reference book about poets and poetry in the 20th Century. There were others too. I was firing off in all directions. This was a foolish thing to have done, I recognised later. No publisher likes to be told that you have *several* books that you could write for them. One is more than enough.

Here is the synopsis of that book, almost exactly as I wrote it then.

Ezra Pound and Venice: the Synopsis of a Book

Ezra Pound returned repeatedly to Venice in the course of his life. He wrote of it in poems and essays, and he also lived there, intermittently when young, for much longer stretches of time in the 1930s, and after he was released from St Elizabeth's Hospital, Washington, D.C., in 1956.

And, finally, after his death he was buried across the water from Venice itself on the cemetery island of San Michele, amidst a group of plots reserved for the Protestant dead, amongst whom is the poet Joseph Brodsky. And beside his simple marble memorial, sculpted by a Japanese artist friend, there is the plot reserved for Olga Rudge, Pound's faithful companion and mistress, mother of his daughter Mary von Rachewiltz, the Italian translator of his Cantos.

Olga's father, a banker, had bought her a tiny cottage in the Dorsoduro district of Venice, and Olga and Pound lived there from the time that he was released from his incarceration until his death in 1972. Pound called this cottage 'the hidden nest'. He was a morose, bitter, broken man in those last years, disavowing his achievements, rebuffing all visitors; but it is of great significance to his life and work that he should have chosen Venice as his final resting place – in life and death.

Venice – its physical embodiment and its symbolic significance as La Serenissima, Queen of the Adriatic, its art and its architecture, its very presence in the Adriatic as an image of the beautiful and a testimony to man's achievements when he works in harmony with nature – was of central importance to Pound's work. He was first taken to Venice in 1898 by his aunt when he was thirteen years old, and his first book of poems, A Lume Spento, was produced and printed there at his own expense in 1908, the year he came to London in pursuit of W.B. Yeats – and the life of a littérateur. This study, the first to be devoted to Ezra Pound and his connections with Venice, will include the following chapters:

1. The young Pound – an account of his early formative visits there, and how they helped to shape his thinking about The Cantos, which he began to write in earnest in 1916.
2. A Lume Spento: the writing and the publication of his first book.
3. Pound and Venetian art. Pound's writings on Venetian art and architecture in particular and the Italian Renaissance (especially the Quattrocento) in general.
4. Venice, Pound and Politics. The Venetian Republic and its influence upon Pound's political thought.
5. Venice and The Cantos. Specific links between The Cantos - especially the so called 'Venetian Cantos' – and the city itself.
6. Pound's Venice. The monuments, the works of art, the particular places he held dear.
7. Pound in old age: his later life in Venice with Olga Rudge. The daily itineraries. Their home: a shrine still preserved in his memory.

The illustrative element – maps, itineraries and photographs – will be very important to the book. Olga Rudge is still alive, though in her ninetieth year. When I visited her in Venice, the gondolier's cottage was exactly as it had been when Pound was still alive – full of drawings by Wyndham Lewis, first editions of Pound's books, busts of the two of them young, etc. It would certainly be desirable to interview her again at length (if she were willing to co-operate) and to photograph the interior and the exterior of the house. There are extant sources of Pound/Venice photographs – see, for example, the wonderful photograph of Pound that was used to accompany my review in Books & Bookmen in the spring of 1984. It was published in Ezra Pound: The Voice of Silence by Alan Levy (Permanent Press). If this picture is as good as it seems, it may do for the jacket. Another photographic source is Vittorio Contino, whose book Ezra Pound in Italy was published by Rizzoli in 1970.

Length: 60,000 words approx. Plus captions

Ib Bellew rejected the book – he also failed to return to me the only copy I owned of that 1984 issue of *Books & Bookmen* which featured the photograph of Pound on its cover. It was too specialised in its appeal, he told me, and for various reasons (which would surely have included relief, frustration, anger and disappointment), my desire to write such a book stalled. Ezra disappeared from view for a while.

Old Ez's Lament

Six years later, in 1990, I happened upon a letter[4] written by Pound in 1964 to his long-time friend and publisher, James Laughlin. It was a touching, pathetic, heartfelt document, cataloguing Pound's obsession with his own increasing infirmities. It is anxious and self-mortifying. As I read this letter, it occurred to me that there might be a long poem to be written about this old man at the end of his life, a tragic, solitary and somewhat broken spirit who had been closely guarded and defended by the heroic Ms Rudge until his death. Would a long poem be more likely to find a publisher than that proposed book about Pound and Venice? My appetite had been quickened by that letter to Laughlin. In time, the poem was written.

Here is that poem, preceded by an edited extract from the letter to Laughlin. It is based on fact; it also includes some fanciful speculation of my own. It incorporates some of Olga words in response to my questions. I have taken liberties with such facts as are known, twisting them to my particular purposes when I so chose, and, where it seemed appropriate, embroidered somewhat, trying, always, to be true to the spirit of the man.

Much of the poem is spoken in the voice of Ezra himself. Ms Rudge's own words to me appear in italics. There is a third voice, that of a professor who occasionally makes general – and usually slighting – references to Yeats and Eliot. His is the voice of that fiercely committed Poundian who descended upon the cottage during our conversation, and chose to throw in his ha'porth of good or bad sense to leaven the whole.

---

[4] pp. 281/2 of the Pound/Laughlin correspondence – see Book List

Preface

Ezra Pound to James Laughlin,
San Ambrogio, Italy,   *18 September 1964*

Olga trying till the last minute to
get me to pull my mind together
and stand up to something.

No memory to speak of

no ability to register
either the pitch of a note,
or remember a sequence
of tones or notes in a tune

complete loss of capacity to

always too slow on uptake

non perception of relations

hen on chalk line

failure to learn english,
i.e. meaning of words in language,
let alone thoroughness in any foreign tongue

lack of price of any form of clothing

parasitic existence

weak bladder from the beginning

have not provided Olga with decent umbrella
or warm clothing in winter
or covering for summer...
***

Keep this lagoon water out of my mouth,
Meister Eckhart.
I call upon you here,
lost in these mists,
amongst all these masked clowns,
my ears beaten down
by the clangour of
old, cracked bells
because your words are surely
worthier than mine.
You always told – and will tell –
more than I can tell.
Your words resist all the greedy
licking and lapping of these waters...

Raise up that marble stoup now, Olga,
I am adrift up to my knees!
Or let that gondolier's boy do it for you.
After all, your father stole this house –
and just in time, I said,
(though I do not say it now,
having wholly repented of my past)
or we would not have as much as we have,
which is, of course, in my case,
tantamount to nothing...

I have lived here since 1929. 252 Calle Querini, San Gregorio, Venezia. My father gave me the money. He was in real estate. It was a good job. I asked him then because, one year later, the year of the crash, he would not have been able to give me a penny. I had not even seen the house when I bought it, but I wanted a little house in Venice – who doesn't? – and American friends who lived on the fondamenta – we used to go to dinner with them – said that these three little gondolier's cottages in the calle were up for sale. So I wrote to my father and asked. We lived in Paris then. Capito?

I want a good lawyer
who will take up his case,
and clear his name.
Some senator from Idaho
who wants to make a name for himself.
Can you do that?

Are you trained in that sort of thing?
I don't care how long it takes.
Do they care about him now?
He may be dead to you,
but here he remains alive
in that chair over there.
And I don't care
if he doesn't speak to me.
That is his right.
He has a right to silence.
If you had been bruised that badly,
by the country that you loved,
would you too not demand such a right?
He did it for them, all that he said!
He has been so badly misunderstood
and misread.

He put on his best suit —
his mother loved to see him like that.
It was the last time she was to see him.
He wanted to walk down to the village
to give himself up. I went down first.
When I arrived, there they all were,
the Americans, poring over their maps,
not interested in me at all.

They wanted to get to Genoa.
They had to pore over maps!
Why could they not just follow their noses?
So I went away, and when Ezra went down,
they had all gone — to Genoa, one presumes —
with the exception of one negro.
Ezra spoke to him — Ezra was fond of negroes —
and he produced a bicycle.
He wanted to sell Ezra a second-hand bicycle!
He'd probably stolen it.
Anyway, the last thing Ezra wanted was
a second-hand bicycle.

Having very few books at my disposal,
I had to depend upon

the imperfections of memory.
And so I began – it was a way of
shoring up my sanity –
to sort through the detritus
of my own mind.

At times I could see far.
It was as though I were gazing to
the very bottom of a profound,
crystal-clear stream.
There were the beloved texts
of my most favoured people!
Words, phrases, whole sentences would rise
to the surface of the water,
and I would fish them out,
with such care and tenderness,
and lay them down on the page,
still damp and squirming.
At other times, nothing but
mist and slipperiness,
infamous unclarities,
and voices calling,
spiteful, wronged, beleaguered voices,
calling, calling – which, at times,
I would choose to recognise,
and then, at other times,
when I too felt costive and spiteful,
resoundingly fail to recognise.

Eliot did a very nasty thing. He wrote in a letter to Leavis that no more than six lines of the Cantos were good poetry. He could not bring himself to make such a statement in a straightforward way – and yet he wanted to ensure that those who mattered were aware of his real feelings. It is typical of his weakness, his deviousness, to behave in that way...

If you begin a sentence with 'ma...ma', it shows doubt, hesitation. They used to say – as a joke – that if you were caught by the Fascists saying such a thing, they would take you straight off to the confino, no questions asked... Mussolini used to collect jokes like that, against the Fascists. He would have enjoyed that one. He had a good sense of humour.

I knew he had been taken by the partigiani,
but I was afraid to approach them.
So I went to where the English
had their headquarters, believing that
my good English accent would see me in good
stead. The English sergeant-major was helpful,
and confirmed that he was there.
I asked him to come looking for me
if I hadn't returned within half an hour.
I found him there.
Later, I returned to him with the food
that the English gave me –
white bread and other delicious foodstuffs
that we hadn't seen for years.
Ezra and I ate quietly in a corner.

If I close my eyes –
even for a single moment –
I can begin to pretend
that I am no longer here.

The voices recede.
Those scrawny roosters
no longer bother me.
Even a pesky mosquito can land
on this membrane of skin
which protects my eye...

Let it do its worst, I say.
It cannot do worse to me
than I have done to myself.
I have been swollen of head.
Let me now be swollen of eye.

But when I open my eyes
to the accusatory blaze
of the setting sun, this rage
begins to build and build in me.
It is a rage against myself
for being so foolish.

It is also a rage against them
for condemning such foolishness so harshly.
Do they not understand
that I must have been a little crazed
in the head to say such things?
It is a rage against this cage
in which I am being held like an animal –
see how they push the food at me,
with their fingers, between the bars –
just as if I were some pent animal.

It is a rage against myself
for uttering the words
which were not precisely the words
I had it in mind to utter.
How can that be so?
Why was it that intemperance
seized hold of me,
scattering my sanity
to the four winds?

Why did I not hold on to myself?
Why had I not lashed my reason to a spar?
How was it that my mind,
when it listened to the words
which were issuing from my mouth,
did not cry out: hold back! Hold back!
The pivot is wobbling!
Why did my mind not say that to me?
Was it in cahoots then with my words?
But, if so, why? For what good reason?

She came, and she brought me the white bread.
I did not hear her coming.
She must have been carried to me
like dust blown up from the ground.
One minute I was alone here,
the next she was beside me.

Yes, they had already unlocked the door
and let her in. I had not heard a thing.

She seemed so waif-like, so abstracted,
so thin when I glanced at her.
Her nose looked so sharp and so bony –
as if it might peck at the dust of the ground –
and her skin as fragile as paper.

Eat this, she said. Nothing more.
I pushed it away from me.
Eat it, she said. She was speaking
scarcely above a whisper.
I don't want this filthy food, I said.
It is not filthy food, she replied,
so patiently, so evenly.
It is from the English Sergeant-Major.
He has sent you this food
with his best wishes...

Which turned my thoughts, immediately,
to England and old Billyum
whom I had gone to meet in 1909,
London. Old Billyum, in that drawing room,
Kensington; those oracular tones of his,
that measured grace...

He was the greatest of the greats, that man.
And I had knocked him into shape.
Ez, he'd said to me, you know me better
than I know myself. You had better be
my secretary. I sat at his feet.
He patronised me for my hokum ways.
He laughed. We laughed together.
And I survived.
I whupped him into shape.
Now look at me, some beast pent in a cage.

Take this white bread, she said,
(Olga, 1945, Pisa Detention Camp),
and eat, for your own soul's sake – and mine.
I ate.

Many were the nights
when we would sit together,
not saying one word to each other.
He did not want to speak.
He was altogether too depressed to speak.
His words were like ash in his mouth.
They taste of ashes, he would say that.
He would spit them out into the open fire.
He would gather up the phlegm in his throat,
and gob the spit into the fire.
Words, words, worthless, treacherous words,
he would say. I would simply nod and look away.

They would come, many of them.
They would want to visit him.
The Italians were the kindest –
young men for the most part,
who would want nothing but
to hold his hand in front of the fire.
Yes, he would let them hold his hand.
He would let them.
He would stare at it later,
after they had left,
as if it did not belong to him.
They would not question him, of course.
He did not want to be questioned.

But when *they* came, all those Americans,
clutching their papers,
in those earnest, round spectacles of theirs,
all high, gleaming brows and nervous attention,
he would say that he felt too sick –
sick unto death, he would whisper to me –
even to greet them.
And so he would retire upstairs,
and sit with his face to the wall.
They would glance nervously up the stairs
from time to time,
and wonder whether he would grace them
with his presence.

He was never quite silent up there.
He would sniff a great deal
and shift his feet about.
They would know. They would know.
And so I would be obliged to entertain them.
I would give each one of them in turn
two or three thick slabs of *pannetone*
and several cups of weak tea
from this child-size teapot of my grandmother's
which they would gulp down gratefully,
gracefully, because it was almost always cold
when they came.

We knew about the cold, Ezra and I.
We had learnt to resist the cold.
Whereas those young Americans
had no backbone for that sort of thing.

Soon I shall be gone,
swept on as far as
Santa Maria dei Miracoli,
my jewel casket of a church... –
(Renaissance, and much of its time,
though far beyond and above
in so many respects) –
and that will be no bad thing,
to melt against its grey, stark walls...

Your words resist water, Meister,
mine absorb it,
sinking to the bottom of the lagoon
until I cannot find them.
I cannot repeat them to myself
– except, of course, for the worst of my words...
So many bad and foolish words,
so many intemperate words,
so little attention to accuracy.
I mistook and misnamed so much.
Forgive me, *goodly fere*,
forgive me for my tragic dishonesty.

When he did not wish to talk, I would not talk either.
One should not speak for one's husband. Let him speak
for himself. I was not much of a talker when he was alive.
Now look at me...

I have taken this final vow
to shut off my mouth.
There has always been too much prattle
issuing from it.
None of it has done me any good.
And none of it did *them* any good,
those whom I would have wished to educate.

I gave them nothing of my own
because, inside, I was nothing.
I was a mish-mash of tongues,
others' mish-mashed tongues,
tongues of the dead and the dying.
Perhaps I should have been *there* instead.
This was not the place for me,
though Muss got one or two things right
before they strung him up on the gallows' tree...

Let him not stand shoulder to shoulder
with despots and lovers of power,
but with KUNG, and those who love ORDER.
Let him be called the supreme ARTIFEX,
the restorer of the glories of Italy
unto Italy, she who had lost her way
in our day. It was she who shouldered
her burdens like an ox mounting
the steep slopes of the field
in that time-honoured way.
It was he who shook himself free of cliché,
seeing clear and far and true.
He alone had the will to make it new.
To re-awaken the animal life of Italy,
To make a nation rise up and sing,
rise up on its toes, dancing, like a young bull
in the Cordova ring. He alone must we praise.
Yet what did that peasant say

when she saw how the train ran on time?
God help us! We have been Prussianised!
Of such stuff are we made.
Which is why we must be re-made
in the image of all that is vigorous
and swift and true, the eagle's image.
Cut all that cackle
in the milleniar Roman sun.
Now we must run and run,
wrenched from the bureaucratic boozum.
There is no other way.
May the bird sing abundant in the olive-yards!
May the Pontine Marches be drained
of the pus of centuries!
Let us let him reclaim our *gerarchia*.
Right reason must rule. And we must obey.
There is no other way.

It does me little good to listen to
all these voices inside my head.
And yet there is nowhere else to go.
I am condemned to be myself
for a little while longer at least.
Yes, I must go on being myself
until this lagoon water fills my mouth.

It is coming, it is coming, Olga!
Raise up that marble stoup!

In '63 it came as high as the table.
We did not mind. It was lovely, so peaceful.
Only the sound of lapping waters.
I cooked upstairs on the open fire.

That little Jew arrived –
he was the first to arrive –
to sketch him, in the chapel,
the morning after he died –
he was lying in state,
in that little chapel...

He stood to one side,
and leant over,
examining him so minutely,
almost touching his beard with his nose.

He was such a good and faithful friend,
to the end, and Ezra likewise.
Ezra would have done the same for him.
He had no quarrel with his friends,
and so many of them were Jews.

They clasped hands.
They joked and whispered together.
They broke bread.
They were such true and faithful friends –
whatever the wise world might have said.

Of course he denounced the evils of usury!
But not the Jews themselves.
They must learn
that he was not anti-semitic.
Why did his Jewish friends, Cournos and Levy,
not rat on him?
They all remained loyal to the end.
Ezra betrayed no one.

He stayed in Italy
because he had his old mother to look after.
She wanted to go back to America,
but no one wanted her,
the poor old soul...

I was very surprised
that he decided not to defend himself.
If he had had a few weeks of peace and quiet
to gather his thoughts,
he could have done it,
ma...

I was with him in spirit,
in the courtroom, on that day.

He was not himself all the same.

When he stood up to stare at the judge,
he saw swallows winging before his eyes,
and he imagined them singing.

His words were not coming out straight and right
because between him and those words of his,
small swallows were singing,
their voices true and light.

He wanted so much to join them
in flights of song,
but he knew that it would be wrong.
He knew that he must go on.

So there he stood, alone, on his legs,
and, from the point of view of flight,
quite helpless.

And yet he thought they might be helping him
to be understood. That is why
he made his words so swift and light
in his turn,
in partial emulation of them.

He paid no heed to the eyes
which drilled into his,
so many sombre pairs of eyes.
He despised them all,
and he supposed that they despised him.
He was probably right, I concluded,
he was almost certainly right.

And what about Papa Hemingway?
Has the story broken in England yet?
That he was a double-agent,
receiving money every week
from the Cubans, and working for the CIA?
He was as bad as the rest — a rotter.
And Bill Williams too.

Only E.E. Cummings kept faith with Ezra.
He stood by him to the end...
He had such a mouth on him, Hem,
and such swagger too.
He could have swallowed all of us
without any difficulty.
And yet the voice, when he spoke,
sometimes came out small and weaselly,
as if it knew that it wasn't speaking
the entire and honest truth.

Is that the way fiction writers are?
So many different people inside them,
and each one clamouring to be let out;
each one a mouth pack full with lies.
I have never read the Russkies.
I've not even read Dusty Yepsky, not all through.
Though I've blabbed on about Flaubert
and the rest. Truth to tell,
I don't go much for the sprawl of fiction.
Fiction gets everywhere. It's so messy,
so diffuse. I admire the jewel-like concision
of great poetry.

Where did they take him to?
We never knew, not for seven long months.
They caused him to suffer such cruel and
unnatural punishments in that cage
beneath the broiling Italian sun.

The orders came direct from Washington.
It was not the local Americans.
They were absolutely charming.
And yet it was against the Constitution.
What are those words?
'That one shall not cause a man to suffer
cruel and unnatural punishments'?
And yet that is precisely what they did to him.

A shrine for the Poundian,
that tiny house, you might say.

Framed extracts from *The Cantos*
hang on the walls, initials illuminated
in flaming red, like precious Psalters.
Logs burn in the grate beneath a stone alcove,
beside which an ancient flat iron is propped.
In the corner: a pen-and-ink portrait
of Wyndham Lewis; a Gaudier nude, in marble;
Chinese ideograms framed behind glass.
And, on the high mantelpiece above the fire,
two life masks, in plaster, of Ezra and Olga,
circa 1929.

A steep staircase,
with a simple wooden balustrade,
ascends to the tiny upstairs bedroom...

The flood waters shall not reach me in this room.
It is here that I shall sit,
hanging above the world's waters.
Wood-smoke alone shall reach my nostrils,
nothing but the sweet density of wood-smoke.

I would walk a little way with him,
just along the *calle*,
when the rains held off.

He would walk happily enough
when wreathed in mist,
but the rains never pleased him.

He moved very slowly towards the end,
each step a separate consideration before he took it,
and without once raising his head,
his face entirely hidden
by the generous brim of his hat.

They would greet him, often loudly,
his friends the street traders,
knowing him by his cloak and his hat,
and, in acknowledgment, he would raise
his walking stick from the ground,

just a little, to indicate that he knew
he had been spoken to;
to indicate some measure of gratitude
for the fact that they had not forgotten him,
il grande poeta, that same poet who had presided,
every evening, at the table in Rapallo,
in the company of the great hieratic head,
(Gaudier's great head,
hewn from a single block of marble)
over his own Ezuversity...

How his voice had rung out in those years;
how they had flocked to hear him,
hungry as seabirds, from everywhere.
Now all that was gone.
Now he would open his mouth only to eat –
and nothing more.
His needs were simple at the end –
polenta, and a single glass of water.
He had never been a drinking man.

And yet it was Yeats who did the most damage,
Yeats, whom he loved and revered, and whom we had
entertained at Rapallo. Ezra always said to me
that his remarks about The Cantos *had harmed him*
more than anything else.

Travel broadens the mind,
said Great-Aunt Frank,
she who'd danced with General Grant,
and brought me here, at age 13,
after Paris, Brussels, Nuremberg, Mainz...

Let me introduce you, she said,
as if bringing on a friend,
to the Queen of the Adriatic...

I remember: a low, threatening sky;
the slop of mud-grey water
against mooring posts; and,
along the canale grande,

palazzi lurching, forwards and sideways,
as if about to fall into the lagoon -
gestures of desperation in stone;
greatness half gone, but still visible
beneath the depredations of extreme old age;
and, more local and transitory,
though still just as memorable:
cat-slink, hackles risen, along the *calle*.
Or perched like miniature stone lions
on balconies, waiting to be fed...
(And, all my life, I would feed them,
and they would know me
for their lord and protector.)

Yes, to *der alte Venezia*, when young,
with Great-Aunt Frank, she, of blessed memory,
who had danced with General Grant
in her heyday, and later, turned *object
of pious memory*, in Tangiers...

On that small, frail mule
in Tangiers, beneath the broiling sun,
like some queen herself: broad, immense,
slow-moving, white-bodiced...
Even a cat might have worshipped her.
As I do still, though she be bodiless.

Complete loss of capacity to...
lift a hand – like so. You see,
I cannot, must not, do it.
Do what though?
Drive the pen across the page
in the customary fashion.
Nor open my old ears to
the Lady Audiart, the lovely Lady Audiart,
she of simplest wishes
and matchless accoutrements...

When I was naked, she covered me,
the Lady Audiart,
that kindest lady of my heart,

yet I have not covered her,
not with the least fine thread
of a garment.

In fact, I have harmed her.
I have not kept the winds
from driving across her until
they freeze her sparrow bones.
(She is a small-boned woman.
The bones stick out like spikes
in the worst of times,
and we have known such times.)

I have heard the sirens –
in the night, in the half-light,
at all hours of the day –
acqua alta! acqua alta! –
and I have not raised a finger
to stop the waters rising.
Rather, it is always she
who has covered me,
leading me up the stairs,
singing to me,
sometimes even
pushing me from behind as we go,
so cheerfully...
It is she who does it, not me,
always she...
She is plenitude itself, my lady,
and I am the empty vessel,
left here, alive though dead,
to wrestle with these phantoms in my head.

I would have gone back
and left her here, the girl,
but she would not do it,
and so, consequently,
I made it clear
that I would not do it either.

But in the first instance,

my lord, I was prepared to do it.
I am not worthy to be a father,
and that is why she too hates me
like all the rest.
And I deserve that hatred.
I am up to my neck
in the filth of my words,
and I deserve her hatred,
all their hatreds.
I cannot save her from drowning.
I cannot save myself
from the hell
of my own deserving,
and I must not either.

And still the waters,
faithful to the uttermost,
are resolute in their rising.

She strove to bring order out of debris,
and yet still I did not try
to clothe her nakedness.

I spouted upwards of a million words
in my time,
and not a single one of them
saved one man or one woman from drowning.
I ought to be ashamed of my life.

I spoke of ORDER, ORDER, ORDER,
and yet I could not order my thoughts
or my words. My *Cantos* were a mess,
a botched job. My letters were ridiculous,
my prose incoherent at the best of times.
(And most of my times were the worst of times.)

Where did I learn so badly to be myself?
Homer was a modest, truth-telling man.
Why did I not stay in Pennsylvania
and teach literature to the kids back home?
It would have been better that way.

What was it that betrayed me?
It was my mouth, and the size of my mouth.
My mouth took the measure of
Pound's incipient greatness
too early on.

I conquered London, Paris, Rome.
My mouth drove me on, on, on
as far as Radio Rome...
I was enslaved to my mouth.
I mistook myself for an oracle.
Will I ever be rid of
these miseries of the self?
No, says my shrivelled heart,
not before death.

Then let me defy my mouth,
even though it is dumb now,
and run, with a spirit of hope and youthfulness –
do I have some of that left
this late in my life –
toward death?

I am a man of wounds and unsound mind.
I have built up so many notions in the air.
See how they tremble and fall now in this heat.
(O heat, my chief accuser,
          which crushes me to the ground.)

To be of unsound mind is not to say overmuch.
It is to say: here, nothing; there, nothing.
Or: nothing that can be said is worth a fig.
So say it then, again, and make them grin.

Let your mind be a circus ring, with,
at the centre, unreason cracking its whip:
on! on! on! it screams –
such a heartfelt, hellish cry.
If there were tears to be shed,
I would shed them,
but my tear ducts are dry.

Now in she comes again
with that swollen offering of the bread,
and I have not the heart to glance at her —
thou, Olga, sweetest melodist of my uproar.

I have no wish to be photographed, not *solus*...
Or perhaps I should say *sola*
because we are within earshot of him,
and he does pick up on that sort of thing.

I am of little intrinsic interest myself —
beside him, that is. I have played my part.
I have played the violin to a certain standard.
I helped to rescue those precious scores,
Vivaldi's, from the Dresden catastrophe.

And now I protect him. And that is enough for me.
He does — or did (not any more) — the talking.
And I do the listening. May I suggest
that you do a little listening too?
There is much to be learnt
if you listen carefully.
There is much to be learnt from his poetry.

He was a great poet in his time, you know —
Eliot said so, and we all know what that means —
and I do not believe that he has been forgotten
by those who have troubled to remember him.

Many others have supported him too,
though not so wholeheartedly towards the end.
One should never trust fair-weather friends.
One should do one's best to identify
fair-weather friends in order to
score their names from the book of memory.

I have folded my blankets, that is all.
It is sufficient unto the heat of this day,
I have done no harm to the roaches either —
Were there roaches here?

O hear me, intercessor, say, fist on breast bone:
I did no harm to any living thing on this day!

I spoke not one word
to that curious, scrawny henfolk,
straying, prying.
I offered no word of advice or warning.
I merely blessed them with my stony eye.

So you may set down this
for a truth absolute:
Old Ez folded his blankets
in this camp at Pisa
as life was shifting around him,
so slowly, and with so little
conviction to stop the heart
that it might have been death dancing.

And yet they gave me the wherewithal
to write something.
And here I am, you have caught me at it,
writing, the *Pisan Cantos*...
This sight of my hand moving across the page
keeps me alive because if there is a motion,
there must be life –
albeit of a mechanistic kind.
And so, on this day, October 4, 1945,
I am a mechanical, and I am writing
the *Pisan Cantos*, line by line,
out of my heart.
Having no book, I can but consult
my heart – see how it palpitates!

By a certain light,
at a certain hour of day,
I fancy I hear
Antheil on the keys,
practising impossible harmonies...

And I hang at his elbow,
marvelling at that fingerwork of his,

so unpredictable, so fancy-free...
It cannot, alas, be
(though it may once have been)
because today, at this hour,
by that same falling light,

there is a kitten pawing
at those self-same keys
and, if I strain around,
I catch a glimpse,
the merest hint,
of its outstretched tail.
And then it is gone again.

As once passed the great Antheil this way,
he of most blessed memory.

Every new day, this waking to nothingness,
inside and beyond...
The dull sheen of waters enveloping me,
and she too enveloping me
with her scrawny arm,
and piping at me in that voice of hers,
a very English accent for an American girl...

I am fully prepared to go on that journey.
I take nothing with me.
I go as I was made.
I have folded my blankets.
I shall go as I was made.

Would that I could prepare myself
to give a full and proper account of myself.
But my words stick in my throat.
Ezra, the grandiose, the gullible,
Ezra, O man without the least best hope.

Once I remembered that I remembered.
This is not so any more.
Now I am as an open door
that the wind blows through.

I flap at the mercy of the wind.
I am no longer remarked upon.
I am simply a means to an end.

Once I believed myself to be a gate of wisdom,
but such wisdom as I had –
if I had any then –
fell away, crumbling
in my fingers as I watched
like unfired clay...
O kitten on the keys,
make such harmonies
as pass beyond mere human sense.
Prowling night-puss, close my ears.
I am drowning in my tears.

I see birds on the middle wire,
poised to fly,
like notes on a stave,
taking their song from me.
My fatigue goes as deep
as the grave.
Let there be no mercy.
We save but to throw away.

These men who pass by,
between here and the sunset,
they are nothing but shadows.

I shall tell them to leave
this tent of mine because,
though insubstantial,
they have the power to torment me.

I shall set Olga as a guard at my entranceway.
I shall force her down, down on all fours
until she possesses the cruelty
and the rapacity of great Cerberus,
all appetites unslaked...

If I could only find and re-enter my books,
I could change them as I pleased,
and then walk beside them,
gods beside man, privy to their ways,
advising, reproaching as I know I can.

This cage is no place for me,
though I may still be a man.
Do you understand,
you who pace here so restlessly,
as though before some beast?

The Verdict

Not long after the poem was completed, I showed it to my old friend Philip Morre, poet, bookseller, publisher and long-time Venetian resident. He expressed some doubt. Had I *really* caught Pound's voice and manner? Had I added too much by way of literary embellishment?

Those few brief words of condemnation stung me to the quick. If I had not captured the essence of the man or the poet, who exactly had I captured? A phantasm, real only to myself? Ideas began to swarm. Is it easier – or harder – to deal with the dead than the living? The living being is a forever moving target. What is more, if I had actually met Pound, would he always have seemed to me to be a lesser thing because I would have been inclined to batten down on to his foibles as a mere human being? Are words untethered from the living more inclined to resonate and shine? Does not the very idea of a Poem raise itself up for admiration?

Disheartened, if not winded, by his lack of enthusiasm, I thrust the poem into a drawer to mature for a few years, and decided to make a start on the writing of the book that Ib Bellew had rejected... Perhaps it was to be Ezra in Venice then...

Ezra Starts Out With Some Stale Cream Puffs

In Search of *A Lume Spento*

Ezra published *A Lume Spento*, his first book of poems, in 1908, at the age of 23. It was launched in an upstairs room in Venice, facing an old boatyard near the church of San Trovaso, within a short walk of that gondolier's cottage where he and Olga were to live. Later in the spring of 2012, my wife and I went in pursuit of that upstairs room in the Dorsoduro district.

We walk along the Zattere, past the Gesuiti church, until we meet the point where we turn along the San Trovaso Canal. Yet another site sacred to

Pound mentioned in the *Cantos*, I am thinking to myself as we approach the point where the canal meets the Rio Ogni Santi and the ancient boatyard – the *squero*. Now we are standing facing it across the water, exactly where Pound himself would have stood, in 1908. At my back is number 944 Calle dei Frati, now a bar and osteria. We step inside for a cappuccino and a *crostino*, eaten pinched inside a flimsy paper napkin snatched from a dispenser on the counter. There is music playing: 'Stand by Me'. Ezra, had he been standing beside me now, would probably have preferred Vivaldi. Two elderly, flush-faced Venetians are elbow-leaning at the bar, nursing their camparis and speaking to each other with passion in the Venetian dialect. The room that Pound would have rented in 1908, the room from which he had launched that first book, and where he posed for photographs in 1970 after his return to Venice from America, looking every inch the bearded sage, is directly above this bar.

I go out of the door, look up towards the two windows facing the canal, and wonder which one he would have peered out of. The old green wooden shutters are folded back, quite neatly. The cafe itself stands at the corner of the *calle* – there has been a cafe on this spot for decades. I walk along the *calle*, looking out for the side door by which he would have entered before mounting the stairs to his room. The doors are unnumbered. In fact, all the numbers have been removed because repairs and re-decorating are going on. At the end of the *calle*, it bends sharply to the right. By this point the numbers have re-appeared: 939, 940. I must have passed the door that Pound would have used. I retrace my steps back to the edge of the canal, passing by those two tantalisingly unnumbered doors, and look across the canal more carefully at the old wooden buildings of the boatyard, one of the oldest in Venice.

There's a gondola in dry dock, hauled up onto its wooden trestles. Other boats lie sprawled around on their sides, waiting patiently for some attention. Young men pick their way between them with all the busyness of practised experts. One of them is wearing trainers and casual red trousers, white stripes down the side, with a satiny sheen. The ancient and the modern in rude conjunction. Seagulls wing around mewing in the air at the junction of the waterways. Children are squealing in the nearby churchyard of San Trovaso, colourful lunch packs bouncing against their backs as they run, swerving away from each other. Turning back, I notice again that the green shutters of Pound's window above my head are folded back. There is relatively modern wrought ironwork in front of the window. The usual tangled fuss of cabling that carries the essential utilities hangs beneath it in characteristically unkempt and untidy Venetian fashion. Ezra is long gone. We walk away, with the ghost of his hard, quizzical stare still pursuing us.

A Vexing Conversation Beside a Venetian Canal

You see, I don't really know what it is that I'm doing... I am explaining this to my waspish old friend, the poet and translator Philip Morre, in his apartment overlooking the Ormesini Canal in Venice. It is the spring of 2013. Otherwise all is well here in Cannaregio. How could it not be? There is salad, cheese, boiled eggs and wine on the sun-splashed table, all courtesy of Billa, the local *supermercato*, which is open for business as usual on a Sunday morning. The window is open to the canal. There could be no more agreeable pursuit than to stand on that balcony and look out onto a sunny day such as this one, with the pinnacles of the Madonna dell'Orto (that magnificent church from which a priceless altarpiece by Giovanni Bellini was once stolen) peeking over the rooftops, and the lazy wash of the lagoon beyond....

Philip has read the first fifteen thousand words of my manuscript about Ezra Pound and Venice, and he has made various comments. Some of them are unflattering, which is always helpful. Who would not want to be scratched on the back by a feral Venetian cat, of which there are a few hereabouts? He tells me that I need to discover something new about Pound, that there seems to be no discernible trajectory to the fragment of manuscript that he has read. I explain, very imperfectly, because I feel embarrassed, muddled and slightly befuddled by prosecco, that I want Pound's Venetian story to be interwoven with my own in some way because my discovery of him as a writer has also been a life-long exercise in self-discovery.

He does not fully comprehend what I am saying because I am not making myself particularly clear. He suggests that I do a synopsis of the whole, with a couple of sample chapters. We talk about Ezra's putative late son

Omar, who died in 2010, and lived all his life in the shadow of his father. Putative? Philip has just pulled Humphrey Carpenter's biography of Pound out of the shelf, and read to me the passage in which the biographer muses about Omar's paternity. The following day he tells me that he thinks Omar's father may have been the poet Basil Bunting. Their eyebrows were remarkably similar, he reminds me...

Saturday Morning in a Soho Bookshop

Do you have much Ezra Pound material? I ask the poet Marius Kociejowski. We are standing in the tiny antiquarian bookshop where he works in Cecil Court, Soho. I am paying him my usual Saturday morning visit. His small desk, as usual, is wedged into its far corner, just holding out against the teetering ziggurats of dust-choked volumes. Oh yes, he replies, purposefully sweeping back his hirsute grey hair. He drags his metal steps across to the shelves beside the desk, where some of the rarest books are kept, behind glass. He climbs up and, reaching out balletically, plucks a handful from a high shelf. They are all lovingly protected by cellophane. Very rare indeed, I see, as I begin to examine them: a good first edition of the *Catholic Anthology* of 1912, another of an early collection of poems published by Elkin Matthews called *Umbra*. These are precious objects indeed, and their rarity is reflected in their prices: £1,500, £750.... One of them even has Pound's own signature.

'I'm thinking of writing a book about Ezra and Venice,' I tell him. He looks surprised – and pleased.

'Gosh, Pound, that could be interesting. Who reads him now though?'

'It will also be something to do with his influence on my life, how I've been reading him on and off for years, planning books I might write about him, and never quite doing so... Why has the idea of him always interested me so much? I'm trying to explain it all to myself.'

'You could begin – well, not that you need me to tell you where to begin – by reading a piece that Geoffrey Hill once wrote about him. I think it was probably for *Agenda* magazine. He thinks that Pound is the greatest poet of the twentieth century. Probably worth ringing Christopher Middleton too. He and Guy Davenport went to see Pound when he was in St Elizabeth's.'

'Did you talk to Christopher Middleton about Pound when you did your book-length interview with him?'

He looks slightly puzzled. 'No, I didn't. Goodness knows why. I ought to have done...'

'Was Pound really silent most of the time during the last decade of his life? Or is that a piece of myth-making?'

'Oh no, I think it's true. There's an old lady who lives in Museum Street. She used to go and read to him. Baron Corvo, I think. He never said a word. Not a single word...'

I hand back the precious first editions. He climbs up to slot them back into that empty space on the upper shelf.

'Is it generally agreed, do you think, that Omar Pound was not in fact Ezra's son at all?'

'Oh yes,' he says, with some confidence.

'Who was his real father then? Someone recently told me that it was probably the poet Basil Bunting. Apparently, he and Omar Pound had very similar eyebrows..'

'It was an Egyptian businessman, as far as I know...'

Idling in the Sun-splashed Garden of the Chelsea Arts Club with the Art Critic John McEwen One Friday Lunchtime

'Cambridge? Then?' John McEwen calls across to me. He is walking back across the garden of the Chelsea Arts Club with a couple of brimming glasses of Kir, both held deftly in the one hand, and rather alarmingly on the tilt. We've both been talking about the 1960s, and of some early encounters with Ezra Pound. 'Cambridge then, my dear Michael? Those, surely, were the last of the pre-tourist days.' He falls, sighing, back into his chair. 'I got to know some friends of my brother's soon after I went up. Italians. They were so sophisticated. They taught me so much... Coffee, for example. Who knew about coffee, then, in England? And women...' Raising his head, he opens his mouth and peers into the middle distance.

'Isn't it just marvellous here?' he says, interrupting himself. He looks around a little more, wondering at the scene across the lawn. I count four panama hats sheltering mature, balding pates from the relentless downbeat of the sunlight. One of them is slumped in a deckchair, seemingly dead. 'Could there be a better place to be lunching than here, now?' John adds, warming to his mood of reverie. Then he returns to the matter in hand. 'I clearly remember that there was an exasperated member of the English Faculty who once did a survey amongst the undergraduates. It consisted of one sentence only: who was Ezra Pound? Just that one question: who was Ezra Pound? And, do you know what, Michael, about sixty per cent of them – sixty per cent! – thought that he was a woman! And that was in 1964, the last of the pre-tourist days...'

We walk back through the bar, nodding at Bill Packer, art critic and painter, as we go. He is bent forward over his glass, talking to a co-conspirator. I glance across at the dandified plaster bust of Whistler, raised up on its plinth beside the fireplace. Ah, Whistler! Ezra was a great admirer of Whistler, for his ability to forge a name and an identity for himself as an Amurikan in Europe, that capacity to fight back or even to hold one's own. (Ezra didn't do quite so well. He turned into an embittered ranter against the philistinism of London far too soon.) When Whistler sold the celebrated portrait of his mother to the Luxembourg for a miserly four hundred francs, it was regarded as a triumph. Even Monet had not been allowed entry to the great national collection. As the most distinguished member of the Chelsea Arts Club – and its co-founder into the bargain – Whistler was treated to a banquet in his honour. Sadly, he died in July of 1908, just as Pound was due to arrive in London.

Would Ezra himself have been welcome as a guest here? It seems unlikely. In those days the Club was on the turn against all things newfangled. Stephen Bartley, the club's honorary archivist, confirms this. 'He may have visited, of course – I'll need to check the visitors' book – but it is rather unlikely that his opinions would have found much favour here. The club was vehemently anti-modernist at that time, which is exemplified by their 'spoof' exhibition of 1910, 'Septule and the Racinists', which was a dig at Cubists, Futurists and all the other -ists. It was organised by the then President James Jebusa Shannon, and aided by Henry Mayo Bateman and others...'

Ezra would certainly not have come here to enjoy the booze because he was never much of a drinker – he didn't need alcohol to make him hyperactive. When Swinburne made an ass of himself at the club, Whistler complained to the committee about the club's response. 'You ought to be proud that there is in London a club where the greatest poet of your time *can* get drunk if he wants to, otherwise he might lie in the gutter.' It was Ezra himself who quoted this outburst, in a review of Edmund Gosse's biography of Swinburne, which was published in *Poetry* in 1918.

That Lunchtime Conversation in Venice Continues

What about doing a biography of the children? Philip Morre suggests as we start on the cheese. I feel utterly exasperated when he says that. With him. With myself. I loathe the very idea of working on a biography of anyone. I have always felt like that. Who in their right mind would wish to devote a decade or more to investigating in minute detail the life of someone else? Surely you would be consumed by hatred of your subject long before you had slogged your way to the finishing line? Isn't that exactly what happened to Lawrence Thompson, the man who dogged the footsteps of Robert Frost for more than two decades?

I ought not to feel annoyed with Philip though. It is my fault entirely. He is only trying to help. Only I am to blame for this state of affairs. My mind is still in a complete muddle about my Pound book – as it always has been. All that I know for sure is that some current is still pulling me in the direction of writing such a book, even though it has never been clear to me – and is not clear even now – what book it is that I'm supposed to be writing.

Ezra, Jongleur

No matter where you go, some writers always seem to travel with you. Today, for example, I am sitting, nursing the *Collected Shorter Poems* of Ezra, at a table in the Aude, amongst some gently upsloping fields near Carcassonne. It is early summer again, and a crop of winter wheat is biding its time below irregular clumps of dense, deciduous, hill-topping woodland (like bosses on a shield, I am thinking to myself as I appraise them) from which, in the hunting season still some months on, you can, now and again, see the dead weight of a muscly, compacted, swag-bellied wild boar being carried, upside down, trussed to a long pole, by a couple of hard-faced local men, moving along, quite furtively, with their long-barrelled guns tight-squeezed into their arm pits. The bristly dead carcass slowly sways along – left, right, left – to the rhythm of their walking pace. Old rituals fade away with painstaking difficulty in these parts.

This is Ezra country, where he walked, alone, in 1914, and again in 1920, seeking the ghosts of the Troubadours, those ambulant minstrels, listening out for their songs of thwarted love, written in Provençal in the twelfth century, that strange, skewed tongue, learnt by him in some college in Pennsylvania, as a way of renewing his own writing as a poet in English. He was teaching himself how to write, how to make things new, shucking off the dead load of Victorian malpractice, by part-mimicking and part-re-inventing the writings of an even more ancient tongue. Those interrupted journeyings in Southern France were recorded in a book of maddeningly fragmentary and piecemeal notes and observations – so much about Ezra was always maddening – published many decades later by a devoted and assiduous American scholar called Richard Sieburth under the title of *A Walking Tour in Southern France*.

That harried book *Guide to Kulchur* has its moments of reflective calm. One such recalls those walking tours in Southern France, how unencumbered life seemed to him then, when, in that era before passports, the serendipitous traveller with an international currency in his pocket could experience the freedom of life without constraints...

I look down at the *abri* below the house where we are staying. And the fields beyond. This lovely, sequestered demesne of sixty hectares, often rudely buffeted by howling winds, is called Cantaloup, and in homage to that old name, a metal weather vane squeals, when the wind changes direction, from the roof directly below my line of sight. Above the turning metal arrow stands a metal wolf, in flattened profile, muzzle raised, baying at the faultless blue of the evening sky.

Some years ago, a different poet[5] wrote about this wolf, and the poem that he wrote is attached to a wall, its words burnt into an irregularly shaped gobbet of wood, in the shadow of that forever restlessly turning weather vane. Here are those words of his:

---

[5] i.e. the author of this book

Homage a la Girouette de Cantaloup
During Incendiary Times

When the wolf howls from the South,
There will be drouth.

When the wolf barks from the North,
Let him bark himself hoarse.

When the wolf croons from the West,
Be at rest.

When the wolf bends to the East,
The blessings of sunlight will lie at your feet.

Pound wrote of wolf-madness in an early poem, I recall, turning to it in my book. 'Piere Vidal Old' is spoken by a fevered old man who was widely regarded in his day as the Fool of Provence *par excellence*, and it re-enacts his pursuit of the lady Loba of Penautier – the chateau of Penautier is just a short drive from this house – in a fit of love-sick, love-lorn distraction. Hunters with dogs went after him, pursuing him through the mountains of Cabaret, and carried him, as good as dead, to the dwelling place of the woman whose unearthly beauty had driven him to distraction. And there he was looked after, by the lady and her kindly lord; and there he raved and raged on about her qualities, life-long, into extreme old age, crazed as a wolf. A pet of sorts then, whose story was told and re-told by the *jongleurs* of this region.

The poem itself is one of Pound's many early voice-projections or instances of assumed identity, in which he tries on this character or that, forever in pursuit of the poet and the man that he was, in time, to become. Here the voice is shrill, high-pitched, impassioned, weirdly antique in its flavour. As a young man, Pound spent many years learning to be old.

That same evening I am sitting out on the terrace in pre-prandial mood, idly communing with a glass of excellent local rosé. Then a most remarkable thing happens. Out of the corner of my eye, directly across the adjacent field of winter wheat, I suddenly see a certain something, appearing and then disappearing, so fleeting, so soon gone. My wife stands up, pushing her chair away, which scrapes along the ground with the unlovely sound of an old fogey clearing a plaque of phlegm from his throat. She has seen it too, and our friend, who owns this field, together with that rising clump of woodland beyond, also jab-points in the same direction, exclaiming. It was a pair of bouncing, leaping ears that we saw, all of us, so tall, so spry, so unusually pointed, and much taller than any animal's ears I have ever seen before. A lynx! my friend exclaims.

Ah yes, I might have guessed, it was one of Ezra's many lynxes – his writings are haunted by lynxes, and one of them had just paid a call on us, as if on his behalf, to assure itself that justice was being done by his memory, his forever shaky reputation.

Many of those lynxes had prowled back and forth across the *Pisan Cantos*, sustaining creatures of myth, at that moment in his life when Ezra felt closest to death. Held in a metal cage six feet by six for part of his period of incarceration, he was about to be returned to America and arraigned on a charge of treason for having made pro-fascist broadcasts over Radio Rome. It was then, in 1945, after Mussolini's body had been displayed in public in a square in Milan, strung up by the heels like a dead boar, that Ezra had written of lynxes, lynxes, lynxes, to an almost obsessive degree.

A Remarkable Photograph of Ezra in Extreme Old Age Turns up in a Venetian Bookshop

About a year or so before I began that rather untidy conversation with Philip Morre, I had walked into Old World Books, his second-hand bookshop in the Venetian Ghetto, for yet another glass or two of prosecco. It was the usual evening ritual: poking about for the bottle in the door of the fridge behind the curtain; easing off the cork with the edge of the thumb; then giving the insides of the two or three glasses a good, vigorous polish with a tea cloth before filling them to the brim, just as trading (such trading as there was; it was seldom much, at that or any other hour of the day) was drawing to a close. It was then that we would stand or sit around – he would sit; I would stand or loll against a stack or two of books about the history of the Venetian Republic – nattering about this and that – who had arrived and who had just left – whilst gently sipping from our flutes. His desk would be the usual chaotic clutter of books and papers and this and that, stockaded around its perimeter by an untidy encirclement of cardboard boxes, from which yet more books would be carelessly brimming. And there he would be, sitting or sprawling amongst it all, affably spread-legged as usual, in his rather appealingly tired looking brown corduroy jacket, catching up on an article from some old issue of the *TLS*. He spent much of his day catching up with the *TLS* – when, that is, he wasn't pretending to sell interesting books. There was always so much catching up to be done.

Something new had turned up on the wall that day, I noticed, occupying a space next to a letter by Paul Verlaine about the sale of a print that I had read repeatedly. Where did you get this marvellous photo of Ezra in old age? I asked him.

Charity auction, he told me in that drawly way of his, as if it was as much as he could do to bother to answer me at all. It had cost him an absolute fortune, he added, but it had been worth it.

This was Ezra, near skeletal, with his wild shock of back-combed hair, caught in the gloom of those final years of almost uninterrupted taciturnity, sitting in the upstairs bedroom of that gondolier's cottage in Dorsoduro in a chair (probably made by himself) into which he seems to be shrinking even as we look, fiercely protected by Olga Rudge, his mistress, who is probably sitting in the kitchen downstairs – there was one room to each floor of that tiny house.

It was the portrait of a once great mind now turned in upon itself, brooding upon the colossal tragedy of his own life, and the botched enterprise that his great epic poem *The Cantos* had become. I took a photograph of it there and then on my camera phone, not a good one – the image of the photographer is even reflected in the photograph – but it was sufficient to record the momentary shock of seeing that magnificent face, that great eminence of a head...

The Religion of Poetry

It has often been said that poetry might serve as a substitute for religion, that when the sea of faith withdraws, the consolatory power of verse (or the consolatory look of its fabricator) steps up. Could this have been the case with me? Did Ezra become my substitute God? It is not entirely implausible. There are both trivial and serious reasons for believing that this might even be the case.

Let us consider that look of the Ezra Pound in old age. Is he not the tortured prophet in that photograph tacked to the wall of Philip Morre's bookshop in the Venetian Ghetto, all that anguish in his eyes and the foaming, unruly beard? He had devoted his life, unswervingly, to the ancient art of poetry, and the world – in the person of the American authorities – had caged, persecuted and vilified him. The world had pronounced him a madman. His very name, Ezra, was biblical in its resonance. Was there not a book of Ezra in the Old Testament? What is more, his daughter Mary had once described *The Cantos* as 'biblical'. What exactly had she meant by that? And, if it were true, would that not have given me, who, when I first encountered Ezra, had been reading the Bible assiduously for several years, a powerful reason to take his words seriously?

The Book of Ezra

In the fifteenth book of the Old Testament, the prophet Ezra is much given to lamenting over various bad decisions taken by the Israelites. Shechaniah, the son of Jehiel, himself one of the sons of Elam, admits to having trespassed against their God by taking *strange wives of the people of the land*. What to do by way of recompense? First of all, and having first put all those wives away, to confess to all that wrongdoing, and then for the guilty sons of *priests to offer a ram of the flock for their trespass*. Broadcasting over Radio Rome in 1940, Ezra the poet praised Hitler's wise words in *Mein Kampf*, where he advocates a more rigorous approach to racial purification, though we have no evidence that Ezra was ever aware of the horrors of the consequences of that malign cast of mind at the time that they were being put into practice.

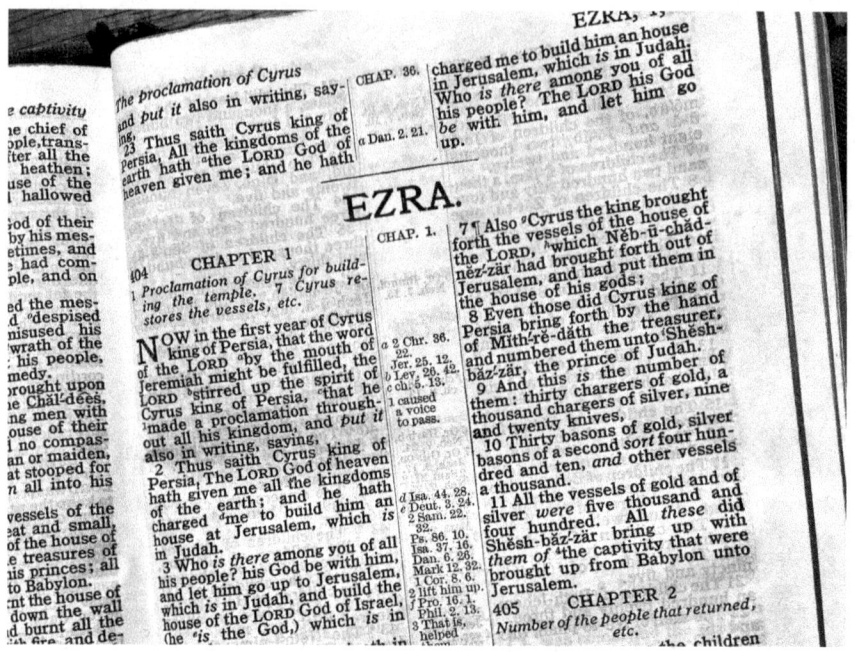

The Badness of Ezra

I am aware that one of the difficulties of writing such a book as this one has been caused by the volatile nature of my relationship with Ezra. This means at least three things: my relationship with the idea of the man, my relationship with his life and the way that he lived it, and my relationship with all that he wrote and published. One of the problems with Ezra is that he had the capacity to write *so badly*. He vexes and disappoints quite as much as he pleases. The quality is so uneven. You can blame much of the bad writing of the 1930s and 1940s – all those tedious rants against usury – on a colossal failure of judgement induced by a mood of perpetual frenzy about the misjudgments of governments. No relationship with another human being is ever easy, not even a literary one. You could argue that a literary relationship might be abandoned much more easily than any human partner – after all, books can be disposed of. No one else will be there to protest.

Not so simple, I fear. Some books, some authors, are with you for life even when you treat them unfairly. Books disappear, only to return in slightly different editions, perkily accusatory as ever. They linger – and they malinger. It is also difficult to shake off some of the many preoccupations you and any favoured author may have in common. Take money, for example.

Ah, Money!

Ah, money! Ezra Pound and I have spent much time being exercised by the idea of money. To wake up thinking of money. To go to bed worrying about the near absence of money. All this sounds very human. Money defines and underpins all that we do, all that we are. It is the silent companion at our shoulder, pointing to this, that or the other, when we walk through this fantastical, consumerist world.

I lay the blame for my obsession with money upon family circumstances. I never experienced desperate poverty as a child, but the fear of an imminent lack of money – that terror of forever skirting close to the edge of pennilessness – has been with me all my life, inculcated into me by my maternal grandfather, Harold Hickson. In our small kitchen in north-east Sheffield during the 1950s, he used to bring out the black tin box (the one whose key he kept in his pocket) on Friday evenings. It always rattled with small change. Friday was reckoning-up night, when my mother and my grandmother, cowed and defensive, were held to account for how they had spent the weekly housekeeping, every last penny of it. The air was painted blue with accusation and counter-accusation. Promissory notes were screwed into tight balls in the fist.

Ezra was very close to money too, though you could say that his family had more of a professional interest in the subject. His father Homer was an assistant assayer at the Philadelphia Mint, and father and son would often hold coins up to the light, scrutinising them closely, appraising their worth, and assessing their aesthetic value as well turned artefacts. This was not the taking of pleasure in the ownership of money alone. It was an appreciation of money as a species of artistic endeavour.

Ezra was generous with his own money (even when he had relatively little of it), and he was always prepared to help others. In a letter of 1916, he told a correspondent that he had earned just £45 that year. In spite of the fact that he himself was often in financial straits, he spent a great deal of selfless time raising money for writers, who, in his opinion, ought to be free of financial burdens. In 1915, he was instrumental in persuading the British Government to pay a Civil List pension of £100 to an unpublished Irish writer who was living in exile in Trieste. That man was James Joyce.

The theme of money's misuse at the hands of international bankers engaged and increasingly enraged him for much of his later life. The subject spread like a stain through his writing, poetry and prose alike. In time, the lyric poet went into deep freeze. The political spilled over into the personal. In his opinion, there was no greater sin than usury, the lending out of money at interest. Ezra, like any right-thinking individual, knew that every human being on earth needed money to stay alive; that there was no literary production without money, no free-floating aesthetic world that was not finally made possible by hard lucre. Writers, for example, were supported by patrons. And there had always been an inextricable link between high culture and high finance. Picture frames came gilded at a price. The great patrons of the arts in Florence during the Renaissance had themselves been bankers. So money had its place. What troubled Ezra was the mis-use of money by those pernicious individuals who regarded the amassing of money as an end in itself. At that point the world begins to fall apart. In Ezra's opinion, that happened during his own lifetime.

Ezra raged against the fact that in 1917 the US Government stopped printing their own money, that they became slaves to private banking. That abrogation of responsibility set everything out of joint. The Florentines on the other hand, in the way-back-whens of the 1500s or thereabouts, had been very good at banking. They had been responsible and exemplary bankers. They had not invited the filthy Sienese to do their banking for them. By the 1930s Ezra was obsessed by the subject.

Ezra was regarded as an oddball for paying so much attention to money. By the 1930s, publishers were beginning to look askance at him, to regard him as a crank and a literary misfit. What was a lyric poet doing fussing over money? Why should he be concerned with such unpoetical matters? What was wrong with paying attention to the human heart? Wasn't that what poets were supposed to be for? Oh no, Ezra disagreed with all that. He had set aside his lyricism, he explained, precisely in order to give to the world a wake-up call about the evils of the misuse of money. Nothing would stop him. He became an evangelical for the cause. It was just too important to be ignored.

He has a point, I suppose. You could say that, generally speaking, writers talk too little about money, and that Ezra was merely bringing out into the open what needed to be discussed as a matter of urgency. Why not talk about it anyway? Why pretend that it doesn't exist? Writers are nowhere without money. Without money they cannot survive. And when they deliberately choose not to talk about it, they are involved in a game of emotional dissimulation. They are pretending that there is a world of writing, some pure, quasi-paradisal zone, that exists beyond the reach of stinking money, and that what they have written is a million miles from financial considerations. This is all a lie, of course. Money – grants, hand-outs, state subsidies, prizes, awards – give you the wherewithal – the space, the time, the hours free of the burden of exhausting work of other kinds – in which to write. To pretend otherwise is a nonsense. Ezra saw that. He knew that writers needed money. And yet the money racket was poisoning the well of civilisation. That was why he felt that he had to shout so loudly and for so long.

Ezra Vies for my Attention With the Youthful Vincent Van Dogh During a Visit to my Son in Norwich in the Winter of 2021

It's been a challenging weekend up here in Norwich for two reasons: a truly alarming encounter with Ezra, and another with a skittery zipper of a young canine newly christened Vincent Van Dogh (who is a young Jack Russell terrier, and the latest addition to my son's household). In order to distract myself from his leaping and rendings – Vincent never leaves you in peace. He takes flying jumps at any newspaper you might try to open. I watch him helplessly as he makes off with a ragged twenty-five percent of a full-page review in this week's *TLS* of a new gathering of books by William Faulkner – I take a trip upstairs and out of harm's way.

I am currently sitting in the attic bedroom, door closed, trying to distract myself from the practical difficulties of the day – how not to get bitten or tripped up, for example – by having a little fun at the expense of a dead American academic called Leonard Doob. 'Scooby' Doob raises a half smile when I mention the possibility later to my son, who is a doctor. My son knows the source of half my woes. He is finding Vincent difficult, too. Did the breeder separate him from his mother too soon? Probably. The peaceful attic room's dormer window looks out onto the ancient tower of Norwich Cathedral. The idea of the consolations, the healing balm, of religion float into and out of my head. Then the furious scratchings at the door begin again.

Actually, Harvard-educated Doob was a very serious man, author of many books, and a cognitive psychologist into the bargain. Amongst his public duties had been to serve as director of overseas intelligence for the United States Office of War Information during World War Two. That's why I have him with me this weekend. Doob edited a fat orange book of Ezra's wartime radio speeches, delivered over Radio Rome between 1941 and 1943, called *Ezra Pound Speaking*. It was not published until 1978, six years after Ezra's death.

This is a book I had known about for most of my life, and had never read. Never chosen to read? Possibly. Within its almost five hundred pages you encounter the very worst of Pound, the most hysterical, the most unhinged, the most repellent, the most vitriolically slapdash. It is as if Ezra has taken leave of his senses. He makes Vincent van Dogh, that paper-render of a wild pup, seem, by comparison, like a sober-suited, seventeenth-century prelate. Can this really have been written to bring Americans and their European allies to their senses? I glance down at the words I jotted down in my red notebook as I was reading it: coarse, vituperative, crudely denunciatory; extravagant verbal tomfoolery; crazed wordplay; more a sequence of spasms than an argument. How can a man who blithely talks of justice and equity, and who bemoans the death of classical scholarship, be writing in words so hysterical and out of control? He offers Adolf Hitler his personal congratulations for having spoken out so forcibly about the need for racial purity in *Mein Kampf*...

What caused him to deliver this series of vituperative rants? He needed the money, Olga had told me in the winter of 1984. All other sources of income had dried up. Those were desperate days indeed...

A Conversation Beside the Sea about Ezra's Madness

It is a Saturday in late April, and I am in the doldrums. I seem to have reached an impasse, a state of suspension, a mood of complete bafflement. I do not really know what went wrong with Ezra during and immediately after the First World War, what exactly set him off in the direction which eventually caused him to fall into a kind of slipshod, slightly hysterical manner of writing that seemed to be at odds with everything by which, as a young man freshly arrived in London in 1908, he had set so much store: clarity of meaning, sharpness of perception, a lack of emotional slither. These are the very virtues for which I used to commend him when, in my early 20s at the end of the 1960s, I was first beginning to read him, and they were the very ones he had insisted that every young poet must pay attention to if he is not to fall into bad habits as a writer.

I have just been re-reading the so called *Malatesta Cantos*, in which Ezra engages in a kind of historical re-presentation of episodes from Italian Renaissance history of the fifteenth century. The way in which he redacts or summarises sequences of historical events in these *Cantos* seems at best ill-judged and at worst incompetent, shrill, wild, clumsy, almost ridiculous. He gives the principal players in this drama of Renaissance realpolitik – Sigismundo Malatesta and Federico de Urbino, for example – implausible nicknames, which are slangy, westernized versions of the originals: Siggy, Feddy. And is there not something even more troubling about that nickname Siggy? Is anti-semitism not buried somewhere inside it? In all, he seems to be offering us crude, clumsily staccato versions of what he is trying to explain: the nature (and the failure) of good governance.

And is this really verse that he thinks he is writing? The way it is arranged down the page certainly looks a bit like verse. Unfortunately, it reads like ill-digested, spewed forth gobbets of stuff, tin-eared – as he himself might have said, witheringly. What was going so badly wrong?

In pursuit of an answer I travel, one sunny weekend in April, to the South Coast of England, to the somnolent 19th-century seaside town of Eastbourne, for some enlightenment. It is there that my old friend Alistair Davies lives, an academic who has spent a good part of his career at Sussex University, teaching English and American studies. We were exact contemporaries at Cambridge University, both students of English literature with a modicum of unhealthy addiction to the complicated poetry of Ezra.

We talk over a bottle of Merlot and a plate of pasta in his kitchen.

'He went mad,' that's what happened,' Alistair says. 'The First World War drove him mad. The best minds of his generation – the philosopher T.E. Hulme, the sculptor Henri Gaudier-Brezska, for example – were killed, and completely unnecessarily. We needn't have joined the war at all – Niall Ferguson argues this in *The Pity of War*. We had no particular reason to defend the sovereignty of Belgium. It was the merchants – that is Wyndham Lewis' term – who were pushing for our engagement. German manufacturers were overtaking ours. Something had to be done about it. The arms manufacturers forced the hand of the government. I believe that

Pound, even though he may not have been privy to sensitive information, sensed that this was happening, on his pulses, that England was pitching herself into an act of madness that would not only bring her close to bankruptcy, but which would sweep away all the structures of pre-war England, including the kind of aristocratic patronage upon which he depended. It was a wrong and catastrophic decision. Who was left after all that carnage? Clive Bell and the simpering Bloomsburys. I believe he felt the carnage of the First World War as a personal tragedy. And what was it all for? A botched civilisation, as he writes in "Hugh Selwyn Mauberley"...'

I nod. This makes a good deal of sense even though I had flinched at that use of the no-holds-barred word madness. The trouble is that good conversation turns me off my food. I just can't seem to concentrate on two things at once. I push my half-full plate aside, a mite sheepishly.

'Ezra always seems to me to be writing with such impatience,' I interject, 'and he gets worse and worse as he heads into the 1930s. He becomes hysterical. He won't take no for an answer. When *Jefferson/And Or Mussolini* is rejected – 40 times – during the early 1930s, it does not occur to him to think that it might be something to do with the sloppiness of the writing. He thinks that it is only his unacceptable ideas which are being attacked. The enemy is everywhere. How different his tone of voice is from T.S. Eliot's, for example, who is so measured, so smoothly patrician, so lofty...'

'What you mustn't forget, Michael, is that Pound was – and regarded himself as – an outsider – just as Wyndham Lewis did. He was proud to be an outsider.'

'It's true that he was forever trashing academics and academic institutions, but it's also true to say that, while he happily played at being an outsider, he could also be a bit of an insider too when it was of some advantage to him. He would remind people that his grandfather was a lumber merchant. He would also mention that his mother's family, the Westons, came over to America in the 17th century, and name the boat. Pound could express himself carefully when he chose to do so, but he could also transform himself into a bar-room brawler at the drop of a hat, complete with cranky spelling. How much is this issue of money to do with his general sense of hysterical insecurity do you think, Alistair?'
'A lot. What he regarded as the pernicious behaviour of Jewish financiers gets woven into his arguments quite early on, but he himself was very

much aware of the need for money. Old patrons disappeared. John Quinn died young. There is also, I suspect, the related issue of patronage and jealousy. Did you know that Joyce had a patron called Harriet Weaver whose investments gave him an income, over time, of about $1.7 million dollars? The point I'm trying to make, the key point if you like, is that Pound and Lewis lacked regular income from a wealthy patron while Joyce had a regular, very secure and very considerable income by comparison.'

'No wonder he didn't have to worry about the prospect of readers... Ezra's father Homer gave him an allowance of sorts for many years. I don't know when that stopped. At the time of Homer's death in 1941? I do remember Ezra's daughter writing in her memoir *Discretions* that at the time he was doing his notorious broadcasts over Radio Rome, this was their only source of income. What is more, the question of how to survive is constantly being broached in that book...'

'Michael, these men – Pound and Lewis – did not go to the best universities. They did not come up through the public school system. Pound was not a scholar of a traditional kind. Nor was Lewis either, although he had a brilliant, magpie mind. How the real scholars jumped on Pound when they thought they had caught him out making elementary mistakes in his translations from other languages! Eliot, on the other hand, that man with the impeccable Harvard education, would have got his Greek right....'

'What I don't quite understand, Alistair, is why it was Pound, Eliot, Lewis and Yeats, those ferocious political reactionaries, who seduced us as young students, especially given that we were '68-ers ourselves, amongst the vanguard of the revolutionary young. How do we explain that one away? Why did we look to those hieratic, élitist old men when we could have taken Stan Barstow or Arnold Wesker as our role models?

Lago di Maggiore: Fascist Ranting Beside the Hotel Pool

This morning, I'm re-reading my old copy[6] of Ezra's *Jefferson and/or Mussolini* beside the pool. It's an extended rant from the Rapallo years (1935 or A.F. XIII, depending upon whether or not you take your cue from the new Fascist Calendar, and most inhabitants of Rapallo, being

---

[6] First published by Stanley Nott in 1935, and re-published in paperback by Liveright in 1970 – see Book List

Fascist almost to a man, would have done so) that Ezra found very difficult to get treated seriously by an English or an American publishing house. When you read it, you understand why. My copy of the book – it's a paperback – is in pretty poor shape. It falls open – in fact, it falls in half – at a pre-determined place because its spine got broken long ago. Did I break that spine? Could I have been that careless with one of my books? On closer inspection, it's evident that it was a lousy, on-the-cheap piece of book-making in the first place, which was almost bound to fall to pieces, crack clean in half, when opened. The paper it's printed on is terrible too. The more I read its bilious, slap-happy prose, with its superficial judgements about Mussolini – he was a man with a sense of history, apparently – and much overuse of CAPITALIZATION to indicate that Ezra is bawling at the top of his voice in order to get the point across **just in case you hadn't heard** – the more I think that the quality of the book suits its content. Crap book for crap ideas. It's for this reason that I don't even care too much if these crazy kids splash it with a bit of pool water. It's as much as it deserves. They don't though.

Muss (yet another of Ezra's silly abbreviations) is an ARTIFEX, an artist, a man given to ACTION, a man almost destined to rule because he alone was capable of re-awakening a sense of responsibility. This man with an 'editorial eye' spoke with clarity, recognising that there was work to be done, and that he was the man to do it. He was never bamboozled by money. He debunked those who deserved it.

It's all so broad-brush and hectic. By now Ezra loathes Europe in general – all he can see, virtuous Italy aside, are unscrupulous bankers and munitions vendors – and London in particular. Its writers and politicians are all tarred with the same brush. London reeks of decay, corruption, snobbery and complacency. Amongst those Ezra damns is the anthologist Arthur Quiller-Couch, compiler of the *Oxford Book of English Verse*. Quiller-Couch snapped back. Writing in a book called *The Poet as Citizen* (also published in 1935), he describes 'Mr Ezra Pound's *Draft of Thirty Cantos* as 'a roomy, thrice-heated oven into which he would shrivel, all things and all men for which he has a righteous contempt. Is it a revolt against prettiness, convention, complacency? That is no new revolt, nor original...'

According to Ezra, a new orientation of the will was required to make the body politic function again. Mussolini understood all that – and Confucius would surely have agreed. Amidst the shrillness and disorder of his prose rant, Ezra appeals for ORDER, ORDER, ORDER.

The Slip, Lash and Slither of the Weather on the South Coast of England

Eastbourne, hurrying, just the two of us, collars up, along one of the older, twistier streets, quite close to the Promenade, on a squally Saturday afternoon in late Spring. Dodging in out of the cold, spitting rain.

Elemental spite, that's what it feels like.

Then I spot it, the second-hand bookshop! Tarpaulin has been loosely flung across the stock outside in the street. In we go. The proprietor, an elderly man of fixed views, sits in state in the midst of it all, in a tiny island of space amidst the leaning towers and the overstuffed, ceiling-grazing shelves, scowling, fearing the worse that is yet to come, eyes alive on all sides for the kleptomaniac. There are so few bookshops like it these days, I am thinking to myself as, having descended to the basement down creaky stairs, I walk gingerly, side on, between the ziggurats of marvellous, dingily lit promise. Now, after much searching, I find the relevant shelves: 20th Century Literature. Making any headway is not easy. There are stacks of books leaning into the very shelf – it's at floor level – that I want to look at, as if in hurried, whispered conversation, far from the madding crowd of such as I. Then I see it. *Interviews with Robert Graves.* Paperback. £4. I riffle through it as far as the index, find the 'ps'. Ezra Pound. Very few entries. Looking at the first, I quickly understand why.

Phoney. Fascist. Faker.

A not uncommon point of view.

Spasmodic Email Conversation With the Poets Marius Kociejowski in London and Norm Sibum in Montreal

Marius Kociejowski: Is it true, what Norm Sibum tells me, that you are writing an *anti*-Ezra piece? I thought it was pro…

Michael Glover: Here's what I wrote to Norm yesterday, when he asked me whether I was dissing Pound: *no, not at all. That would be too crass. I've been preoccupied by him for forty years. Why though? What does it all mean? Those are the questions.*

So what exactly do *you* think of Pound, Marius?

MK: Oh my o my o my … too big a subject … shall we say tragically flawed? If merely flawed, sans the tragic, then he could be consigned to the literary dustbin as the author of some ghastly radio speeches. As it is, the monument to his genius has yet to be constructed, which is not to say he has not had his brilliant commentators, but that he needs to be seen from afar without their support. "To be men not destroyers." Too many people, my dear friends Norm Sibum and Eric Ormsby among them, are not giving him his proper due. They are studying not the clock but only the pendulum. All that the pendulum signifies are knee-jerk reactions. Show me a 20th century prosody more muscular than his. Those who turn away from it settle instead for the superciliousness of Auden & Co who are still very much with us.

MG: Muscular? And what exactly does muscular mean?

MK: It means kicking sand in Auden's face.

MG: Surely it means more than that.

MK: All right then. It means energetic, vigorous, strong, spunky..

MG: Masculine?

MK That too.

And here is what Norm Sibum replied when I asked him for his opinion of Pound…

NS: He's no god to me, but when someone tells me he's a great poet or was, I'm not inclined to willy-nilly disagree. A lot of the foolishness that has been done in his name is not his fault, so I think it. Well, rots of ruck…

MG: And what exactly does that mean, Norm?

NS: It's Chinese for lots of luck. More later. Just up…

NS (later): Ah, Pound. Twagick figure. No, really. From Idaho cowboy to self-imagined courtier. Well, I wouldn't mind a Venetian garden myself. But I don't knock him for it; compared to our world of such pointy-headed wunderkind, he was entitled to the self-anointing… Ezra thought he had all that mattered by way of culture at his fingertips, beck and command. That he knew everything. But that he was haunted by the fact that maybe a Thomas Hardy was closer to the beating heart of it all, and he had failed, being somewhat trumped up as the World's Mentor. In any case, I think the tragedy is to some extent the fact that in another age he would have been respected, as da Vinci was or Michelangelo, and under the thumb of some king or pope. Whereas in his world, it was already beginning to happen: the impossibility of taking any artist seriously unless they were part and parcel of the arts and entertainment industry. Don'tcha get what I mean, jelly bean? That's why I say self-imagined courtier. He had to 'become' the world that was beginning to disappear on him. No wonder he slipped into fascism. Et cetera. All our democratized 'awtistes', irrespective of genre, category, or field, or test-tube born fascists. Was remarking on all this last night with my new neighbour who has trundled in high art places with his camera. Shoots art celebs...

A Very Brief History of the Venetian Forcola Written in the Spring of 2012, and What Ezra Might Have Made of it...

The boatyard at San Trovaso is a working place, one of the few that remain in Venice. A few days later we visit a boatyard which is now hidden away and silent, and which contains examples of the part of a gondola called a *forcola* – a *forcola* is a rowlock that holds the oar in place when the gondolier pushes forward into his stroke. Its shape and form seem to lead directly back to Ezra and modernist sculpture....

We are following a new friend called Paolo down the narrowest of *calle* in Canareggio. Paolo is an engineer, an expert in hydrology, who knows a great deal about flooding, though he is quick to point out to us that Venice does not flood – the water rises and then recedes again. Flooding is very much on his mind though. He has just returned from a conference in Treviso. The main topic under discussion had been how to deal with the flooding of a local river. The answer had been: create a basin. Now it is eight o'clock in the evening, and the light is falling as we hurry along the *calle*. When night falls, spaces such as this seem to get narrower. There is nothing but the slop and slap of canal water ahead of us. All of a sudden, he swivels to the right and stops outside what appears to be a dark and unmarked wooden door, pushes a key into a lock, and gives us entry into a world of ancient Venetian marvels.

This was once his great-grandfather's *squero* or boatyard, and it is now a museum dedicated to the preservation of old Venetian boats and their paraphernalia. You can see this very *squero* in an eighteenth-century painting by Bellotto, Canaletto's nephew. The book containing this image is propped on a small wooden lectern, open at the page, for all visitors to admire. There are very few working boatyards left in Venice, Paolo tells us. How many? Three. I read the pain of loss in his face.

The *squero*, a long, low building constructed entirely from wood, is full of ancient boats and ancient boat parts. The tragedy of Venice, Paolo explains to us, is that it has lost so many of its ancient boats. The reason for this is simple. The number of boats is strictly controlled. Otherwise the canal and the lagoon would be choked with boat traffic. When a fisherman or a gondolier needs a new boat, he is obliged by law to destroy the old one. Almost the only places you will now see an old gondola – most working gondolas are at most twenty years old, he tells us – are in museums in London or New York. So the capital of this once great maritime empire has not remembered its heritage by preserving its ancient craft. Except here.

Here, for example, is a nineteenth-century gondola with a black hood for keeping inclement weather at bay. 'In the nineteenth century,' Paolo explains, 'all the ancient Venetian families would have had their own gondola, and it would be customary for it to be fitted with such a hood as this one. The open gondola of the kind you see today has been created to meet the needs of tourism, which requires that you see out in order to enjoy the architectural marvels of the Grand Canal. What is more, each gondola would once have had two gondoliers to each craft, not one...'

And, in addition to the boats themselves there are preserved bits of boats, and the tools that would have been used to make such crafts as these: mallets, hammers, planes, rudders, furled canvases suspended on beams above our heads, lamps, and, of course, *forcole*, many of them. There are many elegant variants upon the design of the *forcola*. Each one is crafted to meet the needs of its particular user. The length of each one must suit the particular rower's height because the Venetian rower rows standing up, leaning forward into his oar as he pushes ahead, keeping it always part-submerged beneath the water.

I have been acquainted with *forcole* for a matter of days, and the longer I stare into the idea of them – and the fact of them – the more fascinating they become. What exactly is a *forcola*? It is a rowlock. A rower inserts his oar into it in order to gain the necessary purchase to propel himself along. In Venetian rowing, the *forcola* is particularly important. It is also extremely handsome. I came across it for the first time this week when Anna, our hostess, offered to take us out for a row up the Grand Canal with Albino, her *poppa* or steersman. As soon as she steps into the boat with her oar, and prepares to position herself in the standing position to begin the task of rowing us out into the Grand Canal, she tells us that she is having problems with her *forcola*. The fact is that due to wood shrinkage, it simply does not fit properly into its socket any more. In fact, it rattles around. Something will have to be done about it. Fortunately, the master fabricator of her *forcola* lives nearby, and she calls him to her aid. He comes hurrying along the canal, mobile phone pressed to his ear, and gives her a handful of small wooden wedges that she begins to try out for size. But before that she pulls the *forcola* itself out of its socket, and I begin to marvel at it. It is not like any other rowlock I have ever seen in my life.

In fact, its single twisting form, fashioned from walnut, looks to me like a beautiful piece of sleek modernist sculpture. The more I look at it, the less I am convinced that it is an ancient object of utility at all. It reminds me in the flow of its line and the way it seems to double back on itself, like an amalgam of works by Epstein, Gaudier-Brzeska and Boccioni. I let my fanciful speculation wander. Pound, who seems to have spent at least some part of his time in Venetian rivercraft, would have been very familiar with the shapeliness of the *forcola*. Could it have played its part in the development of his own view of modernity, of his own vision of what the sculpture of the present moment was being compelled to be?

Paolo plucks out a *forcola* and smooths its edge against his hand. Walnut is such a hard, dense, compacted wood, he tells us. So homogeneous, he adds, impressing us with his English. So unlike this wood here.... He raps his knuckle against the wooden gates of slatted wood which open out onto the canal, running his finger against a very different kind of surface. See this, he says. This pine is like a saw, soft and hard by turns...

Searching for Mary

Days later, my wife and I are on our way to Pound and Olga's modest cottage in the Dorsoduro again, which now belongs to their daughter, Mary de Rachewiltz. Who exactly was Mary?

Ezra had a daughter by Olga Rudge. Born in 1925, Mary was put out for adoption on a farm in the Tyrol. Now and again, two rather exotic and well dressed strangers came to visit her from Venice. She called them Babbo and Mamile. She was very fond of Babbo. He spoke to her in broken German. Mamile was more troubling. She was aloof, demanding, and somewhat disapproving. Babbo was quite modest in his self-presentation. She discovered that he was a writer, of books. He didn't call himself a poet. Mamile, on the other hand, played the violin, very well. Babbo bought Mary a diapason. It was a rather disappointing gift for a small child. She had expected sweets at the very least. He also spoke to her of the need to work, work hard. Everyone must work, he said, in his broken German....

These details are taken from *Discretions*, a memoir of her father written by Mary that was published in 1971, the year before Ezra died. I remember giving that new book a cursory glance – not much more than that – in the English Faculty Library at Cambridge in the summer of that year. I knew that it was brand new because it was displayed, face forward, on a special shelf reserved for such treats. A recently acquired copy of William Burroughs' *The Naked Lunch* was also on offer on that shelf on another day, shockingly, thrillingly. I opened *Discretions* and read a few sentences – no more than that. Why no more than that though? Because it quickly exasperated me. Even now, nearly half a century later, I can recall my exasperation when I began to read Mary's prose. I found it staccato, jarring, obtuse. She sounded too much like her father when at his most irritating, as if she wanted to wear her cleverness on her sleeve. I found the photograph on the cover rather jarring and unsympathetic too. It showed a bearded, middle-aged man, in profile. He was wearing an expensive looking coat, and hat tilted to keep at bay the prying eye of the sun. Could that be an astrakhan collar? Sitting on the parapet of the bridge against which he was leaning was a plumpish looking, pretty girl of about five or six years old, ankles crossed, showing off her pudgy knees. She too was well dressed. They may have been brushing up against each other, but you could scarcely call the pose intimate. He was staring into the middle distance, as if thinking bookish thoughts; she was squinting a bit grumpily into the camera. They looked the very picture of bourgeois respectability.

Drawing of Ezra with daughter Mary by Julia Bright

What could this memoir have to do with Pound the poet? I found myself asking as I stood there reading the odd paragraph or two in the English Faculty Library on Sidgwick Avenue. What could the day-to-day inessentials of biography have to do with the serious analysis of great poetry? So I put it aside as essentially unserious. And yet the idea of it stayed with me. As with all the other books I have ever seen by or about Ezra, some part of me felt that I ought to give it some attention; some part of me also experienced a genuine twinge of regret that I had not added it to my personal library of books by or about Ezra.

I experienced something similar many years later, in the Indigo Bookstore on Princess Street in downtown Kingston, Ontario, when I found myself circling, over the space of several sultry sunny afternoons, a book of letters to and from one of Pound's many correspondents that I had never seen before, let alone read, which was on display on a table of discounted hardbacks next to the Starbucks outlet. I failed to buy that book too, and now I regret it. Yes, I still regret it even as I write these words. The jigsaw puzzle will never be quite complete.

About twenty years after that visit to the English Faculty Library, I saw *Discretions* again. This time it was for sale in a second-hand bookshop in London for the pleasingly low price of £6.50. The price was softly pencilled in, as if the decision had been a tentative one – or perhaps the book was too precious to risk besmirching it. Beside the price there was a question mark, ringed. It was a first edition. Mary had evidently not grown rich on the proceeds of this memoir of her father. That copy of the book was seized by me without hesitation, and added to my Pound library. It then lived a life of uninterrupted neglect until the notion began to stir that I should write an account of my later life, and the extent to which it had been lived, on-and-off, with the maddening presence of Ezra as a companion.

In the spring of that year, just before embarking on a trip to Venice in pursuit, yet again, of Ezra's ghost, I read it. It was quite the most remarkable and touching book I had ever read about the man, much better than any of the many biographies I have consumed over the years. Some of its details come back to me as I write, and they are all, in the early chapters, the impressions of a child who, in the course of the book, matures into a woman, and in doing so, grows closer to that kindly, vexing enigma she came to know as Babbo. As she matures, so Ezra's own situation as an American in Fascist Italy grows more and more desperate.

Mary's Growing Addiction

The story is one of a growing addiction to Ezra and his writings. He becomes her teacher, her spiritual guide. She listens out for the familiar tap tap of his black malacca cane along the *calle* when he returns from the room he has rented at Signora Scarpi's. She accompanies him on his regular, zestful shopping trips around the neighbourhood. She notices his kindness to beggars. She lovingly recalls his belongings: his patent leather shoes, broad silk cummerbund, velvet dinner jacket, his three sets of rimless pince nezs.

Most of all, he teaches her to THINK. His opinions become her dogma. He inducts her into the art of translating Thomas Hardy into Italian. Then she begins to make efforts to translate his *Cantos* into Italian, having listened to him reading them of an evening in that gondoliers' cottage in Venice, with an audience of friends grouped around him in a reverential semi-circle.... It will turn into a life-consuming project, the translating into Italian of his unfinishable poem in progress, in the course of which Mary will become the apologist of a man who, at a certain point in his life, believed that he was enunciating eternal truths. And then, in time, came to disavow those truths.

A Chance Meeting with Howard, the English Chaplain

A few days later we are at dinner in a *palazzo* quite near the Rialto, and I am explaining to Jane Gorlin, our hostess, my wish to pursue the ghost of Ezra through the serpentine *calles* of Venice, which have already included seeing again that gondolier's cottage – the outside only this time – which my wife and I had finally visited for the first time in 1984, and, in the future perhaps, to meeting some of the people who might have known him during his lifetime.

At dinner that night I happen upon a man who opens yet another door. Howard Levett, a kindly, gentle sort, is the unpaid priest who officiates at the English church in Venice. He has a bad cough. He leaves the table quite frequently to have another cigarette. We get into conversation about Ezra, Olga and Mary. He smiles knowingly at me. I talk at him with some vehemence. His modest home, I discover, happens to be next door to Olga and Ezra's. What is more, he tells me, he knows Mary very well. Yes, he would be more than happy to make an introduction. The following day I drop him a note.

Dear Howard,

It was a great pleasure to meet you last night. I would love to have a discussion about Ezra with Mary if she is happy to do so. That could be in person, by email or a mixture of the two. Whatever she finds most comfortable. As I explained, I have been reading Ezra throughout my life – my absorption began at Cambridge – and I am working towards a book which will endeavour to give some account of how my life and preoccupations have intermeshed with his.

It may interest Mary to know that I had a long and fascinating discussion with Olga at Calle Querini in 1984. My late friend William Cookson, sometime editor of Agenda magazine, put us together.

To which he responded as follows:

Dear Michael,

The pleasure of our meeting was mutual.

In the meantime I have spoken to Mary Rachewiltz (EP's daughter) who would be very happy for you to get in touch with her.

Agonising Over a Note to Mary

I am elated by his response, but we are just about to return to London, and it is too late to contemplate the possibility of meeting Mary in person – she lives in the Tyrol, in Schloss Brunnenburg – even were she to wish me to do so. So I email her instead, but before that I agonise over what I am going to ask her. It is so easy to sound, crass, foolish or fawning. How to strike the right tone....I also find myself asking this: what do I hope to achieve by talking to her? I am not writing a biography. I am not trying to find out answers to conundrums that other biographers have not solved... What, then, is the purpose of this exercise?

It is at least something to do with her memoir, I know. She observed the tragedy of his life so closely as he moved through the 1930s – his involvement with Mussolini, for example (Ezra met him just once), and how Ezra believed him to be some kind of saviour of mankind for the most insubstantial of reasons; his broadcasts over Radio Rome during the Second World War in which he condemned America for involving itself in such a hideous conflict and, also, hit out at international Jewry with wildness and intemperance... She saw it all from the inside. She knew, for example, that one of the reasons for continuing to make those broadcasts was quite a touchingly simple one, far removed from any considerations of political mischief-making: they were his only source of money. The commissions had dried up. He was fast turning himself into an international pariah.

The Email Sent to Ezra Pound's Daughter

Dear Mary,

I am in the throes of trying to write a book which will examine and explain – as much for my own sake as anyone else's – the nature of my life-long fascination with – and perhaps even haunting by if that is not too strong a word – the idea of Ezra, whose work I first started to read as a school boy in South Yorkshire, England, almost half a century ago. (I myself am a poet and art critic for the Independent *in London.) Thanks to the kind intercession of the English poet and editor William Cookson (who wrote a perspicacious notice of the* Rock Drill Cantos *as a school boy, to which Ezra responded with characteristic generosity and encouragement), my wife and I had a conversation with Olga at Calle Querini in December 1984 – at that particular moment I was contemplating the possibility of writing a book about Ezra and Venice.*

At the moment various unbudgeable questions hang in the mind, prompted in part by my re-reading of his memoir Indiscretions in recent weeks. If you feel that you are able to give me a view on any of these matters, I would be very pleased. If you find that my questions are too tiresome and too often asked, please forgive me and ignore them. The better part is often silence, as W.B. Yeats once said. I shall understand. I'm sure you have been pestered by questioners for the greater part of your long life.

I find it difficult to reconcile Ezra's passion for Confucian values and all that this entails with his frequent bouts of verbal intemperance. He so often writes as if he has barely the time to spit out the words, let alone hone them into smooth and elegant sentences. This intrigues me, this mood of perpetual exasperation at the world and its wobbly values. Sometimes, and especially in the letters, he is testily colloquial to the point of self-parody. He uses jarring and bizarre colloquialisms. He often seems to write precisely in order to jolt, jar, shock. It is all so different from the slyly burnished prose of T.S. Eliot.

Can this be ascribed, at least in part, to his exasperation that a poet is not quite enough of a man of action? I remember a signed editorial from an issue of Exile *(number 4, I believe) of 1925, in which he speaks praisingly of Lenin and Mussolini because of their 'sense of time'. Lenin almost evolved a new medium, Ezra writes, a sort of expression half way between writing and action. Does this mean that poetry felt inadequate because it somehow always hung suspended above the rough and tumble of the world? I was re-reading* The Cantos *in Venice last week, and I was struck so forcibly that its language – like Venice itself – felt suspended on water. Like poetry itself. Eternal truths can never be temporal truths. (There is so much water in* The Cantos.*)*

You speak of your brother Omar intermittently. Were you close? Did you collaborate at all in your endeavours on behalf of your father?

In a letter of 1964 to James Laughlin, Ezra speaks remorsefully of his misjudgements. Was he predominantly remorseful in those years? And is it really true that he said little? Or was it that he merely refused to have anything to do with ignorant American journalists? Your account of your shopping trips together before the war paints quite a different picture. But then all that happened long before the horrors of Pisa and his incarceration....

You speak of your passion for The Cantos *as biblical. Are they a sacred text for you?*

That is quite enough for the moment, I feel. If you do have the time and the inclination to write back to me, please let me know whether you would be happy for me to follow up your responses with further questions.

warm wishes to you, Mary

Michael Glover

P.S. According to your memoir, Ezra seems to have taken great pleasure in films. This is something we seldom hear about. Could you say a little more about this?

Mary Writes Back, Promptly

From: Mary Rudge de Rachewiltz

Dear Michael,

I wonder if the first thing my mother told you in 1984 was that she had a very good friend called Etta Glover ?

I'll try to answer your questions as best I can (because of our good neighbor in Venice and the familiarity of your name). Also: William Cookson was one of the sincerest and most generous Pound scholars, the best 'influence' you could have had. God bless him for Agenda.

The 'verbal intemperance' is indeed hard to accept in time of 'political correctness'. I tend to quote Goethe: 'der Zorn der den Dichter macht' and EP himself repeating again and again that most literature stems from hatred but what remains is born out of love. And lines in the Cantos confirm it (Orage held the basic was pity, CXI)

Congenital irascibility. The URGE to attend to his work, i.e Poetry/ Cantos. *(The production IS the beloved, CIV).*

The bizarre colloquialisms, yes. He tried to salvage his American background. Indiscretions *needs careful reading, and moreover it is fun.*

Constantly interrupted and misunderstood, grasping to get his meaning across. I tried to explain his need for action in Agenda *special issue, 1979/80. Have you considered the humility of the short 1972 introduction to* Selected Prose?

I like your 'suspended on water' and hopefully there will be a chance for conversation in Venice before you have finished writing your book, though 'there is no end to talking....' and having returned from a funeral of a friend younger than I am, I feel the pressure of time.

No, I was not close to Omar, though I would have liked a brother. It was only in 1943 that I learned of DP's and Omar's existence. My father was a chivalrous gentleman, although this may sound strange. He had promised to always protect his wife and did, yet he was ahead of his time also in his private life, not only as an artist – as was my mother. To be a 'single mother' is no longer a crime. Perhaps you can look up my introduction to EP: Letters to his Parents. *Since you mention reading* Discretions, *I hope you have New Directions ed. with my Afterword.*

Yes, my father was remorseful and said very little. But he tried to correct wrong statement and to 'have his ideas examined one at a time'. After the triumph of journalists: 'he himself said he botched it', i.e. The Cantos, his last words to Pasolini in the much publicized interview were: 'it's music'.

Which brings me to your last question: film. Yes, it started with Alvin Coburn's Vortographs. And you might find Margaret Fisher's E.P.s Radio Operas, 2002 *helpful.*

All for the moment, I wish you good luck and perseverance, Brancusi's "mais finiiiiir..." IS haunting, so I know how you feel.

Here's hoping ,

Mary

I Reflect upon the Sadness of Some of Mary's Words

No, I was not close to Omar, though I would have liked a brother. Those words of Mary's, the tragedy and the sadness that they seem to encapsulate, have stayed with me since I first read them; that these two human beings, both offsprings of Ezra (though perhaps not Omar), should barely have known each other – to such an extent that she tells me that she would have liked a brother! Surely, had things not been different, a half-brother might have been regarded as a move in that direction, and especially given the fact that they were both, though continents apart physically, life-long Pound scholars, both keepers of the sacred flame... How sad that they were not in touch with each other to the extent that she could have acknowledged and taken comfort in their common paternity. If indeed they had a common paternity. Was Ezra too divisive a figure for that even to be conceivable?

Dutiful Poundians: Omar Pound and Dorothy Shakespear

Yes, there was also a wife, born Dorothy Shakespear, whom Ezra married in 1914, and there was that child of hers too, Omar, whose parentage on the father's side has been disputed by recent biographers – a fact mentioned earlier in this book. The two children were very close in age, but they never met when young, and in later life Omar lived and worked in America where, like Mary, he devoted much of his life to toiling on behalf of his late father – in his case preparing editions of his father's letters for publication. The two of them laboured, patiently dutiful exegetes, on Ezra's behalf, half a world away from each other, never coming close. In the 1970s, they were in fact a little closer than they perhaps knew – or cared to know. During that decade, Omar and his mother lived in Cambridge, England, where he taught literature at what was then known as the Cambridge Technical College. My wife's mother and father also taught there. What is more, they knew Omar. And Omar, as I discovered, had once given them a precious, perhaps talismanic, object.

Ezra's Jade Talisman

The piece of jade we had in our possession was in the shape of a smooth, flattish pebble of sorts. Protected from harm by a small, white cardboard box, it was kept stowed away in my wife's desk, along with other items of family jewellery, in our house in Clapham. One day, I opened the desk – I was probably looking for a post card – and saw it there. I opened the box, plucked out the jade, and smoothed it between thumb and finger – it was very satisfyingly, soothingly smooth to the touch – and asked her about it.

That was once Ezra's, she said.

My wife grew up near Cambridge, and her family lived in the city itself in later life. One afternoon in the 1970s, Omar Pound – in those days he, like my mother-in-law, was teaching at what was then Cambridge Tech, which later became Anglia-Ruskin University – had visited the house and made a gift of it to her mother and father, she told me. It had been Ezra's, Omar told them. He wanted them to have it. It was a kind of worry bead. He liked to hold it in his hand, rub it between thumb and forefinger. It had a smooth dimple of a groove into which your thumb would naturally settle. Dorothy Pound, Ezra's wife, had had tea with them that day too, and Omar's Canadian wife too. I asked my wife how she had found the three of them, and what had been said on that day. They talked a lot about their children's education, and how keen they were to have them learn musical instruments. My wife's mother found a flute in the house in the form of a walking stick, more a gimmick than anything else. Would they like to practise on that? It had a mellow tone. There was lots of laughter, and gushing, high-spirited conversation of a typical Cambridge kind. Omar was very fleshy. He sweated a lot.

Understandably, I was utterly astonished by these discoveries. I stared down at the talisman that I was holding in my left hand, scarcely believing what I was looking at. According to Omar, we had in our possession a piece of jade that Ezra himself had owned, and which he had perhaps used to soothe away cares. Was it in his pocket when he was kept in that cage beneath the burning eye of the Pisan sun? What is more, his very wife and son (or putative son) had paid a visit to the home of my wife's parents. How much nearer was I ever to get to the ghost of Ezra?

And what was it about Ezra and jade anyway? We first hear of him looking for the stuff in 1912, when he reports to his future wife Dorothy Shakespear in a letter that he has been seeking it out in three locations in central London: a pawnbroker's at 55 Long Acre run by William John K. Clark; Charles Collier, the antique dealer based at 31 Edgware Road; and at Samuel Fenton's, a curiosity dealer of 33 Cranbourn Street.

Had Ezra maintained his interest in jade throughout his life? It was certainly precious to the Chinese, and he mentions jade in several of the cantos. The drift of Chinese imagery in Canto 49 includes a mysterious reference to a world entirely covered with jade. Jade has assumed the form of a precious protector. Did Ezra keep this tiny sliver of jade beside him as a form of spiritual solace, to protect him from harm?

In 2022, I returned to Kettle's Yard in Cambridge, that place where, as an undergraduate, I had first seen those drawings by Gaudier in the attic, to write about an exhibition of new work by Ai Wei Wei, China's most famous dissident artist. Its theme was Chinese fakes and forgeries, and how the art of making the new seem old and venerable had been practised by skilled Chinese fabricators for millennia. I noticed, displayed on a table top, a gun made out of jade. What would Ezra have thought about a neutered weapon made from a material quite so precious? Repulsion or veneration?

Perhaps it is to Be Neither This Nor That

A certain lightening of mood has seized hold of me on this Spring morning in south London. I cannot ascribe such a mood swing to the weather, which is truly appalling today, as it has been all week. Yes, even as I write these words, hail stones are flinging themselves against the ever more fragile window panes of my study at the top of the house. The roof tops are all a sickening grey, greasy slick… No, this unexpected lightening, this inward sense of lightsomeness even, to be a tad more flamboyant, has to do with this book about Ezra that I now know, without a flicker of any doubt, that I shall never write in the way that I once expected.

It has just occurred to me why it has been so difficult for me to write it in the past and, and now that I am fully aware of this fact, I feel that I can rest content with what I am doing now, which is to flit about here and there within hailing distance of Pound's orbit, never getting too close, recognizing my abiding interest (which has not, of course, gone away, it probably never will), but also telling myself that it will not be slaked in ways that I have always found unpalatable. What exactly do I mean by all this though?

It has just occurred to me that the book I always felt that I was doomed to write about Ezra, and which I probably never wrote for this very fact, would be a book of literary criticism because that was the sort of thing that might be expected of any human being with an English degree from Cambridge University who had an interest in Ezra Pound. Oh horror of horrors! Were not some of the best and the worst of our days as undergraduates spent, late at night amidst the groaning metal stacks of the Victorian chapel that was Queens' College Library in those days, beneath those dingy, ever flickering strip lights, driving our red eyes back and forth across works of literary criticism – Reader's Guides to… – Companions to… and so forth?

The dreadful thing about books of literary criticism is that they almost always utterly destroy one's appetite for books by the author who is under the critic's scrutiny because the books of literary criticism themselves are so much more tedious, dull and turgid, than the works they are said to be happily companioning and elucidating. Why did we ever fall into the habit of reading such books in the first place? There is a simple answer to that. We did so in order to steal bits and pieces from them for our essays. Being supreme idlers ourselves, they were our crutches.

And now it has slapped me across the face. It did not have to be like that! I did not have to write in this way about Ezra at all. Nor did I have to write a biography either. Who would be fool enough to wish to write a biography of Ezra Pound? As a writer, we yearn to divert ourselves by our writing, to write what pleases us as far as is humanly possible. Why else do it? Who other than the writer deserves to be humoured most of all? How can you possibly faithfully promise to give yourself pleasure if you decide to write a biography of a writer, whose very identity you may come to loathe by the time that you are twelve months into the tedious research for your ten-year (minimum) project?

No, it did not have to be such a thing. But what could it be? Could it really be anything at all? Well, best of all perhaps might be an enterprise such as Fernando Pessoa's *Book of Disquietude*, a glorious medley of conflicting fictional voices which can be opened at any time and at any page, or one of those novels by the wonderful B. S. Jonson which were to be found, early in the spring of 1969, stacked up in a heap on a table in Bowes & Bowes, the Booksellers on King's Parade. The novel itself was unbound. It sat in a box of its own, quietly minding its own uniqueness as a phenomenon. It consisted of goodness knows many pages – it was unbound and entirely unpaginated. You began where you began. You riffled around in it. You seized life by the horns at the moment of your choosing. That is not quite what has happened here – but it is a little like it, this mingling of my life with his which has moved somewhat, though not wholly, in the direction of serendipity.

A Thwarted Conversation by Email with John Ashbery About 'Uncle Ezra'

Date: Wed, 6 Feb 2013

Dear Michael,

Just to reply quickly about Uncle Ezra, I've never been keen on his poetry, except for some of the early lyrics and translations, and have found *The Cantos* impenetrable and annoying. However, I don't especially wish to go on record with these sentiments, so I fear a conversation project is out. I hope you'll understand (my not liking him, I mean, since he apparently means so much to you).

Love to you and Ruth,

John Ashbery

John Ashbery Goes With me to Andalucia in February 2023 to Soothe Away the Cares of Ezra…

There was something so pleasing and so amusing about the fact that John Ashbery had cared so little for Ezra's words that I decided, in early February of 2023, to take a volume of Ashbery's *Collected French Translations: Poetry* with me to Anadalucia in order to rid myself of Ezra's ceaseless pesterings, for a week or so at the very least. I had come across the book in a deep cavity under the front of my writing desk, where I usually park my feet. Several rows of books had managed to organise themselves down there without my even really noticing. Mostly poetry, needless to say. Books do find odd ways of clinging on, and especially when the owner of those books is being encouraged, on an almost daily basis, to reduce them in number. I was a little surprised when I turned to the copyright page and saw just how old the book was: 2014! Could I really have left a volume by Ashbery unread for eight long years? Why? How? What a pleasure and a tonic it was to bury myself alive in that old familiar Ashbery tone of casual insouciance! How little dyspepsia of the ezraical kind John had ever shown!

I had expected some balmy weather by way of accompaniment to our brief time in Andalucia, but it was not quite to be. We huddled indoors, over the wood-burning stove in the salon most days, with my eyes meandering through John's youthful renderings of many, many little known French poets, including the flightily melancholy verses of the almost wholly forgotten (except by John and a smattering of others) Arthur Cravan. Why was a man with an English name writing in French in the first place? And what gave John the wish to translate him back into English?

No matter where I choose to sit or roam, out in our friends' back yard, or in Cabo de Gata park itself, tough-minded, leathery, indomitable cacti seem to be defending their little patches of arid ground. A line or two from Ted Hughes' poem about thistles, always a favourite of mine, came back to me one afternoon, how they *spike the summer air*, burst open under a *blue-black pressure*, and in time have sons *who fight back over the same ground*…

Cacti too will not be gainsaid. I've just been brought up short by a note from my old friend Alistair Davies. Being a close and long suffering friend, he has read my Ezra manuscript again – it was forty thousand words long when he read it last, a couple of years ago. Now it is 70,000 words. Had it improved? Had I paid any attention to what he had said about the earlier draft? He'd wanted me to say more about our teachers at Cambridge. I'd studiedly ignored that advice…

Every day, when the wind doesn't freeze the bones, we take a walk from the house and into the park in order to give us, and our friend's dog Beetle, a chance to run and to run. It's the dog which does all the running and running, needless to say. There is no beauty of a soft or a yielding kind in the Cabo de Gata park. The miniature mountains (it seems wrong to call them hills because they look too fierce to be hills) that flank us as we walk, often peak in sharpish, serrated edges, like chipped teeth. The mountains flanked us as we walked. Their slopes are patchy with tussocks of green never quite luscious enough to be called anything as biddable as grass.

What is most noticeable about the stony track we take are the dead remains of the agave cacti that accompany us almost all the way. They are everywhere, twisty grey roots, fallen sideways, and sprawled out in exaggerated gestures of anguish. I'd seen few natural things die quite so dramatically as these cacti, the way they twisted in seeming agony, keeled over, and then thrust out their huge root growth. What had caused them all to die like this, put on such a spectacle? And in such a context too. There was something about their dying and the palpable visual death agonies, as if most of all they *wanted to be seen dying*. Something that kept pulling me back to Ezra in old age: those photographs of his white-grey hair, how it spilled around or stood up as if electrified in shock, that portrait of him on my desk, eyes screwed up against the prying of the light. Or of him in Venice in the 1960s, deflated, half crushed, taciturn, exhausted.

Message from Amazon.co.uk, 2 August 2014

M T Glover,

You might like to know your copy of *The Pisan Cantos (New Directions Paperbook)* is eligible to trade in at our Trade-In Store.

When you've finished with this book you can trade it in for an Amazon.co.uk Gift Card, which you can then use on millions of items across the store.

Another Face of Ezra, Newly Discovered on the Wall of a Sitting Room in Shepherd's Bush, West London

My host and I are sitting in an upstairs study in West London. The light is low, almost guardedly sullen, on this particular Spring day, which makes the act of seeing this drawing of Ezra on the wall, a drawing that so few people have ever seen, and which has never been catalogued – well, it has to be said that there *is* no *catalogue raisonnée* of Gaudier's drawings, so no one knows with any degree of accuracy quite how many of them survived – feels a marvellously secretive thing to be doing on an otherwise unremarkable day in the middle of the working week.

It is hanging above the owner's right shoulder as he speaks to me. A mutual friend tipped me off about it, quite casually, one Saturday morning, when we happened to be discussing Ezra and his friend, Henri Gaudier-Brzeska. This is not the only drawing by Gaudier on my host's walls. Elsewhere there are pen-and-ink sketches of animals, quick, attent, on-the-wing, hieratic, wonderfully boisterous, as Gaudier so often tended to capture them.

'How did you manage to acquire these drawings?'

'From the Mercury Gallery in London, over the years. No one knows how many survived. There could be a thousand or two.'

'That many! This drawing of Ezra is obviously a study for the hieratic head that Ezra kept with him for much of his life. What is so surprising is how different it is in style and atmosphere from the other surviving preparatory drawings for the head – it was said that he did hundreds – at Kettle's Yard in Cambridge or the Centre Pompidou in Paris. The remaining surviving drawings – aren't there about nine of them in all? – all tend to have a touch of Gaudier's savage angularity about them. They are quite severe in atmosphere – like the hieratic head itself, you might say. Yours seems to have been drawn up from a more tender and yielding part of Gaudier's sensibility. He seems to be admiring Ezra's youthful handsomeness – well, I suppose that, being almost thirty he wasn't all that youthful! But I always think that the marble head itself looks as if it could be a flatteringly stylised representation of a man who was in fact much older, something akin to a bit of imperial flattery perhaps…'

Beside a Venetian Window

I am sitting beside the window of our ground-floor room directly opposite the soaring brick wall of what once was the largest convent in Venice. A metal grill, painted a tasteful light grey, separates me from the outside world. It is a little as if I am trapped inside a luxurious prison. The window is perhaps one metre and a half above the level of the very narrow canal which opens out into the Fondamenta Ormesini just beyond my line of vision. The room in which I sit feels suspended on water, which is murky and unusually turbulent at the moment, washing fiercely backwards and forwards – a barge has just passed along the canal, creating its shock waves. The bricks of the wall are unusually small to my London eye, and proceed in a very orderly horizontal arrangement – end on, side on, end on, side on… The courses of brick, which go from tawny to ochreous to green, to pink, to black and are often badly pitted and thirsting for mortar to repel the encroaching damp, stop a foot or so above the level of the water of the canal.

The part of this great boundary wall that is submerged in water, which shifts in colour from olive-green to turquoise depending upon the time of day and the nature and the quality of the light, consists of solid blocks of stone, and these blocks are encrusted or dully bejewelled with barnacles. Just to the right of my window, about half a metre above the canal, there is a door set into its white, stone-mullioned frame. Well, I guess that it must once have been a door. Now it is a series of green wooden planks, set into place one above the other. Utterly impenetrable. For all that, the long stone step of the phantom door frame is prettily notched, as if wishing to draw attention to itself. Someone must have entered here from the water once.

Amongst a Fraternity of Venetian Rowers

It is a Friday evening, and I am preparing to give a poetry reading to a roomful of members of the *Settemari*, the Venetian rowing club, at a dinner convened in my honour. I have never read to a roomful of rowers, and the very idea of it unnerves me slightly. I think of the snobbery of the Henley Regatta and shudder inwardly.

Poetry is language afloat on water. I begin with those words. The idea, even as I say it, makes me think of Pound's *Cantos*, and how they are engulfed by water from the moment they begin. The very first poem plunges us into the midst of things, without any kind of introductory explanation. Odysseus is voyaging back from the Trojan Wars. He is in mid-sea, a perilous situation.

Poetry is language afloat on water. I say this before I present a handful of poems from my new book. The audience consists of thirty boisterous, cheerful, receptive people, gathered around two long tables. I feel so contented to be in their company – irrespective of the fact that they are showing me such warmth and generosity.

Later it occurs to me that this is one of the reasons why Pound himself would have wished to return to Venice throughout his life, that the fact of this unreal city afloat on water, perpetually threatened by the possibility of its own dissolution, somehow would have thrown back at him the core of his own endeavours as a poet, and the essential paradox of poetry itself. It would have imaged poetry as language afloat on water, always shifting, always re-formulating its own meanings in a city part real and part unreal, ever shifting, ever changing – in spite of all appearances to the contrary. Did not a friend once tell me how difficult it had been to write about the facades of the *palazzi* on the *Canale Grande* because so many of them had been quietly re-fashioned, time and again? He had abandoned the project. Nothing survives easily when it is afloat on water, precariously pinioned to ceaseless fluidity. *The Cantos* begin with the voyage of Odysseus, another man afloat on water, as he returns, after years of voyaging, from the Trojan Wars. We are thrown into the midst of the turmoil of his voyaging, without fuss or introduction. All is pure phantasmagoria.

Another Venetian Interlude: the Poet Philip Morre Has Practically Given up on Ezra

It is a warm evening in September 2022, and we are back for a Venetian interlude in the company of the poet Philip Morre, which consists of the following: an excellent combination of local white Pinot Grigio fortified with a dash of Cassis; a heaped plate of pasta (with interleaved slivers of zucchini); gelato; and much laughter and conversation. You'll spot the building, he tells me breezily over WhatsApp. Go over the second of the two wooden bridges. It's the tallest and reddest along the canal, quite close to the end…

And so it is. And also, thanks to its position well away from all the street dining, the least noisy – which suits him to a tee. His welcoming mat outside the door of his apartment in Cannaregio reads GO AWAY. (He doesn't go out at night these days.) *I really mean it!* he laughs as he adjusts his braces and beckons us indoors, selectively hospitable as ever. We spend a long and lovely evening over the Ormesini Canal, double windows flung back to let in an intermittent smattering of voices, and the persistently furious barking of one dog. Philip leaps up from the table and yells fuck off! The small dog obliges.

He leans over the table as he talks, massaging his cheeks, working and re-working the sculpting of his hair. He is in love again. Philip is always in love. He opens his laptop so that we can admire her on Youtube, his latest. She's a Latvian singer who treats us to a medley of Offenbach in front of an orchestra intimate in size. Then we skip to a later clip. She's six years older now, but still lovely. Philip is especially fond of the way she cups her ear with her hand when she sings…

Is it ten years ago that we first discussed Pound and my book-in-the-making around this table, when I explained to him, rather pathetically, that I had not the least notion of the book's direction of travel? He mooted the possibility of a biography on that evening. I? A biographer? I smiled at the absurdity of such a notion. Facts slip away from me too readily. A journalist such as I have been all my life contains as much as is ever needful for the passing moment, which is forever falling away, needless to say.

This evening, being forewarned, he offers me a book called *In the Bughouse*, which is a relatively recent account of Pound's incarceration at St Elizabeth's Hospital. I've read it, I own it, I tell him. We talk about the condition of Pound's house in the Dorsoduro, and of the skulduggery that went on in the aftermath of Pound's death, chronicled in a book called *The City of Fallen Angels* – how the house was saved, but not the papers. They ended up at Yale. Who owns it now? I ask. The Guggenheim Foundation? The Comune? Then we pass on to talk of his own poetry, and of books in general. There are always too many of them, needless to say. His wish is to have no more than will fill the wall-to-wall bookcase behind his bed, which is one brisk stride back from the kitchen table. Will that ever be enough though? The books of a bibliophile such as himself do *not* furnish a room, as Virginia Woolf once contended. They quietly and determinedly proceed to overwhelm it. There are books in heaps on the floor, books on the table to be pushed aside when eating (though he eats very little these days), books almost everywhere. Luckily, much of the wall space is taken up with art. Yes, his partial slimming down of the ever growing collection – why do books always seem to turn up, even when uninvited? – looks like an impossible dream.

He carries a single oversize hardback volume to the table and slaps it down. You can have this one, he tells me. He was just about to get rid of it. It's a companion to *The Cantos*, and it's a biceps-builder of a volume. 'I like Pound less and less,' he tells me. '*The Cantos* were a ridiculous mistake, to go on and on like that. Why didn't he just stop and write some decent short poems instead? It's like one of those Italian motorways, which take you beside the sea, in sunlight, for a little way, and then plunge you into long, dark *gallerie* for mile after mile... *The Village Explainer*, that's what Gertrude Stein called him,' he tells me, laughing. 'They knew each other in Paris during the '20s. Do you know Hemingway's *A Moveable Feast*, his account of the Paris years? It's so wonderful that you really want it to be true.'

He pours out another tumbler of Pinot Grigio, clouding it with a dribble of Cassis to give it that extra kick of pleasure. Just before we leave, he reads us 'Whitsun Weddings' by Philip Larkin, one of his especial favourites. We listen to the marvellous words describing all that was to be seen from a train travelling south towards London on that sunlit Saturday afternoon, and then laugh together over Larkin's fiercely class-conscious snobbery. Larkin too would have had a doormat which read GO AWAY.

Can Hemingway be Trusted?

The Cry of the Gondolier in 2022

Ay yoyoyoy yee! The gondolier has just pushed his tourist-laden craft past the stout grill of our window, rising on his heels as he leans into his rowing oar. He makes that cry of warning as he meets the junction with the Misericordia Canal, warning others of his approach. When Ezra Pound sat on the Dogana Steps, they pushed into their oars to a different song: *stretti! stretti!* was the refrain, a snatch of an ancient Spanish *cri d'amour*.

Can I Really Trust Hemingway on Ezra? I am Asking Myself as I Walk Back Along the Ormesini Canal

As I descended the cold concrete steps of Philip Morre's apartment down to the level of the Ormesini canal – it was all so still and so dark and so people-less down there at his end, the end where the canal-side restaurants with their umbrella-flourishes and their table cloths do not presume to go, even though it was barely nine o' clock – I was still thinking about what he'd said about Hemingway and Ezra, how Gertrude Stein had spoken dismissively of Ezra as a *village explainer*. Generally speaking, Hem had been kind to Ezra in that book. He'd shown him to be a crank, but a fairly kindly and certainly a very generous crank.

Why then did Olga tell me, in 1984, during that interview, that he'd been one of those who had betrayed him? And how much should I trust *A Moveable Feast* anyway? A book, written in later life by a writer cushioned by celebrity that describes itself as a memoir has built into it some kind of an admission that it is not necessarily to be trusted to tell the truth. It's a confection of memories of memories, created to entertain, a piece of icing on a cake that's already big enough to fill a room.

A Wild Boar on the Label of a Wine Bottle in England

It is a sun-struck Sunday morning in Deal on the east coast of Kent in the summer of 2014, and I am sitting, facing the sea, at the dining table, in the breakfast room of an old bathhouse. On that long wooden table, there are still remnants of yesterday evening's dinner: a spent wine bottle, flecks of candle wax, and a stone, hollowed out in the middle, which holds sea salt. The house sits almost on the shingle, and it overlooks the English Channel. Sailing boats are prettily weaving in and out in a kind of desultory dance. Just across the water is the coast of France, represented this morning by a long, horizontal smudge of shadow. Last night, chalk cliffs reared up, crisp and white and clear. There is nothing quite so changeable as sea, air, land, and the way they present themselves for the delectation of the human eye.

As I sit there, looking idly at the sea, I find myself thinking about Ezra again, and this time I return to those hours, just a few weeks ago, when I was sitting outside the house of another friend near the village of Arzens in the Aude. I had been reading Ezra's poems, and, in particular, his versions of poems by the Troubadours, those itinerant minstrels who lived in those parts eight centuries ago, and to whom he gave so much time and attention.

At a certain moment – goodness knows why – I must have looked up at the wood, skirted by a field of winter wheat, which rises up the hill. There was no one about. This reminded me that, some months before, two huntsmen had come walking down the track which skirts that wood, carrying a dead boar trussed, upside down, to a long pole... It was in a house just outside Arzens that I had seen that dead boar being carried downfield.

Distracted from my thoughts of those huntsmen by nothing in particular, I lower my eyes from sea to table top. In front of me on the table there sits that single empty wine bottle from yesterday evening, drained of all but its dregs. Its label is turned towards me, as if impatient to be read. Only now do I do so: *Le Sanglier de la Montagne*. I had not given it a second's thought when I was accepting the wine being poured from it just a few hours ago. Beneath those words there is a line drawing of a running boar. Perhaps it is trying to outwit, out-chase the men with their guns, I think to myself, mildly amused, as I recall the dead boar in that wood. Intrigued, I pick up the bottle, and turn it round to read the label on the other side. This is what it says: mis en bouteille par UCF 11290 Arzens France.

Chewing Over Ezra in Sheffield

I lay down the soup spoon, clatteringly, on the wooden table top and try to make myself clear. Oh for some clarity of motive! It is noon or thereabouts, and we are sitting in a small cafe in the centre of Sheffield on a warm summer's day in 2014. The poet John Birtwhistle – I am here to read with him at a local festival – has been asking me to explain myself, to tell him what exactly it is about me and Ezra. Why there is such a link.

Why we have this bond. He has asked me, in emails, to tell him. Best in person, I have replied, dodging. He knows very well that I am not a Pound scholar. He knows that I am not a professional literary critic. He knows that I would not write a biography of the man – or of any other man (or woman) – in a million years. So what exactly was I up to? I waffle a little. I use many words to tell him surprisingly little. As if there is something to hide. Is there though?

'What I am saying to you, John, is that I feel I cannot *not* write this book. In fact, my friend Marius Kociejowski said as much to me, just the other day that, clearly, it is a book I must write – those were his very words – in order to get it out of my system. And yet the whole issue of my obsession with this man still perplexes me. Why should it be so? Why should I feel so wedded to the idea of a man who exasperates and irritates me so much? I loathe his posturing. So much of me feels so frustrated by, by...' Thinking of my own profound exasperation with the man down the decades momentarily robs me of speech.

The conversation then does one of those curious sideways drifts, like a tacking sail boat. We home in on the subject of exasperation – not only how exasperating Pound could be, but also how exasperating his apologists so often were. And continue to be to this day.

'There is a certain kind of Pound specialist,' John says, warming to his theme, '– I suppose it must be true, to an extent, of any devotee, but perhaps Pound somehow seems to encourage it more – who begins to turn into a replica of Pound himself, complete with all that intemperance, intolerance, rigidity and sheer dogmatism...'

John lays his sandwich down and stares at me with serious ferocity.

'Pound's example seems to invest the Poundian with a kind of superior sense of his own moral authority. It gives him a justification for behaving badly. He dismisses his critics with contempt. By comparison with him, they are know-nothings. They simply do not believe that they can be bested in an argument. The Leavisites were rather similar.

'Why is Ezra more prone to this effect than other targets of literary biography? Not only do his nastier sides justify lesser minds in their own petty flights of arrogance, but he supplies them with a theory and a justification for such posturing. He keeps afloat the incompatible rhetorics of ultra-democracy and aristocracy of intellect. To be familiar with him, in the sense of being a cockroach in his archives, is therefore a ticket both to spurious general humanity and to a special intelligence. Once this ticket has been punched by a publication or two, you can be irascible with your students, contemptuous of your critics and (this is part of the Leavisite comparison) ignorant or shallow about large areas of literature (Auden, for instance) because they have been deemed to lack moral fibre.'

I listen to John, nodding, as he warms to his theme. If this is indeed the case, why am I in thrall to such a dogmatist? Could it be that I am one too?

Ezra Set to Flirtatious Music

This walled garden in Devon is a marvellously sequestered spot, I am thinking to myself on a late afternoon in April, 2015. The sun has just burst through into brilliant early spring life at last after days of sullen cloud and persistent drizzle. The garden's rough, high walls are fashioned from compacted clay and wattle, and the clay, being Devonian, is of a deep, rich madder-cum-ochre. Those mingled colours seems to speak to us in ways that are rather difficult to define, rather in the way that the colour of blood seems to speak to us. They seem to partake of us. We seem to partake of them.

After many months of ignoring the presence of Ezra Pound in my life, he has returned again this afternoon to speak a word or two into my ear. The reason for this is not far to seek. The person who owns this garden, and the Georgian house which is just visible beyond its walls, is a professor of English, a specialist in the literature of the *fin de siècle*. She also has on the shelves of her study many books by Ezra Pound, including an edition of his *Selected Poems* published in 1966. This selection was made during the last decade of his life, when he was living in Venice in a state of near complete taciturnity, having come to regard his life's work as a failure, a botch.

As I leaf through it on a garden bench, hard by a newly flowering viburnum bush clamorous with bee hum, I see that the book contains words I had never read before, a brief preface, written by Pound himself on 20 October 1966. He quotes words from the draft of an early canto, first published in 1912, words which were edited out as the poem got revised and revised. They are words descriptive of the life-long enterprise itself which evidently seemed to him, five decades on, and as he neared the end of his writing life, particularly relevant to his present circumstances, and perhaps even sadly prescient in their way. He called it a rag-bag, that great enterprise, something akin to a portmanteau into which all sorts of things might be flung, whether they be descriptive, historical or mythological. What would it all amount to in the end? And who, finally, would be in charge of their ordering, their shaping, their long struggle towards coherence of a kind?

Some days later, the owner of that book returns from her trip to Southern California, and over a pint of Doombar and a glass of Pimm's in a local pub I talk to her about my obsession with Pound, how his presence never leaves me for very long.

You have an impressive collection of well thumbed books by Ezra Pound, I tell her. She nearly devoted her entire academic career to him, she replies. As a young graduate student she was absolutely passionate about his poetry. *Personae* was the most perfect book of poems she had ever read. There were only two poets worth taking seriously, Yeats and Pound. She and her friends set the poems from *A Lume Spento*, Pound's first book, to music. Such lyricism... She was even going to do her doctorate on him, but when she began to study *The Cantos*, she quickly understood that she would be getting herself into a life-long commitment, and she didn't want to do that. Instead, she chose Oscar Wilde, who seemed much more manageable altogether.

She tells me that she met Ezra once in Rapallo when she was very young and he was very old and infirm. This must have been in the mid-1960s, after his release from St Elizabeth's. Had she recorded their conversation? No. Did she remember what he said? They had talked about his poetry. He had been very, very flirtatious.

'What do you think went wrong? How did it happen that he came to align himself with Fascism? How did it happen that he became so discredited?'

'He was seduced, flattered by the attentions of Mussolini. No one else would take him seriously. He thought that Mussolini bought into his entire social program.' Pound was, in short, guilty of naivety on the grand scale.

Oh Those Belles, Those Belles…

Yes, Ezra was very, very flirtatious, young and old. His long suffering wife Dorothy Shakespear had just had to put up with it, somehow. She'd bought into that story of his – how could he possibly help himself, being a great and exotically attired poet of uncontrollable creative juices? – by 1914, when they got married in London. She was twenty-seven at the time, and Ezra twenty-eight. Her mother Dorothy, sometime lover of Yeats the Eagle (as his inner circle often called him), seemed quite pleased to be rid of her at last.

There were many others in between, coming and going, commitments short and long. Women attached themselves to Ezra like burrs to a Harris Tweed jacket, and he made no effort to brush them off. One of the very last lustrous pearls on his string of belles was a young woman called Martha Spann, with whom he edited an anthology of poetry that was published in 1964, fifty years later, after Ezra had returned to Italy, and fallen straight into the end-of-life care of his long-time mistress, Olga Rudge. (Marcella, a former school teacher from Texas, went along too, as his *secretary*.) What of Dorothy though? Wasn't it Dorothy who had seen to his every need over those eleven long years of his incarceration in Washington D.C.? True enough. Olga got him in the end – and *for* and *after* the end – though. They were buried side by side in contiguous plots in Venice, beneath those blue Adriatic skies. And what of Marcella? Oh well…

Confucius to Cummings, an anthology of poetry spanning millennia, was Pound's last, full-scale pedagogical endeavour. Confucius had been a touchstone for decades and, as Olga had reminded me in 1984, Cummings, man of his own era, had never betrayed him – unlike so many of those other fair-weather friends. The book leads off, unsurprisingly, with thunderous words of condemnation-cum-indignation against the American establishment: *My efforts to indicate part of the quality of Chinese metric have been sabotaged by the lethargy, or worse, of American endowments for the suppression of the life of the soul*, he had written, with the usual smoke rising.

So how was it to be done – the writing, that is? Who from the past would be plucked forth to show us how? Ezra and Marcella set out their stall with the names of old familiars, many of them still as under-read now as they were under-read then. Have you sampled Arthur Golding's unmissable

Elizabethan translation of Ovid's *Metamorphoses* yet? And was Ezra himself to be part of the story? Of course! How could he not be, given who was editing this 350-page book? And so, seventy pages in, we find ourselves reading his very own, very musical and muscular version of the 'Seafarer' (from the Anglo-Saxon). In the 1960s he recorded himself performing it on a Caedmon long-playing record, rolling his magnificent *rrrrs*, every inch some gravelly voiced, venerable Scottish sage. Where had he acquired that voice? we do wonder to ourselves. But then Ezra was always good at collecting identities.

That eighth-century seafarer was Ezra himself, of course, faring forth as a young poet-in-the-making from the little gold-mining town of Hailey, Idaho, traversing the salt waves, full of bluster and naked ambition in just about equal measure. In fact, much of the book seems to be speaking to us fairly directly about the passions and the battles and the disappointments of his own writing life. A little poem translated from the sixteenth-century French of Ronsard, is all about the great Pléiade poet imagining others reading his words after his death. Would they? Would they not? Had he written what would deserve to survive? Of his own words, Ezra thought perhaps not.

And is this perhaps, and somewhat perversely, why he has included in this book so much that is greater by full fathom five than the poetry that he himself ever wrote, such as the extraordinary amount of space he gives to the lyric poetry of Shakespeare? There are so many extracts from *A Midsummer Night's Dream!* It is as if Pound is saluting the greater poet's near heaven-charmed lyrical fluency and easeful mastery. Oh that he had written words with the durability of Shakespeare's! There is much mournful bravery here too – the poems that Raleigh wrote in The Tower, for example. And what of the acres of space devoted to the dramatic monologues of Bob Browning? Now *he* was a man of Ezra's stamp... Ezra even owns up at last to the fact that he had been related all along to Longfellow by quoting from his translation of St Teresa of Avila, a Christian saint to be admired for the quality of her endurance... He gives much space to the great Elizabethan lyricists, those poets who were so adept – like Pound's beloved troubadours – at finding singable words.

Yes, there was so much to be envied, from the astonishing, headlong gush of Whitman to the brilliant showman-like patter of the public poetry of Browning, and, everywhere there is such a seeming yearning for sweetness and simplicity, such regrets that he had not quite managed the 'natural phrasing' of Hardy — what a great deal the practice of novel-writing had taught him!

Joseph Re-paints Ezra for the Bathroom

I must have talked to my son Joseph about Ezra's 'Hieratic Head' quite a lot during his childhood, and of the preparatory drawings that Gaudier-Brzeska, made from life before he started work on it. There had been hundreds, Pound had said in the memoir he wrote about his friend after Gaudier's tragic death. Nine survive. I kept a postcard of one of them in the house, bought from Kettle's Yard in Cambridge. Jim Ede, the man who owned Kettle's Yard, had bought many drawings by Gaudier and they were on display in the attic. I used to stare at that image of Ezra, wondering about his nature, and whether or not he represented my idea of a poet, and what exactly that might mean anyway. In the one we had at home, he looks pert and intense — like a raptor. Joseph decided to do something with that drawing. He painted his own version, in blue, in the bathroom, on the floor, just beside the lavatory bowl, when he was about nineteen. It survives to this day. Every time I stand there and stare down, I feel interrogated by his presence. I also think back to the fact that Pound himself wrote those famous lines on poetry which open *The Pisan Cantos* on fragments of lavatory paper.

The Death of Uncle Ken in 2015

My mother's brother Uncle Ken took no pleasure in his own dying. He had no wish to leave this earth (there were no prospects of a paradise ahead of him, a paradise in which he might have found himself in the awkward company of those relatives of his whose presence he had never especially relished during his lifetime) – and no wish to remain either. Life had become a misery to him, I reflected, as I walked around the bedroom of his bungalow in Yorkshire, days after his death. It reeked of urine and long neglect. He had spent the last few weeks of his life in a care home situated on the busy main road between Bradford and Bingley. His dread, he had whispered to me, somewhat hoarsely, during my last visit, was to be taken downstairs to the dayroom, and to be obliged to socialise with many open-mouthed others, in the presence of a large, noisy television set whose images of unremitting jollity would be unceasing. He dreaded the thought of being marooned in such company. His hands were cold to the touch. There was none of the old firmness in his grip. They felt oddly smooth and slender. He might have wished for one or another of his beloved books to keep him company – Ryszard Kapuscinski's account of his life-long passion for Herodotus, for example, about which we had talked a great deal. I would telephone him on a Saturday morning for our weekly conversation. He had read it and re-read it, that book, he often told me. Towards the end of his life, re-reading had become his passion. He knew what he had loved, and he wanted to remain in that familiar company.

That last conversation was a particularly striking one. He became eloquent. He used such well chosen words. And all in the service of a vision of absolute misery. It was as if the writer he had never succeeded in becoming during his lifetime had newly seized hold of him, honing his words and phrases, making that final push for recognition. After his death I read his diaries. His ambition to write – a novel, a good short story – had dwindled, little by little, as he aged into semi-reclusive respectability. During the 1970s and 1980s, when I was working as an editor in London, he was eager to listen to advice about outlets for his stories. The subject diminished in importance as the years passed. Later on he would write with passion about the joys of an evening meal or describe at dry, painstaking length the route of one of his solitary walks in the Peak District. Of marital passion there was little sign. He had never developed a passion for Ezra either. He did not know how or where to begin with Ezra Pound, he once told me. I was out on my own there.

Handel on Loop in the Chapel of the Bingley Crematorium, Dolmetsch on the Clavichord

At the end of Uncle Ken's cremation, a fragment from Handel's *Messiah* seemed to be stuck on loop. We all began to leave the pews, and then stopped when we saw what was happening. My aunt, she who would survive him for years, had paused, and was standing in front of the raised casket in Bingley Crematorium's Chapel of Rest, leaning on her stick. She stared and she stared. No one could leave before she left. She kept on staring. The chorus went on and on. Fifty odd stood frozen at her back. She had sung in *The Messiah* ten times, she told me, for the local choral society. That's what the women in her social circle did if you had a half-decent voice, even if you weren't a regular chapel-goer. Ten long Christmases of Handel on loop.

I could see out of the door and into the car park just beyond the stacked bouquets of flowers. They were already there, the supporters of the next client in line, clustered around the perimeter, old men in dark suits with their other halves, suitably morbid in their mood, a little restive, though not indecently so. One of them was checking his watch. Another one ran his finger around the inside of his starched white collar. It was a warm day, a fine day for a cremation, you could say. That was in 2015.

In November 1972, Ezra's body was borne across the lagoon to the cemetery island of San Michele by two gondoliers. It had been a simple ceremony. Had there been some Vivaldi, that composer whose works — many of them at least — had been rescued from oblivion by Ezra and Olga? Desmond O'Grady was at the graveside that day. He tossed a fistful of clay onto the coffin.

I had chosen the music for Ken's service. My favourite choice had been an aria from *St Matthew's Passion* by Bach, as sung by Kathleen Ferrier. The bluff and breezy organiser of Ken's funeral had come round to the house to ascertain our musical needs. No, he had not heard of Kathleen Ferrier, but he would ask his uncle, who knew about everything musical. Was Ezra tone deaf, as some have said? That hadn't stopped him writing an opera about Villon, one of his favourite outsiders, or of being generally opinionated in this area too. He loved listening to Dolmestch on the clavichord. And Olga on the violin, of course.

The Chinoiserie of Cathay

Is there any work by Pound that could be praised without reservation? Yes. *The Cathay* poems of 1915. If there was a point of rest in Ezra's tumultuous and ever turning world, this would surely be it. These were poems that I had reverenced, unreservedly, from the start. And the fact is that I had never written about them, not until now. Why? Perhaps I had always wanted to guard my privacy, never to acknowledge publicly what they had meant to me. And yet there was also a problem. They were not exactly Ezra's poems at all. They were also someone else's. He had been given a bundle of documents by the widow of a Japanese-American scholar called Ernest Fenellosa, rough and ready versions of poems from the Chinese. He had read them, fiddled with them, worked on them, and turned them into a small suite of poems of breathtaking loveliness.

Was this to be regarded as Ezra's achievement or Fenellosa's? They are poems of exile, poems of longing for a homeland. They express such moods of sorrow, overwhelming sorrow, yearning and perplexity. They are poems remote and ancient in feel which also seem to belong to the present. They are not ruined by antique phraseology. I have read them again and again. They are inexhaustible and, in the end, unfathomable. And they do not lack for clarity of address. They are not pretentious. They do not send you hurrying to other sources in order to try to unlock their meaning. By the 1950s, by which time chinoiserie was part of Pound's stock in trade, and he was working on the *Classic Anthology Defined by Confucius*, Ezra's angle on the Chinese had turned folksy and bluesy.

The Cathay poems were published at a time when war was raging on the Western Front. Ezra felt the losses of that war very personally, and these poems, for all the remoteness of their settings, feel like broodings that are taking in tragedies both near and far. I would have read them first in the 1960s, when the Great War was being re-remembered as never quite before. This was the decade of the bitter-sweetness and the comic lampooning of Joan Littlewood's *Oh, What a Lovely War!* a helter-skelter, very British romp on the conflict, which seemed not quite to know whether to laugh or to cry. Ezra howled – and bellowed.

Ezra the Bad Man

'Adrian beat him at tennis in Rapallo!' my neighbour who lives at the other end of our terrace in Clapham tells me, referring to an encounter between Ezra and an English art critic called Adrian Stokes in the 1920s. We'd just met in the street. He was about to take himself off to the Common for the second walk of the day. His walk is very distinctive: hands clasped behind his back, head bowed forward, every inch the Thinker. 'It's in my book. I'm sure it is. I'll go and look!'

He's referring to a book he's just written about influential women in art, having smoothly morphed into an art historian in recent years. He had spent his working life as a physician. I follow him back indoors, watching him as he mounts the stairs at least two at a time. He's just published a book about unsung heroines of the art world. He's an immensely tall, eager, kindly man, and when, a little later, he sits on his sofa talking to me, dangling his wine glass until the stuff almost slops out onto his trousers (but never quite), the entire long length of him leans back in a single long and unbroken line. That's a very good example of a hypotenuse, I often think to myself. Once upon a time he was a surgeon (he still edits – or at least part-edits – a medical journal). Then he created another life for himself, which grew naturally out of his life-long passion for art. He always spent any spare cash on art, even when he was a student. That's why his house is full of it. He got to know many artists too, including Eduardo Paolozzi, who used to greet him with the crushing hug of a friendly bear.

He asks me what I'm up to at the moment, knowing I'd be up to something that would stir a conversation into life. His long face sags into a mock-frown at my reply. 'He was a bad man, Ezra, wasn't he?' 'Was he? I respond, still wanting to hedge my bets. 'Perhaps he was.' When he says that word bad, a few words from a song by Woody Guthrie spring into my head (together with the thin whine of that voice of his, accompanied by his rough and jangly guitar playing), about an outlaw called Stackolee. He was a bad man too. He stole six hundred dollars just to buy one suit of clothes.

Was Ezra a bit of an outlaw, a frontier's drifter in all but name? Hailey, Idaho was a gold-mining town. He and his father, assayer at the Philadelphia mint, used to test gold to see whether it was the real thing… Olga didn't believe that Ezra was a bad man though. She thought he had been unjustly accused. She had wanted me to clear his name. I was the wrong man for the job. Poets tend to get knocked sideways inside Courts of Justice.

This question of his tainted reputation has not gone away though, his Fascist sympathies, his reckless anti-semitic remarks broadcast over Radio Rome in 1940. The idea of Ezra Pound as the defender of Mussolini is still very much alive today, whether or not her man is being justly or unjustly accused. That's why there is a movement of the extreme right in Italy called Casa Pound Italia or CPI, founded by Gianluca Iannone in 2003. The last time it broke cover was in 2019 when, according to the *Washington Post*, it helped to organise anti-immigrant riots. Pound's name lives on in notoriety.

Where Ezra Never Quite Goes Away: a Bookshop in Cecil Court, November 2022

Soho is slow to stir into life at the best of times, but especially so on a Saturday morning. It keeps such late nights, you see. Today, the first Saturday in September, is no exception. First to declare themselves are the coffee shops. They just know it's what we all crave in order to jolt us back into a semblance of drifting life. The pavements of St Martin's Lane are already blocked by a scattering of flimsy chairs and tables, carried out of from the back by a stumble of yawning waiters. Various familiar sights make their presences felt night and day, needless to say. The giant bird's nest is still on top of the canopy of the Palace Theatre at Cambridge Circus, which proves that *Harry Potter and the Cursed Child* is still weaving its tedious West End magic.

There are some signs of early life in Cecil Court though, London's most precious book-dealing alleyway. To my surprise the long shelf that runs at knee height along the length of the shop window of Tindley & Everett, dealers in second-hand 20th century books, is not only down, but full of the usual bargains, all spine up, and leaning into each other in a world-weary way.

Is Ezra anywhere to be found amidst this log-jam of chafed spines and discolouring paper? An anthology called *The Modern Muse* (Oxford University Press, 1934) looks promising. I riffle the pages like a card sharp, and find two by him. I open it and read some familiar words from a poem called 'The Commission', in which the poet urges his words to travel out into the world to give sustenance to the oppressed, the faint of heart, the bored bourgeoisie…

I make my way indoors. James Tindley, proprietor, is already in residence, sitting at his table at the back of the shop, with the Saturday edition of *The Times* spread out flat in front of him. A novel by Ian McEwan is keeping an eye on things as James sifts through the news pages. There is an unusable chair in front of the table stacked with a heap of well seasoned copies of *Private Eye*.

This is our second encounter of the day. I saw him first earlier that morning at the 87 bus stop in Clapham because we happen to live a matter of streets away from each other. Today, as is customary when it is not breezing or, worse, squalling, he is standing just outside the bus shelter, steadfastly staring down. He is basking in the morning sunlight, casting a very long shadow, as antiquarian book dealers tend to do. The trousers are a rich terracotta; his blue carrier bag, an old friend, is courtesy of Southeran's of Sackville Street, another esteemed dealer in antiquarian books. *The Times* is already open in front of him – he reads it very systematically, from first page to last. Or that's how it seems. It blows back and forth, tethered precariously by his spread arms. He almost never looks up. By preference, once aboard, he takes the same seat on the lower deck of the bus for every journey, near the front, on the left.

Today, an hour or two deeper into that same morning, I am standing in front of him in the shop, waiting. He looks up from the newspaper, raising his head at a modest pace, and says, smiling: 'Good Morning, Michael'. Did he already know I was there? I ask him about Pound matters. Is there much movement in the book trade? Is he still read and bought?

'His is a name which will not go away,' James tells me. 'There is always a steady trade, and especially for the earlier books. There's not very much at the moment because they tend to go. He did not improve with age – especially the economics, which is unreadable.' And, witheringly, 'Of course I don't read him...'

There are a few Ezras tucked away in the extreme left-hand corner of one of the lower shelves. He takes me over, points. They look as if they are hiding: the *Selected Prose*, *A ZBC of Ezra Pound*, etc...

Ezra on Economics in the Reading Room
of the London Library

There is always another awkwardly shaped piece to be twitched up between the finger ends... Yes, the ever more maddening Ezra jigsaw will never be finished during my lifetime. Today I am in pursuit of a rare copy of his *ABC of Economics* (written in Rapallo, Anno Fascista XI or 1933) at the London Library. *Rather a borrower than a purchaser b*e, I have concluded.

Why? Because my current account has already chastised me severely for having the gall even to contemplate buying the only copy that seems to be available online today.

Familiar questions drum dully in the skull as I walk across sunny St James's Square on that Saturday morning in the autumn of 2022. Will I enjoy reading it? Will I find it enlightening or even comprehensible? I muse as a bicycle delicately shaves my right flank.

Is it on the open shelves? I am asking myself as I scan the catalogue entries online in the dark room that backs on to the Reading Room on the first floor, having first nodded good morning to a monochromatic photograph of T.S. Eliot's head-in-profile on the main staircase. Yes! But where exactly is it to be found?

I descend the softly carpeted stairs again and enquire at the Front Desk. I am told, humourlessly, that it is on Floor Five, in a distant place unreachable by a lift, living in a category called Political Economy, which is itself next to Political Science. This means that it is in the awful Back Stacks (where few except the cobwebby ever venture), reached only by steep flights of cast-iron stairs through which you can stare down at the flickering strip lighting on the floors beneath as you clangorously ascend. The prospect of gloom-struck, pitiless, under-lit toil looms – and then, just as quickly, it is snatched away again as if by some miracle. Was it really true, what she had just said to me? Would I like the kindly librarian to find it for me and put it into my hands? I bless her and thank her and wait beside the table stacked with good-as-new London Library polythene bags, set down there to protect books from harm once borrowed. It was from a shelf close to just here that those lovely London Library book marks, complete with quotations from eminent former members of the library, were once available, free to all library users. They have now been discontinued because they no longer quite fit the prejudices of the moment. My favourite, a model of egalitarian generosity and warm encouragement, had been a quote from Dame Edith Sitwell: *A Great Many People Now Reading and Writing Would be Better Employed Keeping Rabbits.*

The slender book is placed in my hand. When its removal has been authorised by a stamp, I glance down at that stamped page as I take it: I am the third person to have it out on loan in ten years. It is a very slender book, 74 pages in all, and it begins with Ezra telling us that he will feel much better about life when he has got all this stuff off his chest. I open it in the Reading Room, having first settled into my favourite red leather armchair next to the window that overlooks the square, close to the shelf where a spread of new weeklies is always displayed. I read Ezra. The science of economics must include the will to order. Every individual must have the right to work, and it would be sensible to keep the working day short so that one man does not do the paid work of two or three. I lay the book, face down and open, across my knee for a moment. When I look up again, I am being told, far too brusquely for my liking, that I am the last person in the Reading Room to leave.

A Walk to the Gondolier's Cottage

Doing a bit of the Ezra Trail in Venice...

Does the fact that Ezra spent so much time in Venice, from arriving here for the first time as a boy of thirteen with his Great-Aunt Frank (she who was said to have ridden a mule into the ground in Tangiers) in 1898, to dying here as a wizened sage in November 1972, carried back over the waters of the lagoon to the cemetery island of S Michele after a service held at the great, islanded Palladian church of San Giorgio Maggiore by a brace of gondoliers, mean that Pound Tourism is still in full swing in 2022? Let's call that a rhetorical question.

We embark at the San Marcuola stop, into a pretty little canal-facing piazza named after a church finished in rude horizontal bands of plain rusticated brick. By finished, I mean unfinished. No wealthy donor gave it a stone facade. The church looks much resistant to visitors these days – a small wooden cabin has been parked in front of its entrance in the little square that faces the water.

Yes, here we go again, on Vaporetto Uno, a plucky, indomitable Pound Gang of two, safely wedged side by side into our plastic bucket seats, idling our way up the Grand Canal at mid-morning, strictly Italian speed, as the packed boat swings and jolts and lurches its way from side to side, left bank to right, through the slapping, rearing waters, seeing off faster craft (those deft, sleek weavers) by not changing direction, being avoided by rough-hewn, heavily laden, toiling barges, watching the gondoliers in their gleaming black beauties lean into their strokes in exchange for the 80 euros it costs these days to lie back at almost a dead man's angle and dream through a half-hour jag, and noticing how the vaporetto buffets against the landing stage at each and every stop to show off the entirety of its muscular what's what.

It's a brusque, rude, jostly affair, which could easily make you feel queasy if you had over-egged on the breakfast an hour or two ago, which we have not. The Grand Canal Experience is such a pomp of water-borne facades: armorial shields, arches smoothly rounded or ogival, the palazzo where Byron lived, the palazzo where Wagner died, the mosaics, the remnants of murals, the salmon pink walls, the stone gods, the stone lions, the triumphal flag poles, the balconies opening out from the *piano nobile* where you would stand to see and be seen, the faded green blinds unfurled against the morning sun…

Along we sputter, admiring the candy-striped mooring posts that cluster about the waterside entrances of the palazzi, or the stouter ones, bonded like crossed staves, which stride further out into the water, and on past the unseemly glitter of the Ca' d'Oro whose ham-fisted restoration-cum-destruction in the 19th century was so hated by John Ruskin, beneath the long, low, gracious overhang of the Rialto Bridge, all the way up to the Accademia boat stop, where we get off along with far too many others. Are they all Poundians too? Not necessarily.

We're in Dorsoduro now, the old English quarter, where Pound often lived, and where he spent his last years. Should we begin with a visit to the Accademia to admire the Carpaccios, those day-to-day Venetian scenes from the 16th century, that Pound so admired? Not today. Today we are trying to retrace his steps, see what he saw, idle a little where he idled. And so off we walk to the east, in the general direction of the great Salute church, until, having turned almost immediately into Piscina Venier, we are standing opposite what is said to be the green doorway (no 852) through which Pound would have passed in 1910 on the way to the room he was renting as a young man of 25. An unlovely, indomitable iron doorway, ferociously graffitoed, these days. A miserable, desecrated sight. No homage there. No recognition at all.

And so we walk on, weaving our way through calle after calle, and then passing along the Piscina del Forner until we cross over the bridge into Campo San Vio. The English Church faces us now, and a broad view of the Grand Canal at the square's bottom end. It is into these waters that Pound threatened to chuck the script of his first book of poems, *A Lume Spento*, such was his dissatisfaction with his lame and derivative youthful efforts. A friend advised caution, and Pound, having re-considered, published it at his own expense at a printer's a short walk from here. Pound knew the Scots minister of the English church once, remembering how he thundered against Catholicism, the Whore of Babylon, from the pulpit, all those ferocious rolling *rrrrrs*... It is also here where Pound and Olga, always too poor to take a leisurely trip on a gondola, took the 50 cents trip across the water to the San Marco side. That cheap-skate's gondola ride is still on offer, but today it costs two euros.

And now having tacked further east still, we are standing at the side of the Grand Canal, directly in front of the broad flights of marble steps of the Salute church itself, where the canal broadens and opens out into the lagoon. From here we can see the building of the Customs House at the very end point of the island, and across the water, St Mark's Square and the salmon-pink loveliness of the Doge's Palace, whose lagoon-facing facade is fully visible. There are tourists idling on the steps of the Salute, swigging from their little plastic bottles of water, munching on a sandwich.

The Salute church itself is *in restauro*, closed to visitors other than the ones in hard yellow hats, and as tightly wrapped against the intruding eye as any building under treatment by Christo. Instead of the Salute itself, we stare up at a huge photographic dreamscape of twilit Venice, conjured up by the advertising men. Skimming the rooftops of the palazzi on the right bank of the Grand Canal (the Salute church itself, with its two domes, is just in view in the far distance) is the name of the sponsor of all this restoration work: CARTIER. The Cartier panther is reared up, overlooking the scene. Pound might have found that detail diverting. He had a lot of time for Big Cats – especially lynxes and panthers.

Pound wrote about his first trips to Venice in a little memoir called *Indiscretions*, which was first published in Paris in 1923, and later included in *Pavannes & Divagations*, a book of his more occasional writings. It begins with an arch piece of self-conscious reverie, literary in the extreme, written with a kind of knowing, world-weary swagger, in Jamesian sentences of an immense length, not at all the kind of writing that one might have expected from the gunslinger jokily referred to in the epigraph of that book as the Idaho Kid... Later on the style changes, and then changes again, to the staccato spit. Pound is nothing if not several.

We make our way to the rounded spit of the island, where the steps of the Customs House would once have been. The steps have gone. This is where Pound used to sit, on the Dogana's steps, taking in the prospect of the lagoon, and the idea of the fantasy that is Venice, that place where, according to him, all perceptions are heightened, listening to the calls of the gondoliers. *Stretti! Stretti!* The windows of the Customs House at our back are raised high above the ground. For all that, a little posse of teenagers is sitting, perched all in a row at an improbable height, on the windowsill, contented as a flight of birds paused between here and there.

For years it has been impossible to walk around the building of the Customs House – too much building work always came between. Not so today. Today, as we round the end of the island with ease, we take in San Giorgio Maggiore just across the water, the great Palladian Church from which Pound's body was taken on its final journey. And then we walk back along the Zattere, facing the Giudecca canal, towards the gondolier's cottage where Pound lived at the end of his life with Olga Rudge. The address is 252 Calle Querini.

In Venice it is entirely customary, within a matter of seconds, to pass from scenes of noise and crowdedness to utter silence, and the company of nothing but the sound of one's own ringing footsteps across the gently canted, and so often enshadowed, stone slabs. And so it is today, when we turn off from the Fondamenta de Ca' Bala into Calle Querini. The *calle* is a dead end – there is a pair of wooden doors, closed and locked, at its furthest point. Stravinsky once lived in a property behind these doors.

The little house of Olga – it was always Olga's house – is on the right hand side of the *calle*, half way along. The exterior walls of the house, lumpy and weathered, are a rusty terracotta red in colour, the door a deep, murky, under-sea green. Electricity cables, crudely tacked to the upper wall, swing and loop acrobatically above the white stone encasement of the door.

It is not easy to return to the house of Ezra Pound in 2022, almost forty years after our first visit. Olga Rudge, that fiercely determined old woman with her slabs of pannetone who had longed for me to be someone else, was long dead. The house was empty. The history of the despoliation of its treasures has already been told in a book called *The City of Fallen Angels*, and it will not be re-told here. I did not re-enter the house after those long years of absence. That would have been impossible. I merely walked up the *calle* and stared at it again, and then examined its fabric.

It is thirty-eight years since Olga Rudge cautioned us to step with great care over the high marble stoup which blocked the foot of the door on that inclement winter afternoon in 1984. Remember the great floods of '63! she cautioned as we did our comic high steps directly into the little room where she and Pound would have spent much of their time. Olga's name is still inscribed on the metal door plate, above a lion, and then again, together with the address of the house, on the door bell, written this time in her own hand on a white label, which thanks to much rain dousing and finger-rubbing, is shredding off.

The house has changed, dramatically. It is utterly neglected, and uninhabited. The painted plaster is blistered, almost as if badly diseased. Much of it has fallen away. A couple of days later I mention this to my friend, the poet Philip Morre. 'You mean the *intornaco*,' he tells me. 'Yes, it comes off with the salty air...' There is a plaque above the door, a memorial added by the Comune after Pound's death, which gives much pause for thought.

In Un Mai Spento Amore per Venezia
Ezra Pound
Titano delle Poesia
Questa Casa Abito' Per Mezzo Secolo
Comune di Venezia

> In his undying love for Venice
> Ezra Pound
> Titan of Poetry
> In this house lived for half a century
> The Venice City Council

Such hyperbole! Such inaccuracies too. Pound did not live here for half a century, though he certainly inhabited the house with Olga from time to time, and especially so in his final years. Was he really a Titan amongst poets? Why exaggerate his importance? And what of Fascism and its long-lingering aftermath, the fact that groups of fascists had gathered, with their banners, outside San Giorgio Maggiore, on the day of his funeral, claiming him as one of their own? What influence if any had that had on this decision to honour him? Olga had wanted me to help rid him of that taint by association, but I was not the right person even to contemplate such a thing. Hers had been an impossible dream. And now the house of the Titan looked neglected and even partially ruinous. Venice has turned its attention elsewhere. The Titan is forgotten, unloved, unregarded.

Did Venice give Pound an imaginative lift? How did he cope as a writer with his enthusiasm for the place? The difficulty is that Venice has meant far too much to far too many, and far too many have written very well about the Queen of the Adriatic. What is more, what gobbet of reverential prose or snatch of awe-struck poem could ever hope to do justice to its beauty? Literature palls, shrinks back, beside Venice itself. It cannot hope to compete, as Adrian Stokes acknowledged. And Ezra's efforts to do it justice in words were a failure too, much of it odds and sods of damp-squibbery.

Venice appears, often, in snatches of reminiscence embedded within *The Cantos*, and especially so in the often desperate pages of the *Pisan Cantos* of 1948, where Pound looks back longingly at all that could be snatched away from him. None of these minor acts of evocation is memorable for its own sake. They resemble half-sentences scissored, almost at random, out of a newspaper, fragmentary phrases. Adrian Stokes often failed Venice too, though in a slightly different way. Stokes poeticises the blowsy Queen of the Adriatic in a way that Ezra does not try to do. Where Ezra galumphs along prosaically, Adrian tries to make his words soar. They don't soar quite high enough. They feel too self-conscious.

Lunch beckons just around the corner, in the company of two gondoliers.

Happening upon the Miracle of Santa Maria dei Miracoli one Friday morning in September 2022

Many of the great Venetian churches are such spectacles because the beginning of any encounter with them happens from some distance away. They reveal themselves little by little: from the end of a piazza, or across the lagoon or a smallish canal. Others feel richer in detailing, and altogether more surprising, for being happened upon by chance, at the crossing of a bridge or the turn out from a *calle*. Such is Santa Maria dei

Miracoli, that church of the mellifluous name, which also happened to be Pound's especial favourite. He called it his jewel casket. When incarcerated at St Elizabeth's Hospital in Washington D.C., he asked for a picture of its facade to be sent to him as an aid to meditation on precious things that he might never see again. That image, though old enough, looks illusory, the west end that we stare at much wider and taller than it actually is. A casket is a relatively small thing, surely.

And such is this Venetian one. You come upon it after walking to the west away from S. Giovanni e Paolo, that great church which abuts the Ospedale, in the square which contains Verocchio's great rearing condottiere, raised up to his monstrous height on its over-size plinth. After crossing a couple of bridges, tacking gently to the left as you go, you reach a confluence of water, *calle*, and a small square called the Campiello Santa Maria Nova. The Miracoli church is tucked in just to the left of you as you cross the Ponte S. Maria Nova, which takes you into the square of the same name. The church seems to fit so tightly and so snugly into the space that it has been allotted. As you walk across the bridge you also notice that its far side runs alongside the canal. Close packed in on every side then, it looks like a ship that has nudged its way through and deftly berthed itself – and has only stopped because a minor bridge has had the impertinence to block its way.

You can sit in the Campiello Santa Maria Nova on an orange bench and view the apsidal end of the church, side on. Seize this opportunity for the church's sake – and your own. It is rare to find sun-shaded benches to sit on in Venice. It is rare not to be obliged to plonk yourself down, hunched over, on the stone surround of a well head, and be slowly beaten into submission by the sun. The church is relatively small, but its presence, the spiritual weight of the material fact of it here, in this particular place, is so much greater than its size. The colour of its marbles, often buttery and veiny, works so well in tandem with the greyness of the surrounds of its blind arcades, and the restraint of its shallow pilasters. If you now stand up and walk back to the bridge you have just stepped off, and look at the church apsidal end on, you will see how the barrel-vaulted roof seems to over-brim the walls of the church – that is exactly what the lid of a jewel casket so often does.

Now cross over to the Campiello dei Miracoli and walk around to the church entrance. More surprises. There is no elaborate entrance way, nothing between you and a sudden eruption into the body of the church, with its restrained harmonies of marble and porphyry. It is higher-ceilinged than you had been led to expect. In part, this is to do with the extraordinarily long and steep flight of steps which, you notice, looking ahead to that far, apsidal end, carries you up from the nave to the extraordinarily high choir, fourteen marble steps in all. Those steps give an illusion of elevation. In making you look up and consider the long climb, you imagine you might been carried further than you could have deemed possible.

There is much to admire about this exquisite interior, and not least the carvings by the brothers Lombardi, detailed work, part floral, part mythological, that rise up in continuous sequences of intricate interweavings through the niches on each face of column after column. So much that will not be said could be said about any one of these columns. But I am here today to look out for one detail alone, one detail about which Pound wrote repeatedly. I am looking for Pound's sirens – his 'serenes' as he called them. They appear in the *Pisan Cantos*, for example. They are never far from his thinking.

Where exactly are they though? I ask the young man inside the glass-panelled booth from whom I buy my tickets of entry. He could scarcely be more unhelpful. He is not in the least interested. He wafts his hand in front of him in the direction of nowhere in particular. I wonder about the carvings on the faces of the columns that flank the entrance to the choir, at the point where you reach the very top of that long flight of marble steps. Could they be up there?

This poses problems of its own, problems of actually seeing what Pound might himself have been able to see back in 1913, when he hurried his friend, the poet H.D., over here as soon as she had arrived in Venice, through *calles*, over bridges, across small *campos*, as she describes in her memoir *An End to Torment*, in order to give her, immediately, without even a moment to catch her breath, the very best that was on offer, which might well have included, I am now wondering, something that we are not quite able to see any longer.

Why? Because at the top of that flight of marble steps in the year 2022, there is a chunky red cord, and various bits of church lumber, preventing humans penetrating any further into the choir. And so I must stand at the top of those steps and, very slowly, climb with my eye up and up, through stylised garlandings, urn-like forms, and sphinx-like, dragon-like creatures, all these elements fantastically interwoven into a single, continuous pattern of visual marvellousness…

And then, eventually, I think I do see them, the ones that correspond to the image I have of them in the little blue book I am carrying. They are at the base of a pillar, almost interlinked in their movements, child-like, mermaid-like forms, cresting the waves on which they ride, looking as if they are being rocked on nursery rocking horses, strange amalgams of this and that out of folklore or mythology.…

In 1995 the Artist Margaret Mellis Gives Me a Harris Tweed Jacket Which I call Adrian Forever After

Margaret Mellis, painter and fabricator of constructions from driftwood, stepped back a pace or two, appraising me. We were standing around in her back kitchen at Lydstep House in Southwold, that house near the sea, politely waiting for the next thing to happen, as one so often does when one is a guest of someone else, and therefore completely at the mercy of their least whim. I was backed up against the fridge. She was working her lips as she looked up at me, which meant that she was thinking, hard. The coffee and porridge were already over, with all that beautifully treacly dark brown sugar worked into it, and we'd almost reached the hour of the morning walk – out of the back door, and then downhill towards the pier in the Walberswick direction, on the prowl for driftwood, always walking at a furious pace, her pace, not necessarily always ours.

She'd been like that in Paris too, when we'd invited her to stay with us in Montmartre, not longer after the children were born. Margaret always had her own agenda, which was not necessarily mine or Ruth's. She had a phrase for it. If we suggested a visit to here or there, she would counter with: *more to the point*. And then grin, and give a spluttery mischievous giggle, as if she wanted it to be known that she was being a bit of a rogue, who would surely always be forgiven, but especially so when she had her best finery on, complete with a brilliant flash of red lipstick. Today, as every day in Southwold, it was all about driftwood. Margaret was always on the prowl for driftwood. That was what she made her art from these days when she wasn't flattening out an old used envelope and painting a flower across its inside surface, the part which was not defaced by writing. I loved the best of those paintings, how she painted a flower shape inside the strange, irregular shape you create from an opened out envelope. They looked as if they were absolutely made for each other.

I was standing facing her, underneath a collage by Francis – Francis Davison, her second husband, that wonderful collagist – when she spoke and gave me that look. 'You're about Adrian's size, aren't you?' she said. We knew that she had once been married to the art critic Adrian Stokes – that was during the war years, when they were both together in Cornwall, welcoming such uninvited guests into the house as Ben Nicolson, together with his wife Barbara Hepworth and their twins – who had then, later, changed his mind and married her sister Ann. That must have been quite tricky, we both thought, though we never talked about quite how tricky it must have been because it was all so long ago and Margaret was Margaret now, slim, teeming with energy and *more-to-the-points*.

'Am I?' I said, a bit puzzled, having not a clue about Adrian's size, although I do remember having once seen a picture of his face in profile. Quite handsome, I'd thought. Margaret darted off upstairs. She was sure of it.

Moments later she came back with it, across her arm. 'This was Adrian's,' she said. 'He left it behind. I don't believe he ever wore it. It's as good as new. Try it on.'

She held it up for me to see. It was a very handsome, brown, close-weave Harris Tweed jacket. When did Adrian buy it? I asked myself. 1940? Around then, perhaps. Which must mean that it had reached its half-century by now… I tried it on. It was a perfect fit. It was wearing its age very well. I myself was about 40, five years younger than the jacket.

It was around this time that I first began to write about art, for the *Financial Times* – I reviewed a show of wild paintings by Basquiat, in Lausanne, where Ruth and I happened to be staying. I had no qualifications for the job whatsoever. All I knew was that my wife was an artist, and that I had often thought I would quite like – in fact, I would relish – the challenge of writing about a painting (or several paintings) in a gallery. I was sick of writing about poetry and fiction and mediocre biographies. I even used to walk around galleries with that challenge in mind, asking myself this question: *which five adjectives would you choose if someone were to invite you to review this show?*

And then I thought of an absolutely brilliant wheeze. I had written regularly about literary matters for the *FT*, and the editor trusted me to do a good job. We liked each other. Why not mention it to him? And so when I asked him, quite casually, about doing a review of the Basquiat show – I thought it would be best not to make too much of it – a few weeks before we went to Switzerland, he replied *why not?* And then went on watering his plants. After which, we moved on to something else, something more pressing. The review was published, to the usual deafening silence – everyone must have thought that it was neither better nor worse than the average art review in the *FT*. And so a new career was born.

And Adrian the jacket stayed with me. I got into the habit of wearing it on gallery occasions. When I was taking it out of the wardrobe, I even used to call to mind from time to time a line from a rather unsettling poem by Yeats about a rape called 'Leda and the Swan': *did she put on his knowledge with his power?* Being a fantasist of sorts, some part of me must have thought that to be inhabiting Adrian's jacket by wearing it would add to my credibility, my knowledgeability, and even my store of wisdom as an art critic. It certainly helped me to look the part. We live and breathe by such little foolishnesses.

Adrian and Ezra bonded over a single building. It was a gothic church in Rimini which was re-modelled during the Renaissance by the architect Alberti. You could say that he classicised it – except that to speak of what he did in that way is to diminish it. The building became known as the Tempio Malatestiano, and it is the cathedral church of Rimini on the Adriatic coast. Sigismundo Malatesta paid for the job. It would be a tribute to himself and Isotta, the woman he loved. Sigisimundo was a leader of mercenary armies and the war lord of Rimini, and Pound admired him hugely. Like Mussolini, he was an ACTION man.

Did Adrian, who wrote at length about the enigmas of that building in a book called *Stones of Rimini* (1934), admire the building more than he admired the man? Pound wrote a sequence of poems called the *Malatesta Cantos*, which is a kind of crude, part versified digest of Sigisimundo's goings on. Adrian found these poems inspiring. He mentions in *Stones of Rimini* that their example would be likely to serve as a spur to further labours on yet another book about the history and significance of the church and its founder. That did not happen. Pound regarded *Stones of Rimini* as one of great books of the 20th century. These two men had much in common, and much that, in time, drove them apart. Adrian did not share Pound's admiration for Sigismundo's muscularity. He loved nothing better than the Tempio Malatestiano and its sculptor, Agostino di Duccio though. Few critics have overpraised that artist more. Adrian was also a great admirer of the Jewel Casket.

The Afterlife of a Jacket Called Adrian

Seven years after the death of Uncle Ken, my Aunt Ena, his wife, died too, peacefully, at the age of 99, in a small, comfortable, overheated room in a care home on a steep hill in Ranmoor, Sheffield, surrounded by family photographs. Her niece sent me one, taken in her final year. Her hair still looks magnificently permed. She is still clutching her favourite teddy bear. Months later, having let a posse of eager solicitors loose on the intricate difficulties of winding up the estate, I inherited some money from my uncle and aunt. Ken was always very careful with money. He could not bear to leave a room without first turning off a radiator. The money, having travelled at leisure, finally arrived. What to spend some of it on as a token of their passing, some gesture which they might regard as sympathetic?

I think of Adrian. He has been a little neglected in recent months, and when I find him again, squeezed in amongst so many others in the far corner of the tall, red cupboard on the topmost landing, I regret that neglect, albeit mildly, because I do regard Adrian as a kind of companion or soul mate of sorts. We have been apart for a very particular reason. The broiling heat of summer and Adrian were incompatible.

I hold Adrian up in front of me. Moth holes. Frayings at the cuff. Lining ripped, as if brutally knife-slashed by a rival art critic. The dry cleaner in Clapham Old Town who doubles as a tailor – it's just across the road from where the red buses stop – gives me a quotation for a complete overhaul. Wincingly, I agree. I feel that I owe it to Adrian. I even tell him a little bit about the jacket and the man. Goodness knows why. The words seem to spill out of my mouth of their own accord in a tidal wave of emotion. *I hope you will think that it is worth your while to spend so much money on an old jacket,* he says, with chilling sternness, folding it brusquely over his forearm before stuffing it into a large plastic bag.

For the Love of Gaudier-Brzeska

I am re-reading Ezra's memoir of Gaudier – it was the very first book to be written about the man, and it appeared in 1916, soon after the sculptor's death at the age of 23 – on bonfire night in 2022, and that stench of burning wood in the local churchyard, together with the fizzing here-and-gone rage of fireworks in the air overhead, seem fitting. It was an impassioned friendship, cut cruelly short by the careless and uncaring brutality of death. Did Ezra love this man as he never really loved any of the many women who fawned over him? They met at an art show in Kensington Town Hall in 1914. Ezra saw the name of the artist beside an example of his work and, like so many before and since, made a ridiculous, sputtery effort to pronounce it: BRZSSEZSKA... Or some such.

As if by magic, Gaudier stepped out from behind a pillar and set him straight. They became fast friends. Gaudier contributed an explosive editorial to BLAST!, a little pink mag (not so little in size though), edited by Wyndham Lewis, that growly enemy to so many, that man Hemingway thought wickedness personified. Blasting the old and heralding the new art of VORTICISM, that was the intent. Gaudier defined the meaning of the VORTEX in a fiery manifesto of partial comprehensibility, and set it, with tremendous intellectual panache, in its historical context. Ezra was awestruck by how well read this young sculptor seemed to be.

He spent time at his cold and squalid little studio underneath the arches at Putney, listening to his compulsive, staccato, rat-a-tat talk. He watched Gaudier hand-carving in stone. Such labour! Such quattrocento devotion! Such direct attack! He saw him hand-carving and sharpening his chisels. He admired his toughness – Gaudier carried a bunch of stone chisels in his pocket in preparation for a second meeting with the local roughs who had assaulted him. Pound sat for what became the hieratic head – the labour amounted to two solid months of cutting into marble – watching himself gradually becoming immortalised in *planes in conjunction with each other*.

Then Gaudier responded to the call to go to war. They conducted a correspondence from the Western Front. He'd taken Pound's *Cathay* poems with him to the trenches. Gaudier's letters show him off as fearless to the point of recklessness. He writes with an almost chilling matter-off-factness about the horrors of the trenches. He needs three things only, he tells Pound: chocolate, cigarettes and poems.

Pound is frank about the extent of his loss – the world's loss too – when Gaudier is killed. The destruction of Reims Cathedral is as nothing beside this. Gaudier's death represents not only a generational but also a civilisational loss, the snuffing out of genius. This was a man who was making art equal to the best of the cinquecento. Pound never wavered in this belief.

Goodbye to the Mask-Making

Ingmar Bergman's *Persona* went on general release in 1966, but it was not until the autumn of 1968 that I first saw it at the Arts Cinema in Cambridge, during the first term of my freshman year. The film anatomises how a single fragile human being can bifurcate, peel away from itself, and merge with another. We see it happening on screen, when the celebrated actress Elisabeth Vogler, played by Liv Ullmann, seems to take on the identity of her nurse, Anna (played by Bibi Andersson), who becomes her carer and companion at a remote beach house on the Baltic Sea. Or is it that the nurse has assumed the identity of Elisabeth? They are both one and the other. Or perhaps they are really neither.

Elisabeth has been sent there to recover from the aftermath of a moment of crisis during a live performance. Her mind goes blank. She lapses into silence. The longer the two women spend time alone together, the more their identities seem to merge. In one scene, the screen itself appears to fissure down the middle as their two faces meld into one. The sight of that fissuring, in all its raggedly smudgy ditheryness, is profoundly disturbing and even painful to watch, bloodless surgery of a very particular kind.

When I first bought a copy of the *Collected Shorter Poems of Ezra Pound* in 1968, it had been called nothing but that. When I came to buy a revised and amplified edition of that same book thirty years later, it had changed its name back to *Personae*, the title Ezra had given the collection in 1926. He had chosen to call it that in acknowledgement of the fact that so many of those earlier pieces had been voice projections, assumptions of a range of identities quite separate from his own. You could call this decision a way of drawing a rule under his younger self. For the rest of his writing life – aside from his multiple harangues in prose and some later works in translation – Pound was striving to bring to completion and perfection a long-form, long-term, life-defining project called *The Cantos*. One of the reasons for the failure of this project was Pound's inability to find a consistent and credible speaking voice. His mask-making had abandoned him. Or perhaps he had chosen to abandon it.

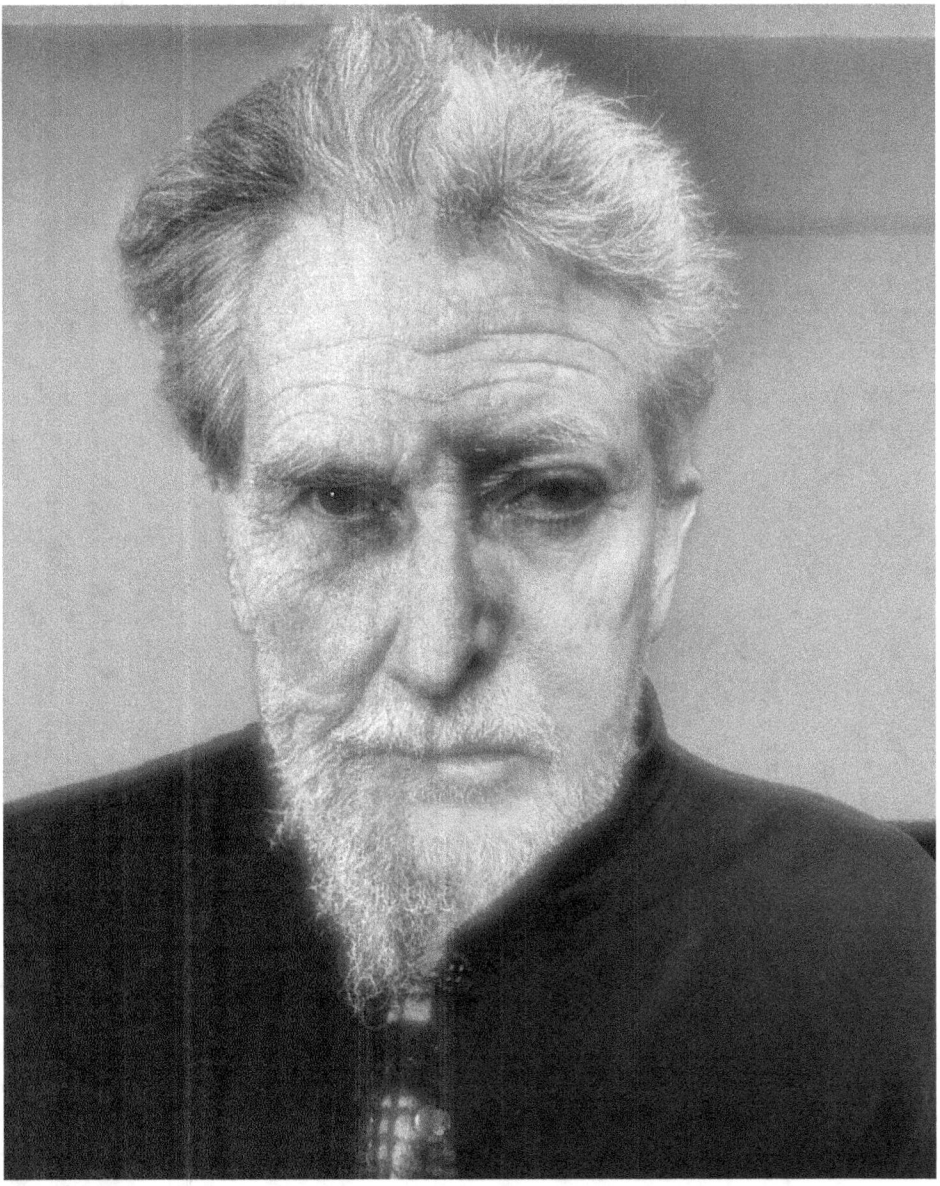

Duelling Personae

Il Grande Poeta:
Italy's Love Affair with Ezra Continues

Has Pound's love affair with Italy in general and Venice in particular been reciprocated? Is it flourishing in the neo-fascist era of Giorgia Meloni? On 23 November 2022, Ca'Foscari University of Venice staged an Ezra Pound Conference. Its main event was a reading, in English and Italian, of a new translation by Patrizia Valduga of the first seven *Cantos*, published by Mondadori in 2022. I asked Angelo Goldmann, husband of the organiser of that conference, whether Pound's name was still tainted by his continuing association with Fascism, and whether he was still regarded as *Il Grande Poeta* in Italy.

Anyone doubting Pound's continuing importance to Italian letters has only to look at the number of translations of his *Cantos* into Italian that there have been, he told me. Pound the poet was very much alive in Italy, his influence still 'strong and very felt'. What is more, his poetry is completely free of any sympathies for Fascism. And, no, there was no enduring taint. Most Italians believe that Pound did penance enough by suffering all those miserable years of incarceration in America. It had cleansed him in the eyes of Italy.

So the sign above that door in Venice is good for some years yet.

Dylan and Ezra Come to Blows in Andalucia
During the Winter of 2022

It's about 5pm – my goodness, how suddenly the chill descends on a late afternoon in February in Andalucia, and how quickly the heat of the sun disappears from the face of the earth, as if it has been little more than a fantasy!

My son and I are sitting in the salon one late afternoon, facing into the corner in order to pay homage to Ben and Neil's highly effective wood-burning stove, around which black altar four humans, two dogs, and a cat called Peggy are already all clustered to pay their homage to the flames, given off by burning logs, that are licking up behind the sealed glass into which we peer, enthralled by their ever changing dance, soon after the sun has disappeared behind the mountain.

'In which song do the words "blue-eyed son" appear?', Joe asks me, by way of a tease, because he knows full well that I, of all people, should know. Shamefully, I'm truly flummoxed for a moment. They are almost overwhelmingly familiar, those three words, that noun tied to that compound adjective, and yet they wholly elude me just then… He's already asked Alexa to play the song over the music system, and when that first metallic jangle of a downbeat strikes my ear, I'm transported once again by Bob Dylan's 'Hard Rain…', at least sixty years young today, I quickly calculate, and a thing of such youthful urgency still, that anthem of a song that never stops giving and giving, no matter how many hundreds of times you may have listened to it before.

As I listen, a thought strikes me for the very first time during the long, maddening and interrupted writing of this patchwork of a book-in-all-but-name. How could it ever have happened? How could I have told the story of my obsession with Ezra, the story of my growing up in the company of his shadow for so long, without ever introducing the name and songs of the man who was at the very least his equal in my estimation? Why had I excluded Bob Dylan? Is it not true that Dylan was so much more alive to me as a human being than Ezra could ever have been? Had I not watched him perform on umpteen occasions, the very first time at the City Hall in Sheffield in 1965, when I was a guitar-strumming boy of sixteen myself? Were the two at odds with each other then? Had I kept them apart by design – or accident? It's true that my passion for Dylan had largely preceded my obsession with Pound and his multi-fold obscurities, in so far as it had begun in the basement of a Sheffield music shop in 1963, perhaps before I had even read any of Ezra's poetry. Pound had been more of a university-propelled preoccupation, a pursuit that had gone hand in hand with a burning wish to be an intellectual. Had Dylan and Pound had much to do with each other?

It was Allen Ginsberg, visiting Pound in Venice after his return to Italy from that long incarceration, who had introduced Pound to Dylan. He had brought a few of Dylan's records with him over from America as a gift. Pound was totally unresponsive. And yet the two men had common ground – and reasons to despise each other too. To many American poets – such as Robert Duncan and Charles Olson – Pound was a radical, an innovator, an anti-establishment man. He was teaching the young how to write verse in a new kind of way. He and Dylan were both enemies of the de-humanising war machine. But Dylan spoke to and for the many, Pound to and for the very few. What is more, Pound's anti-semitism was anathema to Ginsberg (a Jew himself), Zukofsky (another Jew) and Robert Zimmerman, too. And the older he got, the more Pound succeeded in aligning himself with political undesirables on the American far right. Dylan seemed to be voicing desires for wider freedoms than Ezra was ever able to encompass.

Return to Lago di Maggiore, Early September 2023

To Hotel Cannero once again, on the lake shore, with pockets and backpacks spilling with the usual pilgrim's burden: a miscellaneous ragbag of Poundiana. Close to the end now. After this there may be a trip to Rapallo, to retrace his steps there, and another to Rimini, to commune with the Tempio Malatestiana, and to listen in to those distant conversations between Ezra and the critic Adrian Stokes....

This year, we have shifted rooms, from front to back, to save money. Last year's view of the sun-blessed lake from the window has been replaced by an inner courtyard, through which, from time to time, glamorous, gleaming, relatively noiseless cars ease through to a car park hidden within the belly of the hotel, part hidden from view. The cobbles underneath our window gleam, rain-slicked on the evening of our arrival. Sleep-disturbing wheelie bins begin to rumble soon after dawn. Unsurprisingly, the mood of the hotel changes with the weather.

When I open the door of Room 161 on that first morning, the characteristically sun-splashed corridor of yesterday evening has turned dark and gloom-struck. The mellow, lemony light which enriched and exalted the pastel yellows of doors and door surrounds is no more. I pace to the end of the corridor, and turn to face the window which looks out onto the lake and the mountains of Switzerland. Nothing but greyness and the dense occlusion of mist. No water. No distant shoreline. Only a memory of mountains. All feels so self-enclosed.

When we take our places at breakfast on the terrace, facing the lake and the *sportello*, where the ferry tickets are sold for excursions to the islands, flags droop listlessly from the landing stage. Rain falls in heavy spits and spats and splashes. A posse of furled, royal-blue umbrellas inside a gilded drum wait for our attention at the bottom of the steps. Only the ticket seller is out there, facing out to the lake, hands in pockets. Where are the customers this morning, those gangs of uproarious Australian cyclists, the couples with their hampers? What is this place without the blessing of sunlight?

When the rain eases off, we venture over to the cluster of tables beside the lake where lunch will be served in the fullness of time. The cormorant is back, atop his mooring post. The same one? I pick up my book, taking up yet again the story that will never end. It is called *The Sons of Ezra*, and it was published in 1995. Its co-author, Michael Alexander, gave me this copy ten years ago, I see from the inscription, which reads: 'To Michael –

who shared some infuriating hours *chez* Mildred with W.C. and Michael.' There then follows a quotation from Ezra: 'there is no need for complete despair,' followed by Michael's good wishes for the new year. It is dated 1 January, 2013.

Infuriating hours? Despair? What exactly was he talking about? I think back to the 1990s, and to a meeting which took place in Mildred Corbet-Singleton's house at the corner of Carlyle Square in Chelsea. A blue plaque reminds us that Sir Osbert Sitwell once lived in the house next door. When we convened that evening, David Frost was still in residence on the far side of the square. What were Michael and I doing there? The Arts Council had set up an informal committee, of which Michael and I were members. We were discussing the precariousness of the *Agenda* situation.

Was William Cookson still a fit person to be in editorial control? Would the Arts Council withdraw its public subsidy? William was due to be present. He did not show up. Nothing got sorted out. The committee proved to be toothless.

Michael went on to publish *Sons of Ezra* in 1995, a book which invited a range of British poets to reflect upon the impact of Ezra on their own writing. It had not been easy to find a taker, he told me. Not a single British house would publish it. Was it that Ezra was too tainted, too unpopular, too much in the margins of modernity? Probably a little of all of those reasons. Eventually he found a small academic publisher called Rodopi, which was part based in Amsterdam and part in Atlanta, Georgia. The book was printed in the Netherlands, number seventeen in an ongoing series called *Studies in Literature*.

I start in on the book by reading the words of Donald Davie, a poet and critic from Barnsley, Yorkshire, whose gruffness sometimes seems to resembles my own. Davie makes dizzying claims for Ezra – the man, he tells us, was uniquely able to understand European culture *in its totality*. I look up and take a prolonged and deep breath of sheer wonderment. The sun is coming out now. The lake water is calm and blue again. Switzerland is back on the far side of the water just as if it had never been away. A man seated on his own at the adjacent table is part way through a puzzle in *La Settimana Enigmistica*. Ezra, argues Davie, was able to conceive of Europe as a cultural whole *in the mind*. How exactly did he conceive it though? Not so much a thing of words as a *crumbling fabric*. Is that thought fatuous or platitudinous or both? I ask myself at the very moment when the cormorant on its post decides to spread its wings. A cormorant's wet, outspread wings do somewhat resemble the wet panels of an umbrella...

I leaf through name after name...The poet Charles Tomlinson, a grammar school boy from Stoke-on-Trent in the Potteries, discovered Ezra twenty years before I did. By the time I went up to Queens' College, Cambridge in 1968, Tomlinson was already a Fellow there. I remember watching him walk diagonally across a snatch of lawn in Old Court, a thing only Fellows were allowed to do. Tomlinson had found things to like about some of Ezra's shorter early poems that I too had enjoyed as a teenager coming new to his poetry: a certain casualness of address, which seemed to suggest that poetry might relate to matters readily spoken of. Nobody spoke of Ezra at Cambridge though, Tomlinson tells us.

A single young man is skiffing across the surface of the lake with perfect and enviable poise and balance, I notice, looking up just then. The sunlight has just scattered a dazzle of jewels at his feet.

Yes, the wind seems to have blown up all of a sudden. The lake water, darker and heavier looking now, is slopping and heaving. The little promenade at our backs has turned noisy too – a delivery cart is rattling across the cobbles. Airborne gulls have broken out into a hideous cackle. A serious-minded waiter in a white coat appears at our shoulder. Do we want lunch? He jabs a menu into our faces. We are occupying what is now a lunch table. We do not. We leave.

I take up the reading again a little later, beneath a well tilted parasol on the terrace that overlooks the pool. Luckily, school holidays are over and the kids are gone. Oldsters, when they swim at all, do so in ones and twos in a dull and slow and orderly fashion. By the time Michael Alexander makes his own visit to Ezra, the old volcano is a spent force of nature. He is a silenced, shrunken creature. He looks tired, frail and aged. Old blabber-mouth can barely string two words together. His reputation has been blasted. He has been mocked, despised, and is now part ignored and part forgotten.

The poet Douglas Dunn, who takes Ezra's Provençal translations to Provence with him, thought he had it all coming to him. The man was a masochist, born to 'extremes and turbulence', who goaded and jibed and reaped the whirlwind of dislike and condemnation as a consequence. He lacked humility – he was always in too much of a hurry. He courted enmity and disaster. No poet should be certain in the way that Ezra was certain.

Another Scottish poet, W.N. Herbert, digs in to the old issue of how much Ezra ever really knew – was he as much of an intimidating polyglot as he seemed to be? He told us himself that he was *iggurant* of Greek. His old friend William Carlos Williams, poet by night and paediatrician by day, wrote some question-begging sense about Ezra's addiction to quoting in languages few of us were ever likely to use during our daylight hours. *I presume they mean something, probably something pertinent to the text, and that the author knows what they mean*, he once ruminated…

The book does a lot of to-ing and fro-ing between those who loathed him and those who learnt from him. Robert Graves despised him. He thought Ezra's pugilism was hand-crafted in order to identify and provoke enemies. Graves had known combat during the Great War, serving as an officer with the Royal Welch Fusiliers. Though Ezra thundered about war, all that fist-shaking had been done from the safety of the sidelines (a house in South Kensington for some of that time).

Old Approaches to New Approaches to Ezra
on 14 October 2023

'Soldier, scholar, horseman he...' This triplet of singing words is lodged in my head as my muzzy, fragile self descends, haltingly, the staircase from the bedroom this morning at 5.30 am, to confront the reassuringly looming presence of the dark mahogany bookcase that sits on the landing outside the bathroom, and rises almost as tall as the landing ceiling.

It is here that various very precious collections of books by or about single authors or artists are gathered for safe keeping, in order to ensure against wanton scattering by an idle hand such as my own. There is Ruskin; there is Dante; there is the odd pairing of Klee and Neo Rauch; and, on the middle shelf, there is an Ezra overspill of a dozen or so volumes that could not be accommodated elsewhere. Why that triplet of words by Yeats though, from his poem addressed to Major Robert Gregory, that man whose cellar he had drained, to the fury of his host?

The fact is that one running triplet has led on to another. What had the first one been then? I had been lying in bed at 4am or thereabouts, thinking of three words easily linked in my mind: *obsessive, enthusiast*, and *scholar*. It must have been the third of these which had caused those words by Yeats to drift down from the sky.

This first triplet of the coming dawn now reappears as I glance sideways, in passing, at the landing bookcase, letting my eyes drift across the spines of many old familiars, one of which is that edition of *New Approaches to Ezra Pound* whose cover I had once stared at, mesmerised, as I sat on the grass beside the Mill in Cambridge, a matter of yards away from Silver Street Bridge, within sight of the corner of Queens', my old college, in 1969, all of fifty something years ago…

I had been trying, once again, to define with some care the nature of my engagement with Ezra, and this morning I have decided that those three words – obsessive, enthusiast and scholar – may be of some use to me. Am I an obsessive, an enthusiast or a scholar? Which?

I am certainly no scholar. My mind is too flighty. No sooner does it alight on something than it wants to be gone again, to pastures new. Am I an enthusiast then? The word sounds a little too light and pallid and fleet of foot, as if it could do just as well for chocolate…Perhaps obsessive then, which suggests some kind of unshakeable, unbudgeable addiction, perhaps even to be under a kind of spell…

I pull out the book and stare once again at the cover, which had once so enthralled me. The old sage is in right profile, hair rising in a tumult of back-blown, grizzled curls, head part emerging from a kind of violet haze…

Had I actually owned that copy at which I stared on that afternoon I idled on the grass beside the Cam? Or had it been it a library book, borrowed from the English Faculty Library in Sidgwick Avenue, no distance at all from where I was then sitting? Published in 1969, perhaps a mere matter of months after I had first gone up to Cambridge as a nineteen-year-old, I have no memory of having borrowed it from the English Faculty Library, of its having had a sheet pasted into the first page to be stamped by the librarian – that's how they did things in those days. I feel now that it was almost certainly a newly purchased book that I had been handling on that afternoon. I had the money to engage in acts of such extravagance in those days. But, if so, what had happened to it? I would never have let it go…

There is a sheet of paper tucked into the copy I am currently holding in my hand today, which is Saturday 14 October, 2023. It tells me that I bought it online, via Amazon, from Kelvinbooks, on 9 May 2012, exactly eleven years ago as I write these words… The flimsy paper invoice is tucked in between pages 124 and 125, which could suggest that I had got only that far in my reading. I have not picked it up since, I am sure of that.

And yet I have no memory of having read even that far. In fact, I have no memory of having actually read this long owned, and longer pondered upon, book, at all – until now. This, I believe, is itself significant, and significant as a mark of an *obsession*, I believe.

By 2012, having perhaps lost it at some point of travel between here and there (if I had indeed really owned it), *I still felt the need to own it again*. But not to *read* it with any degree of urgency. To possess it, that was the crux. I recall now what I thought about the book fifty years ago, and, in particular, of how it described itself: *New Approaches to Ezra Pound*.

As a complete beginner, I would have recognised immediately that it would have been an act of foolishness for me to read a book, then, about *new* approaches to Ezra Pound because, at that point in time, I knew almost nothing of the *old* approaches to Ezra and his *Cantos* – let alone any new ones. I hadn't even read *The Cantos*. Well, I had dipped into them… What I did know though, as a beginning obsessive, was that if I were to own it, I could regard myself as having encompassed, and been bolstered, if not a little aggrandised, by its contents in some way that must have profoundly appealed to me…

So this morning – a Saturday when, as usual, I will take the 87 bus along the Wandsworth Road into town, alighting, as usual, opposite Charing Cross Station, and then proceed up the eastern edge of Trafalgar Square as far as the flight of steep stone steps that will carry me up to the entrance to St Martin-in-the-Fields, and deposit me beneath its magnificent, eighteenth-century portico, from where I will turn into the church itself in order to spend an hour (or perhaps less) in a pew directly facing Shirazeh Houshiary's wonderful East Window, that oh so symbolic canted oval – I prepare myself for that journey into town by pulling out from the shelf *New Approaches to Ezra Pound*. Yes, I will read the introduction to the book in St Martin's….

And what an introduction it proved to be! It was written by Eva Hesse, its editor, and the translator of Ezra into German. It had been her job to choose the scholarly articles that it contained. The book had been published by Faber, Pound's publisher, so it was officially endorsed. Her introduction – the level of her addiction to Ezra – fascinated me from the start. The poetry of a man such as Pound, she argued, should be regarded as a conspiracy, a form of entrapment, from which, once hooked, you can never hope to escape. The mystery will never be solved because there is always yet another layer to be peeled away. Pound is so self-referential. To fully understand him, you would, at the very least, have needed to *be* him, to read every last little thing he had read, to live like a parasite inside the inner dark of his own wayward thought processes. Assuming, of course, that he was in control of the meaning of his own words. *The Cantos* are the ultimate *mysterium*. Once inside, you never escape. The best you can hope for it is to drown in all the explication, which will never end…

The tone of her introduction seems to encompass threat, intimidation, excitement and more than a measure of peacockishness. It is a heady, almost delirious, bout of impassioned advocacy. She herself makes sure that she dazzles like the rest of the Pound gang. Pound experts exist to dazzle and mystify each other in just about equal measure. As an addict (should you succumb), you will find yourself marooned amongst others of your kind, which will mean that you are more than likely to be gorgeously self-preening. Marooned? Of course. He is too difficult for mere mortals. As I read, I think back to that image on the book's cover that I first contemplated beside the Cam, after a pint or two of best bitter, one lunchtime in 1969, and in particular to the purple haze from which it seems to emerge, or through which it seems to float. This is the haze of a cardinal perhaps, or, at the very least – as Gaudier's 'Hieratic Head' suggested – a being sacred and monumental, staring ahead into timelessness.

Eva Hesse strives to show us that Pound has no earthly equals. When she explains that *The Cantos* 'encompass' Homer and Dante, we know that what she is *really* telling us, although not in so many words, is that Pound is not only their equal but their *better*. He has gobbled them up – like that terrible, gobbling mouth painted by Goya in old age to haunt all our dreams. Pound, in her words, is being presented as the soothsayer of soothsayers, who is responsible for the well-being of humanity. He is very, very important because he is very, very profound. He gets to grips with the nature of 'true reality', with which we are all keen to be in touch at significant moments in our lives. That at least is undeniable.

The poem, to quote a couple of her strange turns of phrase, goes from being a 'liquid melt' to a 'finely structured mineral substance.' Who would ever guess, reading her advocacy, that it had been cobbled together from mere words, by a boy from the margins?

Trying to Put Ezra to Sleep Beside the Lake
on 18 September 2023

The Hotel Cannero beside Lake Maggiore is a perfect place to put Ezra to sleep – as I write that word *sleep* I think, fleetingly, of the grisly final scene of Sidney Lumet's great film of 2007, *Before the Devil Knows You're Dead*, in which Charlie Hanson (played by a tortured Albert Finney), finally gets his revenge upon his crooked, murderous son Andy (played by Philip Seymour Hoffman) by smothering him in his hospital bed with a pillow – because it is the purest example that I have ever happened upon of part-real, part-faux antiquity, which manifests itself across its many rooms, each one of which has a slightly different character. Ezra too was often a model of the faux-antique. Was he not pure verbal brocade, and even a baggy lodging house of sorts, crafted out of various bits of this and that? There was never only one Ezra. He was only ever several.

And so it is with the Hotel Cannero, and we recognise that all the more during our second visit because this time we are obliged to move from room to room during our stay. The hotel has three buildings along the lake shore, and they all inter-connect. The northern end had once been the baronial residence of the Sant'Agabio family in the 18th century. Two centuries before that, the middle section had been a monastery. Another building had been a post office in more recent times.

Our first room, Room 161, was a disappointment: too dark, too noisy. We protested, howlingly. Yes, they could move us all right, we were told at reception the morning after our arrival, but there would need to be *several moves* because no single room was available for the remaining six days of our stay. We get shifted along the corridor, moved on to an apartment without any pretence of style or glamour called *Dafne*, overlooking the swimming pool, and finally end up in a regal flourish of a room with a balcony giving on to a side view of the lake, and a prospect of a covered central courtyard which seems to be Gothic, moorish and renaissance in flavour all at once. The bed's headboard boasts a clumsily painted fake heraldic device. Ezra would have taken all this flitting through the changing stylistic innovations of the centuries in his stride.

By the time we are enjoying the side view of the lake from our balcony in Room 218 (which is described by the hotel as a 'king's room'), Ezra is under sustained fire from a poet and essayist of the American South called Allen Tate in a book I am now reading called *Perspectives*, a collection of essays edited by Herbert Read. Tate regarded *The Cantos* as a formless, shapeless mass of incoherence, and Ezra himself incapable of sustained thought. A few pages along, that fervent Scots poet Hugh MacDiarmid, communist, materialist, loather of all things religious, and quite as combative a spirit as Pound himself, took the entirely opposite view. Ezra's bold, capacious and ever venturesome writing had proved itself to be equal to the challenges and the vast complexities of the modern world. In fact, it seemed to embody, in its imaginative comprehensiveness, the spirit of scientific experimentation. Did we not crave such a 'giant synthesis' as *The Cantos* seemed to offer? And so the battle royal continued between the lofty idolaters and the nay-sayers…

It is our final morning beside the lake, and after breakfast, we sit and read on our favourite chairs facing the water, watching the throat-tremble of the cormorant atop his post (he looks as if he is ululating), whilst keeping one eye out for the taxi that will spirit us away and back to Milan. A botheration of sparrows has gathered at our feet. I have just started re-reading the single-volume, American Library Edition of all Ezra's poems barring *The Cantos*, an American version of the Editions Pléiades. In the photograph of Ezra as a young man on the cover, he seems to be wearing a fur stole. The look is imperious. The angle of the head seems to suggest that he is a young man of moment who is already playing hard at being an old master, a poet of high calling, exalted, a backward-facing Modern.

Much change is afoot. The air has cooled so much in recent days. The hotel's guests are leaving. The big, gleaming cars, many of them soft-tops, are creeping forth from the semi-hidden garage beneath the swimming pool, moving in a slow, ceremonious parade, heading home: the Porsches, the Aston Martins, the Jaguars…

Needless to say, Ezra's lynx is not amongst them…

A Momentous Encounter in Room 150

Lago di Maggiore VII

I am still seeking out a room in the Hotel Cannero where it will be possible to read, and to cogitate upon the work and the person of, Ezra, uninterruptedly. I need a fastness, a space of coolness and set-apartness. The sun is forever prying at the windows in our room, the one that faces onto the lake. The sun always needs to know too much, and too early in the day, not even what I may be thinking or half-thinking at such an in-between hour, but also what I am guessing at, all those swirling, half-formed notions, barely before my fragile brain has even begun to swing into action...Too much of too little consequence is happening here, of course, that is a part of the problem, as in every hotel. Even the dog who sits in the courtyard and barely moves from hour to hour, seems to be frustrated by its own boredom. How otherwise explain the slight, testy rumble in its throat when you do not give it sufficiently wide a berth? When so little happens, one's thinking slows down. It seems a little futile to think. No one is waiting for words of illumination. By and large, and especially after lunch, they are all gently dozing, which itself seems to mean: this is life's best pastime. Why don't you join us?

And then, on the second morning of our stay, as we are slowly descending the stairs from our third floor room, admiring as we go the painted ceiling with its barrel vaulting, I find something that quickens me even as it intrigues. Room 150! Its white door is tantalisingly ajar, though only slightly; its brass door knob gleams invitingly. There is a low table for books and random papers. There must also be chairs. No room is complete without chairs. The curtains have been caught back by maroon velvet bows. Too much sun then? Not at all. The fact that the room is not facing out towards Lago Maggiore but into the inner courtyard and the swimming pool, means it is not flooded with sunlight. There is light in plenty in there, enough to see and to read by, but there is not too much light. What a mercy! *Busie old fool unruly Sunne why dost thou thus through windows and through curtains call on us?* None of that, Mr Donne.

It is, of course, a *trompe l'oeil*! I marvel and even smile to myself when I realise that, how easy it is to be outwitted by a painted scene. The room does not exist. How could it? The door is a painted door, and the fragment of that interior, a painted fragment. Nevertheless, there is activity and movement in there, and even raised voices, because I can hear them, and the longer I listen, the more agitated it all sounds. That is why I had paused there in the first place, and not immediately proceeded downstairs to the breakfast room in the customary manner, as on earlier mornings. Should I intervene? There was no one else. And so I stepped inside, apologising as I burst in, asking to be forgiven for turning up in this way, uninvited.

There were just the two of them. The blue uniform, and the general air of officialdom, of the standing man, he who was pointing, and even jabbing, towards the older man seated, cross-legged, in the easy chair at the window, suggested to me that he was one of the hotel's managers, the sort of person who would be employed to ensure that everything proceeded smoothly by behaving aggressively.

The older, seated man was in a mood of extreme agitation. I walked over to him, at which point the standing man shouted at me, as if it were none of my business to walk forward with such boldness into that room. Such a liberty! I ignored him, as did the man in the chair, who seemed, I rather thought, to be expecting me. I say that because when he saw me approaching, he briskly nodded towards a nearby chair, on which I sat down. The manager – if that is indeed who he was – glowered at me. The seated man said to him: he is here to see me, and he does not intend to go away. We suggest that you leave us in peace. He spoke calmly and reasonably. His mood had lightened. The standing man seemed somewhat deflated by his calmness, as if he had expected to be verbally savaged, and the fact that no such thing had happened rather disappointed him. Yes, why don't you go away? I suggested, nodding in the general direction of the door. At which he left, closing the door of room 150 behind him.

Is there much to be said? I asked Ezra. I knew it was Ezra. I knew that I would meet him here. It had always had an air of inevitability about it, this encounter. It is what always happens in the end, when you choose to hound a man down as I had been doing for goodness only knows how many years. He shook his head. There was nothing to be said. I had said it all. He had heard it all. Even as I wrote, he was listening in. You are the cleverer of the two of us, I told him, I must grant you that. He took in a long breath. You are also much the greater fool, old man. At that, he stood up, and gestured towards the swimming pool. The raucous and unruly German children were flinging those inflatables about again. I stood up too, in order to watch them. We were caught up in our mutual disgust at the world. That too had an air of inevitability about it.

Somewhere Between the Whimper and the Stutter

That enterprise called *The Cantos*, half a century in the making and the unmaking, stuttered to a close in the 1960s, unfinished, unfinishable. Sixty years on, the uncertain enterprise of the making of this rag-bag of a book of mine about Ezra is stuttering to a close too, on board a flight to Venice in the spring of 2024. It's Venice Biennale time again, when all the peacocks of the global art world put themselves on show in an orgy of mutual self-admiration.

After all the gab, and the hand-and-arm flicker-show about safety features, from the three members of the blue cabin crew who have spaced themselves out down the central aisle, I settle down to read a brand new purchase, a first edition of *Thrones*, the very last sequence (barring a small volume of drafts and fragments) of *The Cantos*, dated 1960, plucked from the shelves of a book-choked upstairs room of a cosy little shop in Alfriston, East Sussex called Much Ado Books just a couple of weeks ago. As I leant to pull it out of the poetry section on that particular morning, the ancient boards of the floor squeaked and even seemed to lurch a little, as if being half aware of the contrariness of the author they were supporting.

Thrones comes with a health warning from its publisher: the readers need to look out for the presence of Chinese ideograms dotted about here and there like mines in a war zone. Ezra loved the exoticism of Chinese ideograms. What is more, he thought he knew why they were so good for us. The West had gone astray in every conceivable way. Ideograms would remind us not only of the dependable stability and ancientness of Chinese civilisation, but also show us a form of mark-making in which meaning would be immediately evident because ideograms were pictures, and pictures, even multi-layered pictures such as ideograms so often were, could be taken in at a glance, in an instant. At least, that was Ezra's view. And what would happen if in fact we felt utterly baffled, as the publisher evidently half-feared that we might?

I open it at last, and let my eyes drift down the page, looking again at how Ezra organises his words, how he makes a brief run and then breaks off, and then starts off with something else. And I am doing this as the captain breaks in with a word or two of admonition or reassurance. Captains are there in the cockpit to reassure you, so that you know that someone knows all about the direction of travel. You can trust him. He will hold your hand. Metaphorically speaking. Is Ezra like this?

Not a bit of it. Ezra's pauses and continuations, the way any particular line relates to the next, seem arbitrary, as if what drives him forward and on has been plucked from the air. They jerk. They stop. They surge – and then stop. At whose whim? To what end? We keep on asking ourselves. He dredges quotations, often half remembered, or inaccurately remembered, from the depths of his reading, from the depths of his memory. He puts these beside recollections of incidents in his own life, or in the lives of others. Can it ever really hope to cohere? But he carries on because the making of the work has always been like this. Why change now?

Fortunately, a late conversation with Pier Paolo Pasolini gave Ezra the ultimate get-out clause. Relax! Ezra told Italy's famous avant garde *cinéaste*, *The Cantos* were all music anyway – which perhaps lets us know that in the end they mean everything and nothing, somewhere between those two tantalising possibilities. The main thing is this: don't get lost in the detail. Above all, don't WORRY when you collide with an ideogram.

An Andalucian Interlude

What is the value of half-remembered things, scraps of this and that? Why should they be hallowed? Why should we, the reader, be expected to cherish and be a little in awe of the fact that Ezra, in extreme confinement due to his own excess of folly, arrogance and poor judgement, recalls in a poem some cherished moment with 'old Fordie' (ie. the novelist Ford Madox Ford) in London forty years ago? What is more, he tells us no more than this bald, dull fact! Why are his scraps of quotations from the classics teeming wildly down the page, or his litany of obscure names of the writers of the zillions of books he has scanned and now perhaps imperfectly recalls, of more abiding interest to the world than the fact that, sitting as I am today on an early morning in May of 2024, in a garden wrested from the hard-bitten desert landscape of Andalucia where, sixty years ago some of the great spaghetti westerns were filmed, with its extraordinarily dramatic cacti, ugly, spiky, alarming survivors against all the odds, upthrusting into a sky of a completely untroubled blue, I myself recall, goodness only knows why, a fragment of a song written, in the early 1960s by The Searchers, which assaults me, seemingly from nowhere? 'Her eyes are soft and blue,/her eyes are clear and bright,/ but she's not there…' If the Searchers shine brighter in the memory than a line by Catullus on his sunny morning, is it only my vulgarity which is to blame?

What Did Great-Uncle Jack Make of Sextus Propertius?

Philip Morre, poet, is harrumphing around amongst the back stacks of his tiny third floor flat overlooking the Misericordia Canal in Canareggio, Venice, seeking out a book. He's trying to get rid of books these days, but they still have a habit of turning up. In fact, books seem to breed like rabbits.

Yes, we are back in Venice in April 2024 for the Venice Biennale, and Philip has invited us over to his apartment in the most colourful building along the Misericordia Canal. Ochre, since you are asking, a very rich ochre. As you may recall, the mat on the floor outside the door reads: Not Welcome. We have faced down that message once again. We have strode boldly through the door, and he has been unwilling to stop us. Perhaps he wants us here after all. After all, we are old friends.

After the wine, come the chick pea soup (cooked in water from the can), the bread, the terrine and the Camembert, all served at the same time, and at a roar. Half way through, Philip jumps up from the table *a propos* of something or other of relevance. Moments later we are talking about his Great-Uncle Jack Phillimore.

Great-Uncle Jack, Philip tells me from just behind the door, was a big classics man, youngest ever professor at Edinburgh. A bit of a poet too? I ask. Yes, a member of the Belloc circle, he adds.

Younger even than a young man called Friedrich Nietzsche, who was also said to have been the youngest man ever to be appointed a professor of classics? I am asking myself. Maybe we're both wrong. We're certainly both old enough to be wrong.

Back in the dining area beside the window again, he lunges across the table, small blue book in hand, and deftly slides it in between the Cassis bottle and the scattered hunks of bread. The Cassis adds kick and a splash of colour to any glass of the indifferent local white, of which there have been several up to this moment.

Propertius! Philip says, with vehemence. This is a book of Great-Uncle Jack's translations of Sextus Propertius!

We have been talking about the Roman poet Propertius because Ezra is back on the agenda again. Do you like Ezra more than you did last time we talked about him eighteen months ago, when you said that trying to make sense of the progress or regress of *The Cantos* was a bit like entering one of those interminable Italian *galerie*, which seem to get darker and darker and more and more unending the farther you drive? I ask him.

If anything, I like him even less, he replies, spittily.

Ezra should have stuck to writing short poems is what Philip had said to me eighteen months ago. He should have given up on the epic. But he couldn't because he was doomed to carry on writing what he mistakenly thought would be his life's work, and the final guarantor of his greatness. It had him in its grip. What a fool! What an ass!

A little later, I go through the collection of Ezra books in the shelves directly above Philip's double bed, the surface of which also serves as a useful repository of folders of paper and the odd book. Last time I visited, he tried to give me the largest and heaviest guide to *The Cantos* ever written by an American devotee. I declined because I owned a copy already. Somebody must have leaped at the chance though between then and now because it had gone from the shelves.

In fact, he seems to have fewer and fewer books by or about Ezra these days. The one that catches my eye is a rare one indeed: *Quia Pauper Amavi*. It was published in 1919, and I most certainly cannot buy it off him, he tells me in no uncertain terms when I tentatively propose the possibility because it is one of the very few Ezra books in his possession that he really values.

Why? In part, because it contains Ezra's version of Propertius, a long poem called 'Homage to Sextus Propertius', that he wrote in 1917. I like it too, in part because Ezra's version is so defiantly, waywardly preposterous – as a translation, that is. In fact, it's more of a riff than a translation. Ezra is the only 'translator' from the Latin who has ever added a *patent frigidaire* to the vocabulary of a poet who died in Rome in 16 BC.

Back in my seat at the table, I stare at the cover of Uncle Jack's version. Philip tells me that he'd always hoped to find a line in it that Ezra had stolen for *his* version. No luck so far. Let me try, I say. He smiles, palely. I don't take the book away with me though.

The Comings and Goings of the Elusive God

Even though I am no longer a Christian, every Saturday morning when I am in London, my first call is to St Martin-in-the-Fields at the north-east corner of Trafalgar Square where I sit and look and read and contemplate for perhaps half an hour before having a coffee at Notes in St Martin's Lane.

I try to sit in the same pew, half way up the nave, every time I visit, to the right of the central aisle, with my back against one of the processional of great pillars, all of which culminate in the flourish of a Corinthian capital. Why do I do this? Because I find it inexplicably reassuring. This church, the survival of such a structure as this one, rooted here for almost three centuries, its beauty, its symmetry, the colour of the wood of these pews (a rich chestnut, like a conker dandled in a young lad's palm, a lad such as I once was, fresh skeddadled home from Roe Woods before it got too threatening dark), all of these things, when taken together, give me some sense of dependability. For all my atheism.

What is more, where I am sitting affords me an uninterrupted view of exactly what I want to see. James Gibbs's great church was built in the middle of the eighteenth century. It suffered significant war damage by the Luftwaffe – which is why it now has such an extraordinary window at its east end, a window of such simplicity that you can scarcely credit its emotional impact. The Iranian artist Shirazeh Houshiary has created an oval shape, filled it with fogged glass, and canted that oval to the right. The canting has the effect of pulling the plain-glass window's mesh of leading out of shape in such a way that you half-imagine that you are looking at a human form, with arms extended and legs tight squeezed together. In short, it looks like a ghostly evocation of Christ's Crucifixion.

What is it to find a place, a person, a poet, a religion a profound source of dependability, as I now find the church of St Martin-in-the-Fields, though more than half a century has passed since I last declared myself to be a Christian?

Furniture can feel dependable too, and especially the furniture which has always been a defining place to sit, read, eat and study in a family kitchen. Such was our kitchen table at 45 Coningsby Road, my childhood home in Sheffield, set down as it was within reach of the warmth of the open grate with its roaring fire. It is here that I would eat my kippers at tea time, accompanied by toast fresh slipped onto my side plate from the two-pronged, metal toasting fork, and it was almost always here too, at this same table beneath the wireless set raised up on the wall on a shelf of its own, that I would do my homework, and especially my English essays for Stanley Cook, the local poet who taught me English at Firth Park Grammar School.

My religious fervour may have died long ago, but I still credit my Christian faith for having given me an appetite for book-reading and book-learning. The pleasure of book-reading and book-learning has, for me, much to do with secretiveness – a book's messages are imparted silently. To this early habit I owe my detestation of audio-books. Seeing a reader from the outside is to see nothing at all. There is some pleasure in that. For the reader himself, that is. Ruminating upon what is being read takes just as long as it takes. It can take forever. You are accountable to no one. If you are interrupted by being asked exactly what you are reading, there is a wide choice of garden paths available down which to lead the enquirer.

When I was about fourteen years old, some of my favourite moments of reading happened in bed. I would surround myself with a spread of texts, which would include my New English Bible and a biblical commentary, usually a flimsy, modest little pamphlet which would contain a daily reading, almost certainly chosen from the New Testament, and some exegesis. I was aware then that to read and understand the Bible would be a life-long endeavour. In fact, it would never be finished because the gap between what I knew at that moment and all that there was to be known, was infinite. And I often did this furiously dedicated reading at bedtime, reflecting upon passages from the Gospel According to St Matthew about, say, how the meek would inherit the earth. I savoured that notion – but did any part of me ever believe it to be true? Was it not the words themselves which were so lulling, so seductive? What had all this praise of meekness to do with the tough lives of the men from Firth Vickers, the steelworks down Brightside way where my sister once worked as a shorthand typist, men who walked home past our door after yet another exhausting shift, day after day, in the late afternoon usually, not long after the hour at which I usually returned from school, scruffy white mufflers around their necks, faces stony and seamed, troublingly unreachable, if not a little frightening?

Yes, books, sacred or secular, were something altogether elsewhere, something set apart from the daily ruck. And much of this spiritual imbibing happened in secret, in the solitude of my own bedroom – but I had also been told by Christians older than myself that I had a responsibility towards others, towards those who had not seen the light. My very own mother, for example. Was she not the most lost of lost souls – and this in spite of the fact that she only ever looked her usual humdrum self, fetching and carrying, fetching and carrying, in her floral-patterned apron, back and forth across the kitchen from oven to table and back again, and certainly not a naked (god forbid) harried soul on the brink of everlasting torment. What could I, a mere slip of a child/man, do for her then? I must at least do something. And this is where the kitchen table came in.

I was doing all this religious questing fairly quietly, almost off to the side, and certainly not against all the odds. I don't wish to exaggerate. No one persecuted me. I did not have to escape from my persecutors like St Paul, for dear life, by shinning down a rope. No one mocked me or tried to stop me doing what I was doing. You could call the attitude of my family one of resigned perplexity. You see, no one in my family was in the least religious. In fact, if anything, there was more than a mild whiff of scepticism, if not atheism, about the place. My Uncle Ken, for example, who was a bit of a Thinker when he was not being a book-keeper who added up endless columns of figures in big ledgers with marbled edges, owned a bruised and battered paperback copy of Tom Paine's *The Age of Reason*.

I did not read this book then – in fact, I did not read it in its entirety until thirty years later. Why such neglect? Because it frightened me. I already knew the book by repute. I knew that it was a sustained, if not merciless, attack upon the supposed truths of the Bible, and my Christian faith was too fragile and too tender for me to be able to cope with such a headlong assault upon it. In fact, my Christian friends had warned me off it in no uncertain terms. It was the Devil's work, they had told me. It would lead me into temptation, needlessly. Stay away. Do not be tempted!

And so I read books such as *The Christian's Secret of a Happy Life* instead...

For all that, little by little, scepticism had its way with me. It was in fact a poet called Matthew Arnold, writing in the 1860s, who first drew my attention to, and caused me to reflect upon, the importance of the loosening grip of religion upon our world, in a poem called 'Dover Beach', in which he refers to the 'melancholy, long, withdrawing roar' of the Sea of Faith. Sceptics of the nineteenth century had indeed attacked religion on multiple fronts: Darwinism had caused people to question the uniqueness of humankind; German Biblical scholarship had put the Bible and its claims to absolute authority under critical scrutiny as never before. Pioneering geologists had dug ever deeper into physical facts about the age of the earth itself. It was becoming increasingly difficult, for example, to believe that the earth had come into being, as if by some divine miracle, in 4004 BC.

But could poetry really step in to sustain and console in religion's stead? Perhaps. I had seen it in action myself, at least once. Days before my Aunt Esme was cremated, my Uncle Norman, the least religious of men, asked my advice about a reading at the ceremony in the local chapel of rest. Could I perhaps help him to choose a poem which would rise to the gravity and solemnity of the occasion? Of course. I chose a sonnet by Shakespeare. He, who had no religious beliefs, and no interest whatsoever in poetry, felt that a poem was the needful thing!

But could it really be true that Ezra would step in when God had left the stage of my own life? Some part of me must have believed this to be true.

And the grounds for such a belief, the addiction to study which led on, in turn, to my addiction to poetry and Ezra, may have been laid at our kitchen table. One morning I left a tract on the table for my mother to read. I even pushed it towards her when she approached me. It was called 'How to Become a Christian'. Thank you, love, she said, nothing more than that, before sweeping it off the table with the breakfast crumbs. There were no further discussions about the matter. I never had the gall to ask her whether she had given her heart to Jesus. I prayed for her, with fervour, in the privacy of my attic bedroom. She continued to feed me, to love me, to clothe me, and to tolerate, unquestioningly, the full range of my eccentricities.

Two or three years later it was another book that I was reading at that kitchen table with an almost biblical level of fervour, a book to which I have already referred called *The Poetry of Ezra Pound* by the Canadian scholar Hugh Kenner. His near impenetrable exegesis gripped me and enthralled me as *The Bible* had once gripped me and enthralled me. The idea of making sense of Ezra and his interminable poem in the making might become, with sufficient patience and single-minded dedication on my part, a lifelong pursuit of enlightenment as *The Bible* had once promised to be. That great black book on display in Ward's Bookshop would be the key to an alternative religious pursuit of an equally immense gravity.

I date those feelings induced by reading Kenner at the kitchen table to 1967. The book itself had been published in 1951, when Kenner was twenty-eight years of age. I myself was eighteen years old when I read it, and no more capable of stopping myself writing poetry than preventing water gushing from a tap. I filled notebook after notebook with the wretched stuff, outpourings of the soul as embarrassing, I soon recognised, as they were unpublishable. Five years later, in 1972, Kenner returned to the subject of Pound and his influence in a book called *The Pound Era*. Many Critics thought this book Kenner's magnum opus. They praised it to the skies. Reading it again more than half a century after its publication, its preciousness is that of a man who craves to be at least as lofty and obtuse as the man to whose work he had dedicated so much of scholarly life.

The Ant's a Dragon in his Centaur World!

This May morning in Andalucia I believe I am seeing the world as Ezra saw it when incarcerated in that cage near Pisa in 1945, almost eighty years ago. I am sitting in my chair at the breakfast table, and when I look down at my feet, I notice a solitary ant heroically labouring across the pink flagstones as I have never quite seen an ant labour before. It has benefited by my carelessness. I had let a tiny glob of solid yellow egg yoke fall off the edge of my spoon when in transit towards my open mouth. The opportunistic ant had spotted it and claimed it as its own, and now it was pushing or pulling or carrying it along as fast as it was able to move. How far would it travel? Another ant was nearby, not helping. In fact, it seemed to be turning in circles, as if drunk on the smell of that receding gobbet of yellow.

And so it went, on and on, until Neil stepped up to sweep away the breakfast plates, and by the time he had left, the ant had disappeared from view.

When Ezra had been incarcerated in that cage, in the open air outside Pisa, he had almost no reading matter with him whatsoever – a volume of Confucius, and a small English/Chinese dictionary. The consequence for his writing was profound. What he wrote about in the *Pisan Cantos* had much to do with what he could hear and see – the voices of fellow prisoners, the creatures on the ground beneath his feet, snatches of the natural world, the very clouds in the sky.

And, as for me on that breakfast May morning in Andalucia, there had also been the presence of an ant within his purview, whose presence there, at that emotionally heightened moment, coaxed into being a line of poetry which is amongst the best he ever wrote: *an ant's a centaur in his dragon world...* How strangely heroic that tiny creature became for him, raised up, magical, a giant of a presence in a broken poet's utterly shrunken world.

The Drowning of Ezra

Every morning Ezra, the Odyssean wanderer, the drowned Phoenician sailor, suffers the fate he almost certainly deserves: to be entirely submerged in milk at the bottom of my cereal bowl. It seems right, that the image of Ezra should be submerged in this way, an image, scored by my own son into clay, of the poet in 1914, sitting, yet again, for his portrait but in front of his friend Gaudier.

Ezra looks vitally alert and alive, a bristling antenna, a being on the prowl as the drum rolls of a catastrophic war begin to sound in his ears, but when, today, in 2024, one hundred and ten years later, I pour my cocktail of oat milk and semi-skimmed cow's milk over him, idly and carefully, having first loaded up the bowl with a substantial heaped mound of granola, he disappears from view entirely. He is lost, drowned, humiliated, reduced to a detail of my every morning's routine.

The Battle of the Titans

That plaque above the door of the gondolier's cottage in Calle Querini in Venice, where Ezra lived out the years of his decline with his mistress Olga Rudge before he died in 1972, rings out hubristically: Ezra Pound, Titan of Poetry…

Was it true? Does he deserve such praise? How might we judge such a claim? Perhaps memorability might be one useful test. Pound arrived in London in 1908 with one aim in view: to meet and sit at the feet of W.B. Yeats, the man he regarded as the greatest poet then writing in English. Their relationship prospered. In time, Ezra, never, a man to shrink from challenges, even began to suggest editorial changes to Yeats' poems. Yeats often acquiesced. You could argue that Ezra had a crucial role in turning Yeats into a poet equipped to face the new modernity. Ezra helped to blow away decades-long remnants of Celtic miasma…

Some years later, Yeats visited Ezra in Rapallo, by which time the writing of *The Cantos* was in full flood, and Ezra was dating his letters by the time-scale of the bright, young, make-believe world of the Fascist Calendar. Yeats was not a fan of *The Cantos*. In fact, he was perplexed. As he put it in his introduction to *The Oxford Book of Modern Verse* in 1936: 'I discover at present either exquisite or grotesque fragments.'

Yeats died in 1939. Ezra outlived him by thirty-three years. Now that both men are long dead, we ask ourselves: who was the real titan? Who has stood the test of time? And in asking such a question, we return to the issue with which we began: which of the two poets wrote poetry which has lingered on, in the mind and the memory, whose words are still on the lips of even a journalist? There is a continuing urgency about so many of Yeats' turns of phrase. His words live on. They still matter.

Let a single example suffice.

> Turning and turning in the widening gyre
> The falcon cannot hear the falconer;
> Things fall apart; the centre cannot hold;
> Mere anarchy is loosed upon the world,
> The blood-dimmed tide is loosed, and everywhere
> The ceremony of innocence is drowned;
> The best lack all conviction, while the worst
> Are full of passionate intensity…
>
> From *The Second Coming* by W.B. Yeats

Poisoning the Bloodstream

Why do stray lines from poems swim into view in the way they do? It happened when I woke up this morning, to the accompaniment of these words : *slowly the poison the whole bloodstream fills*. I even felt I could hear it being read out to me, with great solemnity, this line from one of William Empson's gnomic sonnets. It sounds a little chilling, doesn't it?

Why pop up today of all days though? I think I know why… Today I am on my way back to the London Library in St James' Square, feeling just a tad shame-faced. Can it really be true that I have hung onto the library's precious copy of Ezra's *ABC of Economics* for almost two years? Did I borrow it on 23 July 2022, as the stamped date of the issue slip tells me?

I console myself with the thought that no other member had demanded its return over that twenty-two month period…

But why this poison? Was Ezra some kind of a disabling disease after all? I think back to the little squib of a poem I wrote decades ago, which you read earlier:

An Epigraph

To the memory of Ezra Pound

>You are standing at my shoulder again,
>Advising me on my literary opinions.
>Your voice is high and shrill.
>You will not take no for an answer.
>
>You have read the best that there is.
>You have witnessed the worst of mankind.
>And now you demand some attention.
>You will not tolerate an empty room.
>
>I look up and stare at you.
>Your eyes are red-rimmed.
>There is dust on your shoulders.
>I would sweep it off if I dared.

Earlier I called this a bit of doggerel, a snatch of pure inconsequence. Why though? Because I knew that this book would end up by being something of an apology of a book. My obsession with Ezra has not caused me to rise to great heights as a writer. I am not awe-struck by him. Ben Jonson criticised his contemporary Shakespeare for over-writing. *Would he had blotted a thousand* (of his lines), he once remarked in a little book called *Timber or Discoveries*. In spite of this qualification, his admiration also enabled him to write a great tribute, in verse, to his matchless contemporary.

Pound has not enabled me to do anything similar. I have not been inspired. His manner of writing is not imitable. In fact, you could say that it is uniquely disabling. It is grotesquely of and for itself. No one could take *The Cantos* as a credible *point de départ* – even though some poets claim to have done so. Such a venture would be ridiculous. Pound has no method but that of grinding accumulation. If anything, he poisons the literary bloodstream.

And then there are the additional reasons for my unwillingness and inability to make him an exemplar. What is there to be done with the horror of his political opinions, the rashness and the folly of so many of his judgements, and his unreadable economic tomfooleries? Nothing. Let them lie where they must, unhonoured, unregarded.

Botched

In 1968, the year I left my home town of Sheffield and went up to start my university life in Cambridge, *Encounter* magazine published an interview with Ezra by Daniel Cory. It was reckoning time. Ezra didn't hold back his punches. The whole thing was a botch, he told Cory, a mess and a botch. He was talking about *The Cantos*, the magnum opus. Or so he had hoped. He'd used the word 'botched' fifty years before that conversation with Cory, in one of the anti-war poems that insert themselves, rather brutally, into the near seamlessly self-conscious, if not precious, aesthetic flow of a long, double sequence of poems called 'Hugh Selwyn Mauberley'.

In those days it was an entire rotten civilisation – our civilisation – that was being thrown to the dogs, by Ezra himself, for its folly, its arrogance, its mediocrity, its grubby warmongering – no one was spared: writers, politicians, they all got tossed into the pit. Ezra was always very good at fury and condemnation. He generally knew best. He also thought he knew how to put the world to rights. He expected to be listened to because he was Mr Pound, the furiously judgmental poet. And then, after his release from St Elizabeth's Hospital and his return to Italy, the long decline into remorse began, from which he never recovered. Who had been the fool after all, the gullible idolator of Mussolini, the poet who had expected the President of the United Stares to shake hands with him and, *well, listen up, Mr President*, or his enemies?

How to do This, That and the Other

How to read. How to write. Pound the pedagogue kept grinding on and on and on, telling us which books to read (very few of which could ever be found in a good library near you), and which writers to learn from. Did his example ever do me any good? Let's split this down the middle: the critical pronouncements in prose, and the poetry itself. Some of those early, snappy judgements seem quite encouraging to any young writer, clear-headed, and even forward thinking. Even 'Make it New' sounds like a clarion call to make you stand up and listen. Who would not yearn to slough off the burdens of the past, rid yourself of your forefathers' sloppy habits of writing?

Unfortunately, Ezra did not quite practise what he preached. The idea of using *The Cantos* as a useful guide for any writer in the making. And even some of those critical pronouncements may sound good in the abstract – melopeia, phanopeia, logopeia – music, images, coherent thinking, to roughly summarise the general drift – but when you are actually in the thick of writing, at the point where the Angel of Mercy actually descends – all that kind of stuff just falls away. And then, leaving aside the botch of *The Cantos*, what of the shorter poems? There are good things here and there, but, taken as a whole, it is only patchily good. And as for those translations from the Provençal! Too often Pound fails because he twists and tortures the English language into such unnatural shapes. If he had wanted to replicate the sound of the music of birds in mimicry of Arnaut Daniel, perhaps he would have done better to learn from the listening habits of another lover of bird song, Olivier Messiaen. Why not just stand under a tree and listen?

Burgess had said reviewers were cheats. The way I reviewed books changed dramatically over the years. At first I was a complete slave to the text, page by page. I had to note down quotations, make brief summaries, all that sort of thing. Then, one evening, I learnt something new. I was sitting beside a reviewer whose name I knew, at the Poetry Society in Earl's Court Square. He was reading a book. We had a bit of a conversation, not much of one. The book was the thing to be attending to. I understand that impulse all too well. He did happen to mention though that he was reviewing it, for the *New Statesman* he added. Did he tell me that in order to raise himself to a slightly higher level? Almost certainly. Seconds later I drifted off to get a re-fill.

Something had struck me about that man though, something that stayed with me. I could sense that he was reading it in a very different way from the way I read books to be reviewed. He lacked the earnestness, the sense of serious dedication to the task in hand, the unshuckable habit – once *my* unshuckable habit – of reading the book at a desk precisely because there had to be paper next to it on which to record all those notes and comments. I made a resolution to myself there and then that I would behave quite differently in the future, that I would do nothing other than read the book itself and trust my memory to retain everything that it needed for just as long as it needed to do so – which would not need to be for very long, surely? I was terrified. Would I do the book justice? Would I really be able to remember the salient bits, the key arguments?

Yes I would, and yes I did. I discovered something else too. I was, as a result of that decision, able to take a more aerial view of the terrain, to relax into the writing as I had never done in the past. My book-reviewing improved in every way. I became a much less constipated writer.

The Wooden Man of Monmouth Street

I had taken us to Monmouth Street Coffee House in Covent Garden on that blistering Saturday afternoon recorded close to the opening of this book for a reason I never quite shared with my friend Alistair Davies: the statue in the front window, the wooden figure of the man in the bowler hat. I had long since decided that this man was a stylised portrait of T.S.Eliot, traitor or staunch defender of Ezra. When W.H. Auden once said that it was not becoming to look too much like a poet, he was thinking of the young Eliot in 1917, posing, in bowler hat, leaning on his cane, for a photograph of himself outside the offices of Faber & Gwyer (later Faber & Faber), the publishing house where he would work for much of his life. They were both posers in their different ways, the face of the respectable insider versus the face of the rebellious bohemian.

What did Eliot really think of Pound? Every Saturday lunch time – it is usually around noon – my wife and I queue patiently outside Monmouth Coffee, waiting to be seated indoors, in the high wooden pews that face the tables at the back, and as I wait, I almost always stare at the wooden, bowler-hatted man in the window, still posing beside the coffee and the packs of brown Costa Rican sugar, still biding his time, still not quite letting on.

Saying Goodbye to Birling Gap in June 2024

Is this to be our very last visit to Birling Gap, that very special place in East Sussex, on the southern coast of England, where the Sussex Downs open out all of a sudden like two spread palms, and a ziggurat of a shuddery metal staircase enables the visitor to experience, at beach level, how the white chalk cliffs meet the sea?

Our son, daughter-in-law, babe – newly leaped into this dangerous world – and, last but scarcely least, their frisky Jack Russell terrier Vincent van Dogh, no longer quite that menace of a pup who once, when they all lived in Norwich, made a flying leap through the pages of my *TLS* like some circus entertainer through a flaming hoop – will be leaving here for Oxfordshire within a couple of months. Tomorrow to fresh deeds and pastures new, as Milton once had it.

So this moment, this mid-June visit, feels both special and valedictory. And the weather this morning is doing its bit to make it so. Seldom have the waves, ply upon ply of them, looked so sullen, minatory and rebarbative. Before I even reach the top of the metal staircase, which seems to be juddering in trepidation, I feel the full force of the wind knocking me sideways and almost lifting me off the ground as if I were not so much man as leaf. The wind's howl in combination with the sea's roar make it almost impossible for me to hear my wife's words… I park myself on one of the National Trust's well secured wooden benches feet away from the top of the stairs, and let them make the descent without me.

By the following morning, the day is much calmer. I descend that metal staircase slowly, but with relative ease. Vincent, deft and speedy as only a small dog can be, makes his own journey up and down several times as if to ease the way, test the difficulties that may lie ahead for mere humankind.

He is right. It is manageable this morning. What is more, all is very different down there at beach level, walking in the shadow of the chalk cliffs. The sea has dredged up from its depths and levelled out a great platform of shingle – gone are the huge, ankle-twisting rocks that usually make this beach perambulation so hazardous. Cleaving to the foot of the white cliffs, we quickly spot Circe's Ingle once again, that cave-like, deep scooping into the chalk cliffs which Ezra's Odysseus, had he been with us here today, would have so feared. This is a perilous place for us too – that scooped out bowl means that a tonnage of white chalk could fall on top of you at any moment if you stepped too close. The Circean Curse endures.

The sea is by no means milk-calm this morning, but the withdrawing tidal waters do, once again, possess some flavour of Matthew Arnold's long, slow and melancholy retreat of the sea of faith. There are swimmers in these waters too – I had spotted them first as we looked out from the top of the staircase, prior to our cautious descent, a great outspread flotilla of human bodies breasting the waves, all wet-suited in black. Their movements put me in mind of Yeats' *long-legged fly upon the stream*, though their agitated arms, and all this circumambient elemental music, do not seem to be at one with the idea of minds moving upon silence….

Long-Legged Fly

That civilisation may not sink,
Its great battle lost,
Quiet the dog, tether the pony
To a distant post.
Our master Caesar is in the tent
Where the maps are spread,
His eyes fixed upon nothing,
A hand upon his head.

Like a long-legged fly upon the stream
His mind moves upon silence.

That the topless towers be burnt
And men recall that face,
Move most gently if move you must
In this lonely place.
She thinks, part woman, three parts a child,
That nobody looks; her feet
Practise a tinker shuffle
Picked up on the street.

Like a long-legged fly upon the stream
Her mind moves upon silence.

That girls at puberty may find
The first Adam in their thought,
Shut the door of the Pope's chapel,
Keep those children out.
There on that scaffolding reclines
Michael Angelo.
With no more sound than the mice make
His hand moves to and fro.

Like a long-legged fly upon the stream
His mind moves upon silence.

W.B. Yeats (1865-1939)

Yeats wrote those lines late in life. In fact, they were amongst his very last poems to be written, more than a couple of decades after he and Ezra had spent their two, pre-war winters together at that cottage in the Ashdown Forest. The poem's strange, if not daring, choice and juxtaposition of images demonstrates, at a stroke, what an influence Ezra had had upon the older man. Had he not helped to turn a maudlin Anglo-Celt into a Modern?

Birling Gap is much more than the dazzle and the drama of its sea-facing, forever dramatically eroding white cliffs. At the top of that flight of steps up from the beach, there is something every visitor looks out for after having experienced a soul-stirring encounter with the elements: a cafe selling hot drinks, Cornish pasties, and outsize sausage rolls. What is more, a giant fridge-freezer, courtesy of Jude's of Battersea, offers handy little bio-degradable tubs of ice cream for dogs. Fortunately, The National Trust, custodians of this stretch of coastline, have provided such a place as this one.

And, once inside, you spot, facing the door by which you have entered, something else too: an entire wall of second-hand books! Yes, this is also a bit of – not a lot of – a second-hand bookshop. I seek out Poetry, and find precisely nothing. Categories that do exist include the following: Sports, Biography, Fiction, Children, Gardening, Travel, Wildlife/Pets, and Quirky.

Now here's a quirky question: how long does it take for any random sample of wildlife to become a pet? And, oh yes: exactly how quirky is Quirky? Titles corralled into that category include *Brush Up Your Pidgin* and *Does Anything Eat Wasps?*

As I browse the books, stationary as a public statue bent in half like a nail, I notice that there are two people forever coming and going within breathing distance. I look up. Their arms are heaped high with books. They both look surprisingly cheerful. Can I help you to find anything? asks the female of the two. I was wondering about Poetry, I tell her. I can't find any, I add, turning out my palms in a gesture of woebegoneness. If there is any, she tells me, brightly, it will almost certainly be amongst the Classics… There is no such category, we agree after a brief rummage. Perhaps there was once, she adds, unfazed. Come with me to the storeroom. If Poetry is anywhere at all, it will be in the storeroom…

The large room occupied by the cafe leads into a second large room, full of air and light and little else. Various boards full of text are on display, supported by free-standing units, which tell us a lot about the local history and the local geography, complete with various photographs, ancient and modern. Occasionally someone, having just had a coffee and a slice of Lemon Drizzle Cake, drifts in from the cafe to have a look, and to take in perhaps a thimbleful of unforgettable local knowledge. Yes, they seldom stay long.

Having led me into this room, the cheerful female book-stacker points to a grey door in the wall that backs onto the book stacks. It is a locked grey door. She unlocks it. This is the stock room, she tells me, where the Poetry will be if it is anywhere, down there amongst the Classics. She points down in the direction of a dark corner. Having first given her a reassuring smile of thanks, I fall to my knees. They are piled one upon another – oh, for the ease of books stacked spine out, upright! I pull out one stack after another, trying to read the titles as I go, in the semi-murk of this hidden fastness. It is all quite exciting really. They are both with me now, at the open door, those male and female book replenishers, standing side by side, hoping to be of some help. Any books in foreign languages? I ask. French perhaps? The male smiles at me grimly. 'We tend to throw those away'. What is to be said in reply to that? I carry on looking, side on, at the Classics… I slither out from the deeper dark of the back of the shelf at least three stacks, clocking titles as I go: *Villette*, *Jane Eyre*, George Borrow's

Wild Wales, and then, finally, some Poetry. Poetry! There is not much of it, granted, but no one would deny that it is the genuine article.

Here for example, is a paperback copy of *The Faber Book of Comic Verse*, edited by Michael Roberts, looking fairly new, as if it were recently published. In fact, it is a paperback reprint of a book first published in 1942, and updated in 1974, tricked out in a lively blue cover with a smily face. Did any poems by Ezra get admitted? Yes, there are a couple. Both forgettable. I have always thought Ezra's light verse second-rate damp squibs.

Then, as I am looking, one by one, with increasing weariness, at the books in the last stack, I spot something of genuine interest: the *Collected Poems of John Masefield*, a man who managed to remain Poet Laureate of England for thirty-seven years, from 1930 until his death in 1967!

I think of Masefield for a moment. Did he have any impact as a poet on my generation? On Ezra's generation? No. Neither. Ezra thought him a stuffed shirt, a Little Englander, a throw-back, one of the despised Georgians. I try to remember the least little thing about him that may have stuck in my memory. A couple of lines emerge, from a poem called 'Cargoes', sung by the high voices of school boys: '…Dirty British coaster with a salt-caked smokestack/ butting through the Channel in the mad March days…' The first line of that poem – it was a free-standing poem before it was set to music – drifts back to me: 'Quinquereme of Nineveh from distant Ophir'. I remember being enthralled by the sound and the sight of *quinquereme*, that mysterious tri-syllabic word, of hurrying to a dictionary to find and to fix its meaning. Yes, by the time I was growing up, Masefield, to me, was that poem, fit to be sung at a school speech day in Sheffield City Hall, and perhaps 'Reynard the Fox'. He was an old fashioned teller of drum-beating tales in verse. In short, he was the distant past, a forgotten figure, an irrelevance.

Fair? Unfair? Reputations die, perhaps to live again. Having just riffled through all nine hundred pages of the book – it is at least the length of *The Cantos* – I would say that I think the man deserves a second look, and go hang Ezra.

We leave the cafe. No, Vincent leads us out of the cafe, twisting his snout seaward as he turns, panting, leash on the strain, out of the door. There are no dirty British smoke-stacks at large in the English Channel this morning, merely the white prow of the Newhaven-Dieppe ferry, plying from right to left, rearing its nose out of the water as it goes like a small Jack Russell on the scent, as it makes its steady way towards the French coastline from where Ezra, in the 1920s, would wanderlust his way down to Provence, that fabled terrain of the Troubadours, without a passport – passports were not necessary in those days – seeking out the future of the past.

The Lost Red Notebook

My life as a writer has been lived through red notebooks. It is in these notebooks, one after another after another, that ideas have germinated, lines of a poem have emerged, ideas for the next project mooted. The idea that a red notebook might be a storehouse of precious things, laid by somewhat secretively, comes from my Uncle Ken, who also kept a small red notebook in his back pocket for much of the time that I lived with him. From time to time I would see it on the kitchen table. That period of time ended when he left the modest terraced house we had shared with my grandfather, grandmother, sister and mother in north-east Sheffield, and moved in with his new wife Ena. I was fourteen years old when that happened.

And it was in such a red notebook that I transcribed, almost immediately (lest I forget any precious detail), the conversation I had with Olga Rudge in Venice one dying day in December of 1984, the conversation you have already read, the very conversation which caused me to write a long poem called *Old Ez's Lament*, which you have also read. Before writing that poem, I extracted Olga's words from the notebook, copying them out, one by one, on sheets of A4 paper. And then, some time after writing the poem itself, the notebook itself went missing. That would have happened more than thirty years ago.

When I came to write this book, horrified by the notebook's disappearance, I ransacked every cupboard, every drawer, every possible hideout. I went through every notebook I have ever filled – and they amount to dozens – but it was not to be. The notebook, inexplicably, had slipped its mooring post. It had gone missing.

Until yesterday, 15 December 2024, almost exactly forty years after that conversation at Calle Querini, when I happened to mention the fact of its disappearance to my wife, who then urged me to look through every red notebook, and every reporter's notebook, that I had ever filled, one last time. I told her that it would be a futile endeavour, that I had done so once too often already. The urging continued. I succumbed.

Why was I so concerned in the first place? Because in spite of the fact that I, by and large, trusted those notes which I had used, how could I really be sure that I had not missed something – or even mis-transcribed the odd word?

And then I came upon it, amongst a very few others of its kind, filed spine up, in a drawer reserved for old cassette-tape recordings of poets reading their own work…

The paper had browned considerably, but every word was still legible. And, yes, there were things I had not so much missed as left out because they did not relate directly to Ezra himself. They dealt with Professor G. Singh, poet and translator, that visitor who had also been been present at the cottage when we spoke to Olga, and who had interjected from time to time…

Pounding on the Door of a Poundian:
Words from the Lost Notebook of 1984, Newly Transcribed

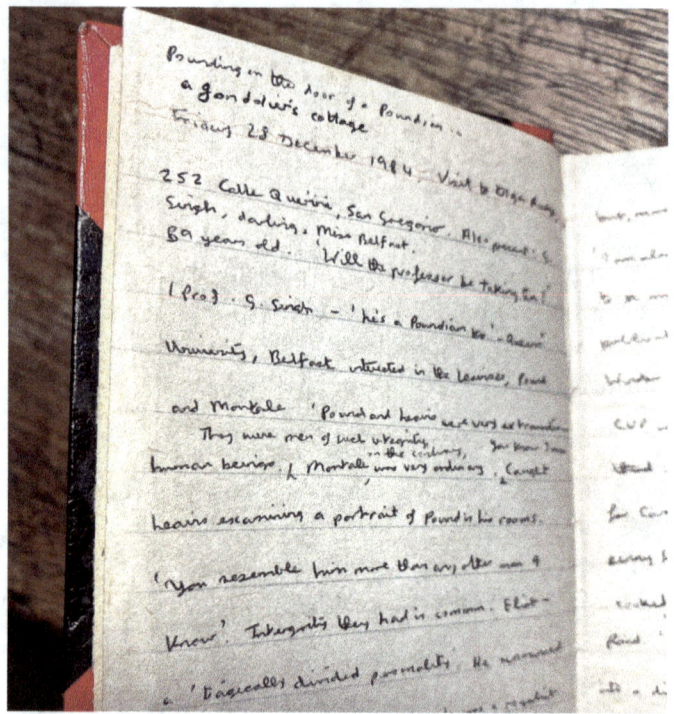

Friday 28 December 1984. Visit to Olga Rudge, 89 years old. Also present: (Prof) G. Singh of Queens' University, Belfast, interested in the Leavises, Pound and Montale. Throughout the conversation, Olga addresses Singh as 'The Professor' – 'Will The Professor be taking tea?', for example – and he addresses her as 'Miss Rudge'.

Miss Rudge (addressing us as he enters): he's a Poundian too…

The Professor: Pound and Leavis were very extraordinary human beings, men of such integrity. Montale, on the contrary, was very ordinary. You know, I once caught Leavis examining a portrait of Pound in his rooms. "You resemble him more than any other man I know". Integrity they had in common. Eliot was a tragically divided personality. He renounced his American citizenship because he was a royalist, but, more important, because he loved Stilton Cheese… I am alone. Can you find me a flat in London to retire to in my old age?

Singh is editing and preparing for publication Leavis' posthumous papers. Chatto & Windus have published *The Critic as Anti-Philosopher.* Cambridge University Press will do the next collection – and perhaps a third. He has also translated a selection of Montale's essays for Carcanet.

The Professor: You know I have not received a penny from them for that publication.

He tells us that the literary critic I. A. Richards, author of *Principles of Literary Criticism*, cooked a meal for him at his home in Chesterton Road, Cambridge.

The Professor: He knew I was a vegetarian. He put a whole cauliflower into a dish and poured cheese all over it. What is this dish called?

I.A.Richards: Cauliflower cheese…

Miss Rudge: My mother never taught me to cook anything. She said it was best not to learn things because then you wouldn't be expected to do them…

We soon return to Olga's abiding preoccupation: removing the taint from a dead man.

Miss Rudge: What I want is a senator from Idaho who wants to make a name for himself. He can take up Ezra's cause, clear his name. This is the most important thing. They must learn that he was not anti-semitic – why did his Jewish friends not rat on him? They all remained loyal to the end. Look at John Cournos – when Cournos turned Catholic, they took his name out of the Jewish Anthology. Ezra betrayed no one. He stayed in Italy because he had his poor mother to look after. She wanted to go back to America, but no one wanted her, the poor old soul. No, no. I want a good lawyer who will take up his case, that is the important thing. I was very surprised that he decided not to defend himself. I thought he would. If he had had a few weeks of peace and quiet to gather his thoughts, he could have done it…

The Professor: On the contrary, I do not think it's a good idea. What Miss Rudge wants is impossible. It is not important any longer. Anyway, no one would publish it.…

Christmas Lunch at Andrew Edmunds Restaurant in Lexington Street, Soho, on 16 December 2024

I am having a late lunch – it starts at 3pm – at Andrew Edmunds restaurant in Soho with a poet friend. I opt for calves' liver, with sprouts and a butter-bean sauce. We each have a single glass of Chianti (175 mls). These are sobering times.

He may be losing his publisher, he tells me. The man is always chasing the next big thing. Needless to say, the next big thing is never poetry. I tell him about another poet friend of mine who is now being treated as if he is an unpublished scribbler – in spite of the fact that he is an 'established author' (his words), with ten books to his name. Perhaps there is no such thing as an established author any longer, I wonder aloud, especially when that author happens to be a poet. Everyone goes to the back of the queue, and, as far as submitting the next book is concerned, is forced to wait for the next window of opportunity.

Needless to say, Ezra is on the menu too. There is so much circumambient clamour that I can barely hear to hear.. He looks sceptical when I mention his name. How many readers for such a book? Is he much read? Is his reputation not too shaky? I acknowledge all this and more – have I not heard it a thousand times before? I try to describe the decades' long struggle to write him out of my system, the nature of the abiding obsession that he has proved to be. What has it all amounted to in the end? I tell him: it is a book about not being able to write a book about Ezra Pound, I tell him. Auto-fiction? he hazards, in sympathy. Would that do?

Goodbye Ezra!

Ezra, That Ghost in the Family Circle

And so Ezra, in spite of all, has formed the nucleus of a book of mine. He has shouldered his way into what perhaps amounts to a spasmodic memoir of sorts of the second part of my life. I couldn't keep him away. He has refused to be written about in ways that I thought I wanted to write about him – perhaps too many people have done that already – and yet he has refused not to be written about because... well, because he is perhaps just as much a part of my life as my relatives. In fact, it would probably be true to say that I have spent more time being irritated by the idea of Ezra – his ridiculousness, his hubris, his extravagant ambitions, his boasting, the scope of his windbaggery, his maddeningly faltering, oh-so-spasmodic brilliance as a poet – than I have spent being irritated by the idea of all my relatives put together. And in some respects, it has to be said, he has been easier to deal with than a relative because I have never had to engage with him in actuality. He has only ever been a man in a book. I have had the luxury of being able to toss him aside when it all got too much. But he always came back, demanding still more attention.

The End in all but Name

Several of the books that I had in mind to write at different times in my life have not been written. They have been part-written, repeatedly, and then abandoned. Some have survived, in spite of all the odds, such as this spasmodic rag-bag of an Ezraical memoir-cum-notebook of sorts, which consists of probings, ruminations, speculations, conversations, some poetry, and, finally, various reasons for having failed to achieve a certain kind of ambition. Pound, meanwhile, remains as inscrutable as ever. There are so many versions of this man. He wore so many different masks, in poetry as in life. We have on the one hand the magnificence of that 'Hieratic Head'. There, you might argue, he looks every inch *Il Grande*

Poeta. Yes, that is what the plaque announces (though not in so many words), the one that is displayed above the door of Olga's cottage at 252 Calle Querini in the Dorsoduro: Titano della Poesia. The mask of this plaque suits him in that place because it sits very easily beside the image of himself as an old man who has returned to Venice, his spiritual home of sorts, something decrepit, fallen, magnificent, an unforgettable part-success of a failure. A dead man's plaque, in all its finality, is so easy to deal with.

Postlude

He is a lesson in life for any writer in general and, more to the point, every aspiring poet in particular. And yet it is not a lesson that is easily swallowed, at any age. He strove so hard for greatness – to be great himself, and to encourage others in the direction of greatness. (You could say that he found more greatness in others than he found in himself. Think of Eliot or Joyce, whose work he championed tirelessly.) And yet, finally, he was never quite good enough, not half so good as some of those whom he championed. This is his sadness or, put more pompously, his tragedy, and it is one he holds in common with so many writers who have died disappointed in themselves. They do not have the talent to embody or realise their own heady dreams of greatness.

Ezra strove to amass esoteric knowledge by the damful, and finally his writing was overwhelmed, even rendered utterly grotesque, by it. He spat it out in unwieldy bits. There was just too much of it for his own powers of organisation, and consequently the building of his mighty epic poem was not channelled or held in check by any sense of proportion. It was not organised with sufficient clarity of purpose. Why? Perhaps he was short on wisdom. Perhaps his flawed character overwhelmed his talents. He was both a brilliant man in the making and a bull-like, tempestuous, empty-headed fool. He wanted too much to be a great poet, and he fell a victim to his own overweening ambitions.

The Curse of Ezra Pound

Your enterprise was absurd, of course. No one believed you. No one understood you. You set sail all the same, across waters of impenetrable opacity. Whose life did you think you were living? That of an Italian Renaissance Prince or some home-spun kid from Idaho with all the blagging cussedness built in? It was your beard that conquered London, your frizz of hair, that cant of the head. And what a mouth! You glanced in my direction once. I glanced back, a bewildered boy from Sheffield numbed by your lightning strike. I was never the same again. Ma...

Vincent van Dogh

Book List

Below is a list of some of the many books that have fed into the writing of *Searching for Ezra*. Almost all of them form a part of my personal library – this will give you some indication of my unhealthy obsession with this man. Not all have been read in their entirety. Some have been read times over. Others have been read in part, and yet others tossed aside in weariness or exasperation. Many are, of course, by Ezra himself; others are biographies or critical commentaries. I could not cite everything that appertains to this disease of a lifetime. That would probably require a book in its own right. So I concentrate on works that I have discussed or alluded to or drawn from or quoted from in order to do those invaluable sources full justice. If I have missed anything, and you have spotted a glaring example of such a lack of gratitude, write to the publisher of this book immediately so that a correction can be made. Please note that for the most part the bibliographical information refers to the particular copy of the book that I myself have read and growled at.

Books by Ezra Pound:

A Selection of Poems, Faber & Faber, London, 1940
A Walking Tour in Southern France: Ezra Pound among the Troubadours, ed. Richard Sieburth, New Directions, New York, 1992
ABC of Reading, Faber & Faber, London, 1968
A Draft of Cantos XXXI-XLI, Faber & Faber, London, 1935
Collected Shorter Poems, Faber & Faber, London, 1968
Confucian Analects, Peter Owen, London, 1980
Confucius: the Great Digest & the Unwobbling Pivot, Peter Owen, London, 1968
The Cantos of Ezra Pound, Faber & Faber, London, 1968
The Cantos of Ezra Pound, Faber & Faber London, 11th paperbound printing, first published by New Directions in 1996
Collected Early Poems, Faber & Faber, London, 1977
Confucius to Cummings: An Anthology of Poetry, ed. Ezra Pound and Marcella Spann, New Directions, New York, 1964
Drafts and Fragments of Cantos CX-CXVII, Faber & Faber, London, 1970
Ezra Pound and Dorothy Shakespeare: Their Letters 1909-1914, ed. Omar Pound & A. Walton Litz, Faber & Faber, London, 1985
Ezra Pound and James Laughlin: Selected Letters, ed. David M. Gordon, Norton, London, 1998
Ezra Pound and Music, Faber & Faber, London, 1978

Ezra Pound and the Visual Arts, ed. Harriet Zinnes, New Directions, New York, 1980
Ezra Pound: Selected Cantos, New Directions, New York, 1970
Ezra Pound: Selected Prose, 1909-1965, ed. William Cookson, Faber & Faber, London, 1973
Ezra Pound to His Parents, Letters 1895-1929, ed. Mary de Rachewiltz, A.David Moody and Joanna Moody, Oxford University Press, Oxford, 2010
Gaudier-Brzeska, The Marvell Press, Hessle, 1960
Guide to Kulchur, Peter Owen, London, 1966
If This Be Treason, Tipo-Litografia Armenia, Venice, 1983
Jefferson And/Or Mussolini, Liveright, New York, 1935
Literary Essays of Ezra Pound, ed. T.S. Eliot, Faber & Faber, 1954
Love Poems of Ancient Egypt, trs. Ezra Pound and Noel Stock, New Directions, New York, 1962
Patria Mia and The Treatise on Harmony, Peter Owen, London, 1962
Pavannes & Divagations, New Directions, New York, 1971
Personae: Collected Shorter Poems, Faber & Faber, London, 2001
Pound/Ford: the Story of a Literary Friendship, Faber & Faber, London, 1982
Pound/Joyce: The Letters of Ezra Pound to James Joyce, New Directions, New York, 1970
Pound/Lewis: The Letters of Ezra Pound and Wyndham Lewis, ed. Timothy Materer, Faber & Faber, London, 1985
Pound: Poems and Translations, The Library of America, 2003
Pound/The Little Review: The Letters of Ezra Pound to Margaret Anderson, ed. Thomas L. Scott and Melvin J. Friedman with the assistance of Jackson R. Bryer, Faber & Faber, London, 1989
Pound/Zukofsky: Selected Letters of Ezra Pound and Louis Zukofsky, ed. Barry Ahearn, Faber & Faber, London, 1987
Posthumous Cantos, ed. Massimo Bacigalupo, Carcanet Press, Manchester, 2015
Selected Poems, ed. T.S. Eliot, Faber & Faber, London, 1939
Selected Poems, intro. by T.S. Eliot, Faber & Faber London 1959
Selected Poems and Translations, ed. Richard Sieburth, Faber & Faber London, 2011
Sophocles Elektra, Ezra Pound and Rudd Fleming, Faber & Faber, London and Boston, 1990
Sophocles Women of Trachis, Faber & Faber, London, 1969
The Classic Anthology defined by Confucius, Faber & Faber, London, 1974
The Classic Noh Theatre of Japan, Ezra Pound and Ernest Fenellosa, New Directions, New York, 1959

The Pisan Cantos, ed. Richard Sieburth, New Directions, New York, 2003
The Selected Letters of Ezra Pound 1907-1941, ed. D.D. Paige, Faber & Faber, London, 1971
The Spirit of Romance, Peter Owen, London, 1970
The Translations of Ezra Pound, Faber & Faber, London, 1970
Thrones: Cantos 96-109, Faber & Faber, London 1960

Critical and biographical studies

A Guide to the Cantos of Ezra Pound, William Cookson, Anvil Press, London, 2001
A Serious Character: The Life of Ezra Pound, Humphrey Carpenter, Faber & Faber, London and Boston, 1988
A ZBC of Ezra Pound, Christine Brooke-Rose, Faber & Faber, London 1971
Agenda: Ezra Pound, 85th birthday issue, Agenda Editions, London, 1970
Agenda: Dante, Ezra Pound and the Contemporary Poet, Agenda Editions London, 1996/7
Agenda: Twenty-First Anniversary Ezra Pound Special Issue, Agenda Editions, London, 1979/80
Discretions, Mary de Rachewiltz, Faber & Faber, London 1971
End to Torment: a memoir of Ezra Pound by H.D., Carcanet Press, 1980
Ezra Pound, Alec Marsh, Reaktion Books, London 2011
Ezra Pound, G.S. Fraser, Oliver & Boyd, Edinburgh and London, 1966
Ezra Pound, ed. J.P. Sullivan, Penguin Critical Anthologies, Penguin Books, Harmondsworth, 1970
Ezra Pound: a close up, Michael Reck, Rupert Hart-Davis, London,1968
Ezra Pound and The Cantos, Harold H. Watts, Routledge & Kegan Paul, London 1952
Ezra Pound Among the Poets, ed. George Bornstein, The University of Chicago Press, Chicago and London, 1985
Ezra Pound and his world, Peter Ackroyd, Thames and Hudson, London, 1980
Ezra Pound and Italian Fascism, Tim Redman, Cambridge University Press, Cambridge, 1991
Ezra Pound & Sextus Propertius, J.P. Sullivan, Faber & Faber, London, 1964
Ezra Pound and the Pisan Cantos, Anthony Woodward, Routledge & Kegan Paul, London, Boston and Henley, 1980
Ezra Pound: Identity in Crisis, Alan Durant, Harvester Press, Brighton, 1983
Ezra Pound Speaking, ed. Leonard W. Doob, Greenwood, Westport, Connecticut, 1978

Ezra Pound: Perspectives, ed. Noel Stock, Regency Press, Chicago, 1965
Ezra Pound: Poet, Vol. I, The Young Genius, 1885-1920, A. David Moody, Oxford University Press, Oxford, 2007
Ezra Pound: Poet, Vol.II, The Epic Years 1921-1939, A. David Moody, Oxford University Press, Oxford, 2018
Ezra Pound: Poet, Vol. III, The Tragic Years 1939-1972, A. David Moody, Oxford University Press, Oxford, 2015
Ezra Pound: Politics, Economics and Writing, Peter Nichols, Macmillan Press, London and Basingstoke, 1984
Ezra Pound: The Critical Heritage, ed. Eric Homberger, Routledge & Kegan Paul, London and Boston, 1972
Ezra Pound: The Last Rower, C. David Hermann, Seaver Books, New York, 1976
Ezra Pound: The London Years, Sheffield University Library, 1976
Ezra Pound: The Solitary Volcano, John Tytell, Bloomsbury, London, 1987
Ezra Pound: The Voice of Silence, Alan Levy, Permanent Press, New York, 1983
Ezra Pound's Chinese Friends, ed. Zhaoming Qian, Oxford, 2008
Ezra Pound's Kensington, Patricia Hutchins, Faber & Faber, London, 1965
Ezra Pound's Radio Operas, Margaret Fisher, The MIT Press, Cambridge, Massachusetts, London, England, 2002
Guide to Ezra Pound's Selected Cantos, George Kearns, Dawson, Folkestone, 1980
Henri Gaudier & Ezra Pound: A Friendship, Richard Cork, Anthony d' Offay, London, 1982
Imagist Poetry, ed., Peter Jones, Penguin Books, Harmondsworth, 1976
New Approaches to Ezra Pound, ed. Eva Hesse, Faber & Faber, London, 1969
Olga Rudge & Ezra Pound, Anne Conover, Yale University Press, New Haven & London, 2001
Pound, Donald David, Fontana, London, 1975
Pound as Wuz: Recollections and Interpretations, James Laughlin, Peter Owen, London, 1989
Pound's Artists: Ezra Pound and the Visual Arts in London, Paris and Italy, The Tate Gallery, London, 1985
The Chinese Written Character as a Medium for Poetry, Ernest Fenollosa, ed. Ezra Pound, City Lights Books, San Francisco, 1968
The Life of Ezra Pound, Noel Stock, Penguin Books, Harmondsworth, 1974
The Poetic Achievement of Ezra Pound, Michael Alexander, Faber & Faber, London, 1979
The Pound Era, Hugh Kenner, Pimlico Publishing, London, 1991

Sons of Ezra: British Poets and Ezra Pound, ed. Michael Alexander and James McGonigal, Editions Rodopi, Amsterdam-Atlanta GA, 1995
Stone Cottage: Pound, Yeats & Modernism, James Longenbach, Oxford University Press, New York, 1988
Studies in Ezra Pound, Donald Davie, Carcanet Press, Manchester, 1991
The Bughouse, Daniel Swift, Harvill Secker, London 2017
The Cambridge Companion to Ezra Pound, ed. Ira B. Nadel, Cambridge University Press, Cambridge, 1999
The Influence of Ezra Pound, K.L.Goodwin, Oxford University Press, Oxford,Toronto, London, 1966
The Master of Those Who Know: Ezra Pound, James Laughlin, City Lights Books, San Francisco, 1986
The Roots of Treason, E. Fuller Torrey, Sidgwick & Jackson, London 1984

Others

A Vision, W.B. Yeats, Macmillan, London, 1969
In Venice and in the Veneto with Ezra Pound, Rosella Mamoli Zorzi, John Gery, Massimo Bacigalupo, Stefano M. Casella, Supernova, Venice, 2007
Pintle 1, Thomas A. Clark and Omar Pound, Blue Room Society, Cambridge, 1973
Stones of Rimini, Adrian Stokes, Schoken Books New York, 1969
The Waste Land: a facsimile and transcript of the original drafts, T.S. Eliot, ed. Valerie Eiot, Faber & Faber 1980

Acknowledgments

This book, which has been many years in the making, the unmaking and the re-making, would not have come into existence without the help, advice, support from and conversations both casual and serious with many friends, loved ones, acquaintances and professional colleagues. I shall name many of them, but in no particular order: Alistair Davies, with whom I have talked about Pound and Pound matters over decades, on times innumerable, and, more formally, on two particular occasions transcribed in this book; Peter Elliott, who read the manuscript more than once many years ago, when it was very short and very ill considered – it was Peter who once told me that this was a book I would never finish, and he was right, of course; Ian Hargreaves, old and dear friend, who pointed out to me how much more pointedly judgemental the book would need to be if it were not to lack all credibility; John Birtwhistle, poet and razor-sharp mind, who spoke to me once, over lunch at Marmadukes in Sheffield, with such an amusing and exhilarating fierceness, about Pound and the monstrous brood of Poundians who have gathered in such a tight cluster around him; John Pitt-Brooke, who has had the patience to give me much quiet and sustained encouragement, usually over beers, throughout the decades of this book's long and unquiet germination; John Francis Phillimore, once a London bookseller and now gaining ground in Venice as a poet beloved by the Italians under the *nom de plume* of Philip Morre, who has given me endless bits of advice which I have always heeded, and often chosen to ignore; Marius Kociejowski and Norm Sibum, also old poet-friends, who I have accosted for opinion, facts and views time and again – bits and pieces of what they have said to me are in this book; John McEwan, art critic, who treated me to an uproarious lunch at the Chelsea Arts Club where Pound was very much on the menu; a hearty thanks to my friend and fellow art critic Adrian Clark, with whom I dined at Andrew Edmunds, and whose advice not to continue with this book I have studiedly ignored; and a thousand thanks must also go to Steve Kay, the ever patient and ever decent and dependable publisher of this book, who agreed to take it on. What a gambler he is, to indulge my wish to go in pursuit of a man as reckless with his gifts as Pound. I thank him for this. I also thank Barry Fantoni, saxophonist, painter, novelist, co-founder of Private Eye and much else, who, writing as legendary poetaster E.J. Thribb, has given me permission to reprint in this book his glorious parody of one of Pound's cantos which was first published in *Poems You May Have Missed* (Gompers Press, 2021). And an especial acknowledgement to the late John Ashbery, for giving me permission to cite his email to me about Uncle Ezra. And, last but scarcely least, I thank my own family – my wife Ruth, my son Joseph, and my daughter Jesse – who have had to suffer the almost daily presence of Pound in their lives as if he were a dreadful relative, never to be shaken off, never off the agenda. They have survived.

About the Author

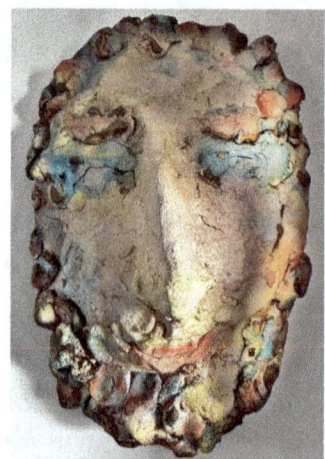

Portrait of author prematurely antiqued, by Ruth Dupré

Michael Glover is a London-based, Sheffield-born, poet, novelist, art critic, editor and publisher who has contributed regularly to the *Financial Times*, *The Economist*, *The Times*, the *New Statesman*, The *Tablet* and *Hyperallergic*.

www.ingramcontent.com/pod-product-compliance
Lightning Source LLC
Chambersburg PA
CBHW071150070526
44584CB00019B/2743